Bone, Robert

The Negro novel
in America

DATE			
OCT. 20 1982			
OCT. 31 1983	NOV. 23 1992		
DEC 1 '88	MAR. 1 9 1993		
NOV 2 8 1988	APR. 1 1993		
OCT. 3 1989			
FEB 16 '90			
SEP 28 '90			
OCT 18 '90			
JAN. 2 1991			
APR. 15 1992			
NOV. 5 1992			

THE NEGRO NOVEL IN AMERICA

By ROBERT BONE

New Haven and London, Yale University Press

Eighth printing, May 1971.

Printed in the United States of America by The Carl Purington Rollins Printing-Office of the Yale University Press, New Haven, Connecticut. Originally published as Yale Publications in American Studies, 3, under the direction of the American Studies Program and with assistance from the William Robertson Coe Fund.

Library of Congress catalog card number: 58–11249
ISBN: 0–300–00316–1 (cloth), 0–300–00024–3 (paper)

Distributed in Great Britain, Europe, and Africa by Yale University Press, Ltd., London; in Canada by McGill-Queen's University Press, Montreal; in Mexico by Centro Interamericano de Libros Académicos, Mexico City; in Central and South America by Kaiman & Polon, Inc., New York City; in Australasia by Australia and New Zealand Book Co., Pty., Ltd., Artarmon, New South Wales; in India by UBS Publishers' Distributors Pvt., Ltd., Delhi; in Japan by John Weatherhill, Inc., Tokyo.

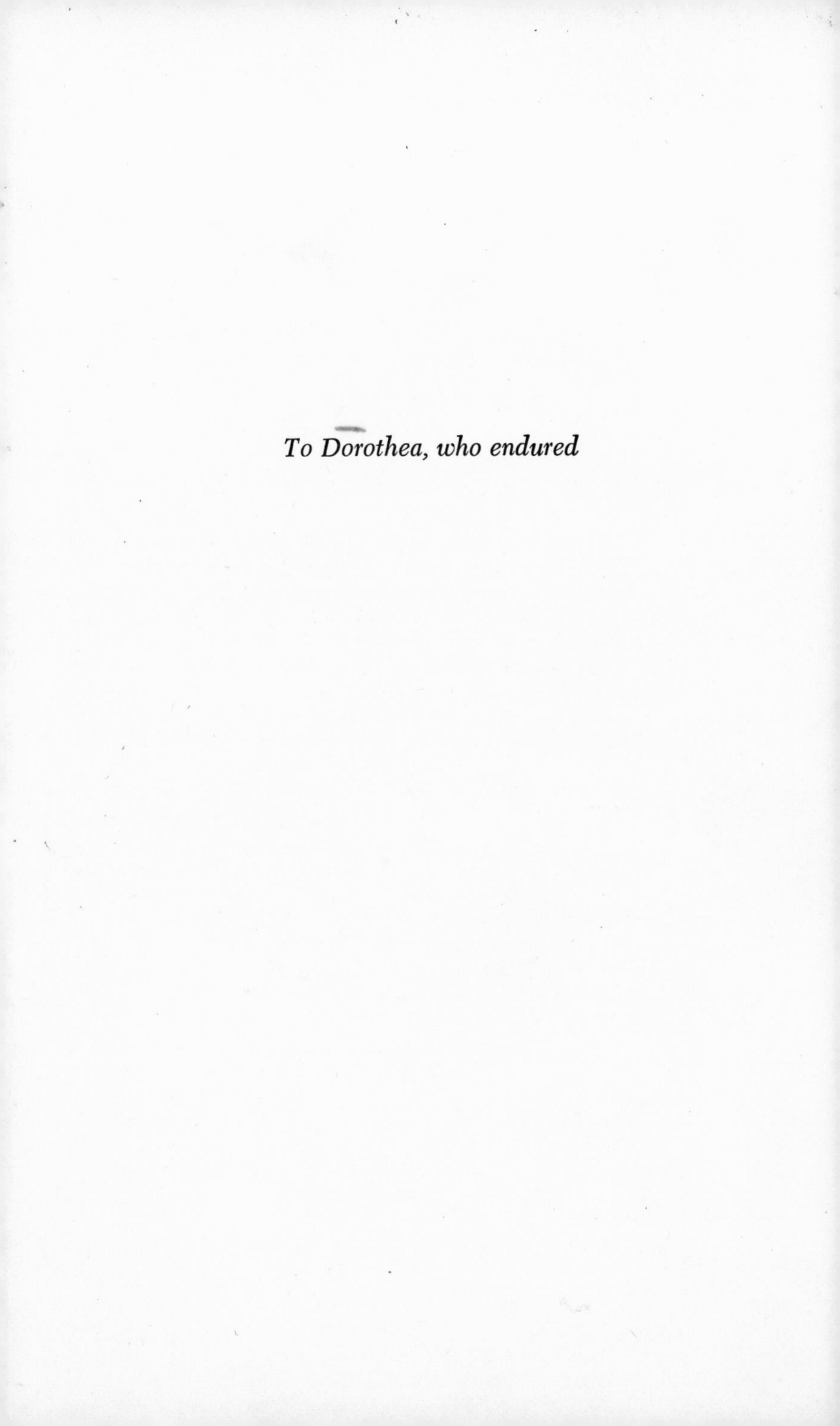

To Dorothea, who endured

Acknowledgments

To the American Council of Learned Societies, whose fellowship aid made the research for this book possible.

To Leonard Prager of Hebrew University, Tel Aviv, for an understanding of assimilationism and Negro nationalism.

To Sterling Brown of Howard University and Norman Holmes Pearson of Yale University, for criticism and advice.

To David Horne, for editorial assistance.

To my colored friends, who taught me what it is not possible to learn in libraries.

Contents

Introduction

Writers are forged in injustice as a sword is forged . . .
ERNEST HEMINGWAY

THE advocates of naive brotherhood will object in advance to the notion of a "Negro" novel. They will deny, usually without having read them, that novels written by American Negroes differ significantly from novels written by other Americans. Is there an "Armenian" novel in America, they ask. Then why single out the Negro?

To this line of argument the classic rebuttal has been advanced by J. Saunders Redding. "Season it as you will," he writes, "the thought that the Negro American is different from other Americans is still unpalatable to most Negroes." [1] Nevertheless, he con-

1. "The Negro Writer: Shadow and Substance," *Phylon* (fourth quarter, 1950), pp. 371–73.

tinues, "the Negro is different. An iron ring of historical circumstance has made him so." As if to restore the balance, he adds, "But the difference is of little depth." With this balanced view I agree. It is a serious mistake to gloss over or ignore strong cultural differences, in order to speed the process of integration.

These differences are the result not of innate "racial" characteristics but of a distinctive group experience in America. They stem from the group past, with its bitter heritage of slavery, and from the group present, with its bitter knowledge of caste. They stem from contact, either immediate or historical, with the folk culture of the Southern Negro, which has left its clear stamp on Negro life in the North. They stem from long experience with separate institutions: with a Negro press and a Negro church, Negro hospitals and Negro colleges. They stem from the fact that most Negroes still spend most of their lives within the geographical and cultural confines of a Negro community. These and similar circumstances have combined to produce a distinctive minority culture which is neither obliterated by the larger culture nor completely separate from it.

The Negro novel, like Negro life in America, is at once alike and different from the novels of white Americans. While it follows, usually after a short lag, the main historical development of the American novel, it has in addition a life of its own, which springs from the soil of a distinctive minority culture. It is no accident that approximately 85 per cent of the novels written by American Negroes deal principally or exclusively with Negro characters in a Negro setting. This racial emphasis is simply a literary echo of cultural reality. Whether this reality is desirable or not is another matter. When and if the Negro minority becomes fully integrated into American life, tendencies toward cultural autonomy will presumably disappear.

Like any other artist, the Negro novelist must achieve universality through a sensitive interpretation of his own culture. The American Negro, however, has not one but two cultures to interpret. He bears a double burden, corresponding to the double environment in which he lives. He must be conversant with Western culture as a whole, and especially with the traditions of English literature of which he is a part, and at the same time be prepared to affirm a Negro quality in his experience, exploiting his Negro heritage as a legitimate contribution to the larger culture. Nor is my espousal of cultural dualism an attempt to segregate the Negro artist in a cultural ghetto. For if his art cuts deep enough, he will find the Negro world to be liberating rather than confining. As Ralph Ellison has remarked, "Negro life is a by-product of Western civilization, and in it, if only one possesses the humanity and humility to see, are to be discovered all those impulses, tendencies, life, and cultural forms to be found elsewhere in Western society." [2]

The phenomenon of cultural dualism is by no means unique to the American Negro. The writers of the Irish Renaissance come immediately to mind, as do Jewish authors who, while writing in English, are nonetheless concerned with their relationship to Jewish life. Outside of certain narrow circles, however, only the sketchiest analytical tools have been developed for dealing with the cultural history of an ethnic minority. The following discussion is an attempt to provide the reader with a theoretical framework from which to approach the history of the Negro novel in America.

When the African slave was torn from his homeland and brought to the New World, he was quickly denuded of his native culture. Tribal organization, language, family structure, religion—all were systematically extirpated. In rebuilding his shattered life, he was compelled to appropriate his materials from a new culture. But his masters permitted him access to Western culture on a very restricted basis. Christianity had its uses, but slaves were forbidden by law to learn to read or write. The process of assimilation was deliberately obstructed by the whites.

The situation has not altered in any fundamental respect under the American caste system. The Negro must still structure his life in terms of a culture to which he is denied full access. He is at once a part of and apart from the wider community in which he lives. His adjustment to the dominant culture is marked by a

2. "Richard Wright's Blues," *Antioch Review*, summer 1945.

conflicting pattern of identification and rejection. His deepest psychological impulses alternate between the magnetic poles of assimilationism and Negro nationalism.

Assimilationism has its roots in what Langston Hughes has called "the urge to whiteness within the race." The mechanism involved has been described by Abram Kardiner and Lionel Livesey in *The Mark of Oppression* (New York, 1951). It begins with an incorporation of the white ideal, when the Negro child asks, "Whom do I want to be like?" His parents are members of a despised group possessing relatively few culture-heroes, and it is perhaps inevitable that he should internalize the dominant cultural ideal. This early idealization may persist throughout adult life as an unconscious desire to be white.

The other side of this coin is an unconscious self-hatred, likewise appropriated from the dominant culture. As Richard Wright describes it, "Hated by whites, and being an organic part of the culture that hated him, the black man grew in time to hate in himself what others hated in him." [3] The manifestations of this self-hatred are legion, ranging from the use of bleaching agents to a statistically dubious claim to "Indian ancestry." Perhaps the hostility directed toward the black masses by the Negro middle class is in large measure a projection of self-hatred.

An unconscious desire to be white, coupled with feelings of revulsion toward the Negro masses, may produce an assimilationist pattern of behavior at the purely personal level. Assimilationism is in this sense a means of escape, a form of flight from "the Problem." It involves a denial of one's racial identity, which may be disguised by such sentiments as "I'm not a Negro but a human being."—as if the two were mutually exclusive. This denial is accompanied by a contrived absence of race consciousness and a belittling of caste barriers. By minimizing the color line, the assimilationist loses touch with the realities of Negro life. Ultimately he identifies with the white group. Assimilationism, viewed as a personal adjustment to being a Negro in America, is a kind of psychological "passing" at the fantasy level.

Assimilationism, however, is more than a mode of personal adjustment. It is primarily a social-class phenomenon. The cultural

3. "Early Days in Chicago," *Negro Digest* (1950), pp. 52–68.

ideal, after all, is not merely to behave like a white person but to behave like a *middle-class* white person. Indeed, becoming middle class is precisely the process of eradicating one's "Negroness." Jazz is replaced by Beethoven, shouting Baptism by staid Episcopalianism, and the matriarchal family by that of the dominant male. This process of assimilation has its biological equivalent in the slogan "lighter and lighter each generation." In the course of rising in the social scale, all traces of "blackness" must be erased. The same situation obtains in the Jewish community, where upper-class Jews place a negative value on "Jewish-ness." The higher the social-class status of a member of an ethnic minority, the more likely that he will be assimilationist in outlook.

A tendency toward assimilationism is at bottom a matter of changing one's reference group, an attempt to abandon ethnic ties and identify with the dominant majority. This identification is so strong that it results in an indiscriminate appropriation of the dominant culture, including even its antiminority prejudices. Thus the phenomenon of the "anti-Semitic" Jew. The assimilationist Negro may likewise direct more hostility toward other Negroes than toward the oppressing white majority.

Negro nationalism is the polar opposite of assimilationism. There is also an urge to blackness within the race, which is essentially defensive in character. Negro Americans are drawn together by their common experience of racial oppression. Segregation creates the conditions of a separate group life, and the common heritage of slavery makes for a separate group tradition. The result is a strong feeling of racial solidarity. W. E. B. DuBois says: "When I went South to Fisk, I became a member of a closed racial group with rites and loyalties, with a history and a corporate future, with an art and philosophy." [4]

This sense of solidarity is reinforced by the growth of race pride. Culture-heroes like Toussaint l'Ouverture, Jackie Robinson, Ralph Bunche, and Louis Armstrong provide a concrete means of group identification. The Negro's self-esteem suffers because he constantly receives an unpleasant image of himself from his environment. Through race pride he tries to rebuild what the whites have torn down. This process of self-magnification may be based

4. *Dusk of Dawn* (New York, Harcourt Brace, 1940), p. 101.

on genuine achievement, inflated achievement, or empty fiction. Race pride may fortify an individual against the buffetings of caste by fostering in him a healthy self-confidence. Or, as Sterling Brown has remarked, it may evoke more applause for a racial bunt than an Aryan homer.

The most cohesive in-group attitude is not race pride but a bitter hatred of whites. The strength and prevalence of antiwhite sentiment among Negroes can scarcely be exaggerated. The colored community, like the white, brings severe sanctions to bear against its members who mix socially "across the line." In making interracial friendships, a Negro may experience an agonizing struggle as he unlearns his universal distrust of white people.

Antiwhite sentiment provides the psychological impetus of Negro nationalism. A negative attitude toward all things white is accompanied by a positive valuation of blackness. Garvey's Back-to-Africa movement, for example, exalted those of "pure African blood," while it excluded light-skinned Negroes. Garvey's organization boasted a brigade of Black Cross Nurses, and his steamship company was christened "The Black Star Line." He even declared in favor of a black Trinity, to spare his followers the humiliation of worshiping white gods.[5]

Militant Negro nationalism is both revolutionary and separatist. It is extralegal in outlook, proposing to meet violence with counterviolence and to take a life for a life. As a political movement, it stresses "self-determination," and resists integration into the dominant culture. Years before the Communist party raised its slogan of a separate Negro nation, Sutton Griggs created in his imagination an "empire within an empire." [6] Garvey's movement, which achieved a considerable mass following, was similarly secessionist in character. Even today one can recognize the impulse toward "national" identity in the advertising slogan of a well-known Harlem bookstore: "Be Patriotic—Buy Race Books."

It would be a mistake to characterize Negro nationalism by its excesses. Yet nationalism cannot be dismissed; it is a necessary part of the Negro day-to-day struggle against segregation. As Du-

5. Cf. Gunnar Myrdal, *An American Dilemma* (New York, 1944), pp. 746–49.

6. *Imperium in Imperio*, 1899. For the place and publisher of all novels cited throughout see the Bibliography, below.

Bois has pointed out, "So long as we are fighting a color line, we must strive by color organization." [7] Essentially, the Negro people must win equality by their own efforts, for in the last analysis, whites can only be allies in the war against Jim Crow. Meanwhile some tendency toward Negro nationalism is inevitable, in order that Negroes may maintain group efficiency, organization, and morale. Paradoxically, the struggle for integration involves the creation of race institutions.

Assimilationism and Negro nationalism, concepts indispensable to understanding the cultural history of the American Negro, are employed throughout the present work not only in interpreting the consciousness of individual authors, but in gauging the temper of whole periods. They help, for example, to unravel the conflicting impulses within the early Negro novel (1890–1920), and to illuminate the nationalist character of the Negro Renaissance (1920–30). They help to account for the success of the "Party line" among Negro intellectuals of the 1930's, and to explain the recent trend toward "raceless" novels in postwar Negro fiction. They provide, in short, a fixed point of reference from which to view the changing racial attitudes of the Negro novelist—attitudes which are often fundamental to the content of his art.

It is the art, in the long run, that matters. Most commentary on the Negro novel, whether by white or colored critics, has followed the Parrington tradition: the novels are treated primarily as social documents, and "evaluated" according to the social bias of the critic. There is nothing wrong, to be sure, with having a social bias, or with making value judgments based upon it. It is essential to understand, however, that these are not *literary* judgments, and that they have nothing to do with the value of a novel as a work of art. The danger is that social theory will become a substitute for literary criticism. While I have my social biases and have not hesitated to express them, I have tried to avoid the Parrington fallacy by placing strong emphasis upon form—attempting to establish the work of art in its own right before viewing it as part of the cultural process.

This is a method designed primarily for the study of major authors, however, and requires modification in a comprehensive

7. *Dusk of Dawn,* p. 311.

literary survey. In general, I have allowed the nature of the material to determine my emphasis. The chapters on the early Negro novel, for example, are predominantly sociohistorical, for the simple reason that the quality of these works does not justify intensive literary analysis. As the quality improves, more and more space is devoted to "formal" literary criticism.

The ultimate aim of this survey is to measure the contribution of the Negro novelist to American letters. Previous work in the field gives the impression of a vast, undifferentiated plateau, where only an occasional rise or hollow disturbs the level terrain. It is the intention here to distinguish the peaks from the valleys, to determine which of these novels are worth remembering and which are best forgotten. "The integration of the Negro artist," writes Sterling Brown of Howard University, "means his acceptance as an individual to be judged on his own merits, with no favor granted and no fault found because of race." It is in this spirit that the present book has been written.

Part I. *The Novel of the Rising Middle Class: 1890–1920*

The boy that learns to sell matches soon learns to sell other things; he learns to make bargains; he becomes a small trader, then a merchant, then a millionaire.

Frank Webb, *The Garies and Their Friends*

1. *Origins of the Early Novel*

IN the beginning was slavery, and it prevented the Word from becoming flesh. Leisure and education are the necessary conditions of literary activity, and the antebellum South did not recklessly indulge its slaves in either. The "peculiar institution," for that matter, seems to have done little to encourage literary pursuits among its beneficiaries, let alone its bondsmen. Literature was never the forte of the Southern aristocracy, and it is perhaps more than a coincidence that the first flowering of American letters occurred in Abolitionist New England. In any case, by its very nature slavery limited the creative expression of the Negro bondsman to folk forms. Broadly speaking, therefore, the cultural history of the American Negro falls into two periods, beginning with folk art before the Emancipation and becoming literary in the full sense about 1890.

The years between Emancipation and 1890 constitute the gestation period of the Negro novelist. During these years an embryonic middle class arose and became differentiated from the mass of freedmen, by virtue of superior educational and economic attainments. In time the rising middle class developed its own ideology, modeled after that of "respectable" whites, and acquired its own grievances, which were different from the grievances of slavery. By the 1890's the Negro middle class had produced several spokesmen who were ready to try their hand at the art of fiction. Their motives, however, were overwhelmingly nonliterary, and the fruits of their labor must be judged accordingly. The early Negro novel has some influential literary ancestors, but its social antecedents are far more important. In this case, the leap from society to literature must be boldly taken, for these novels can best be understood in terms of the aspirations and frustrations of the social class which produced them.

Social Antecedents

The historical origins of the Negro middle class can be traced back to the nocturnal escapades of countless male aristocrats who tried valiantly to wash a whole race whiter than snow. When "Massa" had an illegitimate child by a Negro slavewoman, his attitude toward his offspring was often ambivalent. On the one hand, he desired a better destiny for his child than the cotton patch and the overseer's lash. On the other, manumission was often legally impossible, and in any case it constituted too public an acknowledgment. Above all, it created a free colored population whose very existence threatened the institution of slavery.

Eventually a compromise was effected, by creating a privileged group of mulatto house servants who were relieved of the more arduous duties of the darker field hands. A division of labor resulted, roughly corresponding to complexion, and soon hardened along class lines. The house servants, living in greater proximity to their white masters, enjoyed freer access to the dominant culture. Notwithstanding the letter of the law, they often learned to read and write, and in some cases even assisted with the administration of the plantation. It was this privileged group, together with the free colored population, which formed the nucleus of the Negro middle class.

After Emancipation the rising middle class strove to buttress its position by acquiring the advantages of higher education.

While the masses of freedmen were straining to achieve literacy, the fortunate few attended such newly established Negro colleges as Fisk, Atlanta, Howard, and Hampton. Superior educational attainments enabled the Talented Tenth [1] to entrench themselves as small proprietors, white-collar workers, and independent professionals, in those spheres of the economy—usually involving service to the Negro masses—which were not already occupied by the whites. Gradually they achieved an economic margin and an educational level which brought literary expression within reach. Of crucial significance, in terms of the novels which they were to write, was the ideology of success which they adopted to speed them on their journey up from slavery.

It was inevitable that the Talented Tenth should acquire a boundless faith in the American Dream. They were precipitated by Emancipation into an expanding economy, and into a society whose main prize was success. These were decades of rapid industrialization, of the rise from rags to riches, of Horatio Alger and Silas Lapham. Progress was in the air, and a belief in race progress was an aspect of a basic 19th-century dogma. Racial advancement was regarded as synonymous with individual success, and was simply an expression of the prevailing American *ethos*, in Negro idiom.

The American success ideology finds its way into the early novels in many forms. A strong "inspirational" emphasis, for example, reflects the desire of the Talented Tenth to encourage ambition in the younger generation. Constant stress is placed on the property-acquiring virtues. Thrift and industry, initiative and perseverance, promptness and reliability are the qualities which distinguish hero or heroine from ordinary mortals. Undoubtedly the Negro Church played a cardinal role in encouraging race progress, by providing supernatural sanction for the success virtues. In the early novels these virtues are often reinforced by attitudes which derive from the Calvinist religion of work: a stern regard for duty, injunctions against idleness, and sober warnings against self-indulgence.

Most of the early novelists adopted a strict Protestant asceti-

1. A term coined by W. E. B. DuBois during his controversy with Booker T. Washington over higher education for the classes vs. industrial education for the masses. It is used synonomously with "Negro middle class."

cism, wielding it as a stout club against personal habits which might interfere with the accumulation of property or the achievement of middle-class status. "We must guard ourselves against a sinful growth of any appetite," wrote Pauline Hopkins. It is no accident that several of these authors were active in the temperance cause, devoting ample space in their novels to combating the evils of demon rum. Other proscribed pastimes include dancing and ragtime music, gambling, card-playing, and smoking. The "animal passions," needless to say, were beneath notice, and in polite society, courtship was consummated with a kiss.

As it grew in numbers and confidence, the Talented Tenth came to require of its members certain symbols of status. Home ownership, higher education for the children, and membership in a select religious denomination are stressed repeatedly in the early novels. To these requirements may be added the outward tokens of respectability: neatness, good manners, and conservative dress. Persons who have mastered the "correct standards of deportment" are described as "cultured" or "refined." They join prominent churches or clubs, and visit "fashionable resorts for Afro-Americans" in the summer. They bring out their daughters in the fall, fret over the servant problem, and regard themselves frankly as "the better class of colored persons."

Like other novels of the Gilded Age, those of the Talented Tenth reveal a certain flair for gentility. Having just arrived, the Negro middle class took pains to conceal its lowly origins, above all from itself. The literary reflex of this self-deception is the Genteel Tradition. Trousers become "unmentionables"; every home is a "residence"; every job, a "profitable situation." Shunning realism, avoiding all unpleasantness, the genteel spirit reflects the relative comfort and security which the new way of life has made possible. One of Charles Chesnutt's characters renders this state of mind precisely as he reacts with shocked indignation to the sight of a chain gang: "There were criminals in New York, he knew very well, but he had never seen one. They were not marched down Broadway in stripes and chains. There were certain functions of society, as of the body, which were more decently performed in retirement." [2]

2. *The Colonel's Dream* (1905), p. 226.

In a competitive society success is often accompanied by repressed guilt. In the case of the Negro middle class this sense of guilt is aggravated by the in-group loyalties which result from racial oppression. The form which this guilt assumes in the early novels is a persistent sense of *noblesse oblige,* involving a personal obligation to serve the race. Eventually, however, the Talented Tenth managed to justify its success drive on more impersonal grounds. Pauline Hopkins provided an appropriate formula in her motto *honores mutant mores.* According to this view, the cause of racial justice is best served, through a happy coincidence, by the normal business activities of the Negro middle class: "Greater industry, skill, the sticking quality, honesty and reliability will open the way. . . . If we will only cultivate the saving spirit, cut loose from extravagant habits, work the year round, encourage and assist one another in business, we will acquire wealth, and this will effectively dissipate race prejudice." [3]

The truth is that the early Negro novelist had the soul of a shopkeeper. Yet his world view, which equates wealth with virtue, is understandable enough if we consider his social position. Typically he was of lower-class origin but had himself come up from the ranks to achieve a career as a businessman or professional person.[4] With few exceptions, his life was occupied with business affairs; literature was merely his avocation. Usually his single novel was written during an interlude from the harsh economic struggle. It is little wonder that he held such a stubborn faith in the American Dream.

In addition to its "inspirational" function, the early Negro novel served as an instrument of protest, through which the Talented Tenth could air its grievances and appeal for justice. The early novelist was an advocate; he was pleading a cause, though not always with the high idealism ascribed to him by posterity. To

3. G. Langhorne Pryor, *Neither Bond nor Free* (1902), p. 81.

4. Of the early novelists for whom records are available, the occupations of their *parents* are distributed as follows: professionals, 13 per cent; the "free colored" (freed before Emancipation and frequently artisans), 20 per cent; ex-slaves who were substantial farmers, 40 per cent; and rural folk, (also ex-slaves), 27 per cent. By way of contrast, in terms of their *own* careers, the early novelists are distributed as follows: professionals, 80 per cent; white-collar workers, 20 per cent. The pattern is one of dramatic upward mobility.

understand his motives one must understand the genesis and growth of the American caste system.

Even before slavery was abolished, a new fabric of race relations was being woven to replace it. Caste relations, as distinct from the direct property bond between master and slave, date from the earliest existence of a free colored population. Long before Emancipation, nominally free colored citizens were subjected to segregation in housing and travel, discrimination in employment, and exclusion from places of public accommodation. Although *incipient* caste relations existed under slavery, the American caste *system* did not crystallize until the post-Reconstruction era, when a wave of repression followed the withdrawal of federal troops from the South.

Emancipation caused an economic and social revolution in the Old South. At one stroke it wrecked the plantation economy, severed the master-slave relationship between the races, and threw the former bondsman into the wage market as a legal equal. During the Reconstruction Period which followed, the freedman attempted, under the protection of the federal government, to consolidate his new status against the inevitable reaction which was to come. By 1876 the Republican party had grown tired of being revolutionary and had abandoned the Negro to the white South.

The result was the post-Reconstruction repression. It was a period in which the Negro was systematically stripped of his civil rights in order to assure the restoration of white supremacy. The old plantation economy was revived, based now on sharecropping and tenant farming, peonage, and convict lease. Disfranchisement followed as a means of preventing legal redress. By 1900 Mississippi, Louisiana, and the Carolinas had disfranchised the Negro with the "Grandfather Clause," poll tax, and terror. Where legal methods failed, the Ku Klux Klan and the lynch mob took over. One Negro author observed that "Lynching was instituted to crush the manhood of the enfranchised black."

In the years between 1876 and 1900, the foundations of the American caste system were laid. The new system rested ultimately on the plantation economy of the rural South; it was sustained in custom and in law by *segregation,* an elaborate pattern of caste relations which partly separates the races, permitting them to mingle only under circumstances humiliating to the subordinate caste. During these years segregation laws were enacted in all spheres of life, from education and travel to housing and bans on interracial marriage. These laws, moreover, were promptly ratified by the Supreme Court, in a series of "separate but equal" decisions. Thus black robe and white each made its unique contribution to the establishment of the American caste system.

No sooner did the embryonic Negro middle class emerge from slavery than it ran head-on into these caste barriers. This was the stuff of protest literature. For the most part the novelists of the Talented Tenth responded militantly to the post-Reconstruction repression, bringing every aspect of the caste system under attack. They wrote as participants in a desperate social struggle, defending themselves as best they could against peonage, lynching, disfranchisement, and segregation. Unfortunately, the imperative nature of their struggle caused them to regard the novel primarily as an instrument of propaganda. In the words of Sutton Griggs, "The poem, the novel, the drama must be pressed into service. . . . The bird that would live must thrill the hunter with its song."

Because of the liberal climate that has prevailed in recent years, we are inclined to assume that this early protest literature was egalitarian in outlook, and that its appeal for justice was based on a catholic concern for the brotherhood of man. But as Frazer has remarked in *The Golden Bough,* the disinterested love of liberty is about as common as uncombined oxygen. While the early novels are rich in the rhetoric of human brotherhood, they will be found in fact to contain all the narrow prejudices of their time. They display more than a trace of anti-Semitism, and their characterizations of other nonwhites (American Indians, Asians) are often stereotyped. In typical Know-Nothing fashion, they depict immigrants as "jabbering foreigners," "dagoes," and the like. The anarchist, who was the favorite whipping-boy of the period, receives his share of attention: "The Negro is not plotting in beer-saloons against the peace and order of society. His fingers are not dripping with dynamite, neither is he spitting upon your flag, nor flaunting the red banner of anarchy in your face." [5] No doubt the acquisition of these prejudices was part of the process of Americanization of the Negro middle class. Nevertheless, this attempt to gain status at the expense of popular scapegoats undercuts the early novelist's appeal on behalf of his own group.

More germane in terms of the racial strategy of the Talented Tenth is their open contempt for the Negro masses. Sutton Griggs, for example, refers to "colored people of the lower order—besotted men and slovenly women, denizens of the slums." [6] J. McHenry Jones' heroine in *Hearts of Gold,* reduced by poverty to teaching school in the South, holds her new life at arm's length like a dirty sock: "Reared in an atmosphere of ease and refinement, she was illy prepared for the uncouth side of life she was soon to enter." [7] In several of the early novels there is a stock situation in which a "refined Afro-American" is forced to share a Jim Crow car with dirty, boisterous, and drunken Negroes.

During the period under discussion, hostility toward the Negro masses found expression in the sentiment "The bad Negro keeps the good Negro back." Rather than allow race progress to be impeded in this manner, the early novelist did not scruple to strengthen his own position at the expense of those less fortunate than himself. Sometimes his attitude amounts to outright betrayal. Charles Chesnutt's hero, Dr. Miller, for example, shrinks from a group of farm laborers in a Jim Crow coach: "These people were just as offensive to him as to the whites in the other end of the train." [8] He then suggests that they be segregated, but on a more reasonable basis than color! Otis Shackleford's heroine, Lillian Simmons, carries this argument to its logical conclusion: "She could understand why Jim Crow cars and all other forms of segregation in the South were necessary, but she could not feel that it was fair to treat all colored people alike, because all were not alike." [9]

The color-line is unjust, according to this view, because it does

5. Frances E. W. Harper, *Iola Leroy* (1892), p. 223.
6. *Pointing the Way* (1908), p. 125.
7. *Hearts of Gold* (1896), p. 163.
8. *The Marrow of Tradition* (1901), p. 60.
9. *Lillian Simmons* (1915), p. 139.

not respect class distinctions. The solution is apparent: The Talented Tenth must put as much distance as possible between itself and the black masses, and press for acceptance as a privileged minority. In support of this strategy, the Talented Tenth argued that it was better assimilated, both biologically and culturally, than the black masses, and was thus more deserving of full integration into American life.

It must be understood at once that the early novelists believed substantially in the myth of Anglo-Saxon superiority. Pauline Hopkins writes: "Surely the Negro race must be productive of some valuable specimens, if only from the infusion which amalgamation with a superior race must eventually bring." [10] Heredity therefore plays a cardinal role in the plot and characterization of the early novels, and many of the colored protagonists proudly trace their lineage to some erring member of the white aristocracy. Viewed politically, this obsessive concern with ancestry was a means of strengthening the mulatto's plea for special consideration.

A greater degree of cultural assimilation was also advanced as grounds for special treatment. Whatever may be true of the unlettered ex-slave, the Talented Tenth contended, educated Negroes are "just like white folks." In order to prove this contention, they peopled their novels with colored characters of impeccable deportment, as much like "cultured" and "refined" whites as possible. From their novels, as from their lives, the Talented Tenth sought to eliminate all traces of "Negro-ness," in the hope that cultural uniformity would make them more acceptable to the whites.

Perhaps nothing reveals the parochial character of this early protest literature as much as the audience to whom it was addressed. When all the sound and fury of these novels has evaporated, what remains is an appeal for an alliance between "the better class of colored people" and the "Quality white folks." To this end, the fictional portrait of the Southern aristocracy is universally flattering. As slaveholders they are depicted as kindness

10. *Contending Forces* (1900), p. 87. For other instances of the alleged superiority of "white blood" see Sutton Griggs, *The Hindered Hand* (1905), p. 141; and Charles Chesnutt, *The House behind the Cedars* (1900), p. 163.

personified, while after Emancipation they are assigned the roles of friendly employer, financial benefactor, protector from mob violence, and even social Messiah. A corollary to this policy of exonerating the Southern aristocrat is the use of the "poor white" as a scapegoat for the cumulative evils of the caste system.

In seeking the protection of the former slave-holding class, the Talented Tenth hoped to exempt itself from the worst of the post-Reconstruction repression. By taking advantage of what might loosely be termed their "family connections," they sought to enlist the support of powerful whites in their behalf. In reality, their appeal for fair play was addressed to "their" white folks. Reluctant to abandon the benefits of paternalism, they still hoped to solve the problem of the color line *within the family* (both branches).

Viewed in broader perspective, they were trying to breach caste with class, on the grounds that "whiteness" of appearance and behavior entitled them to special treatment. Perhaps the white folks could be persuaded to abandon the "irrational" application of caste to the Talented Tenth. And why not? There was no historical precedent to the contrary. They had yet to discover the unyielding logic of the caste relations which replaced slavery. When the Talented Tenth became convinced of the necessity for independent struggle, only then was there a concerted effort to close ranks with the Negro masses. But this political realignment, initiated under the leadership of W. E. B. DuBois, was not brought to fruition until 1910. DuBois' program, with its implicit appeal for a united front with the Negro masses, makes no significant impact on the Negro novel until after World War I.

Bearing in mind the racial strategy of the Talented Tenth, as well as its success ideology, we are now in a position to understand the dramatic structure of the early Negro novel. In a typical early novel the colored protagonist is an aspiring, respectable, white-collar or professional person. His antagonist is the American caste system, which acts as a handicap or obstacle to his ambition. The dramatic tension of the novel arises from this conflict between the success ideology of the hero and the inimical effects of caste. With this formula, the early novelist attempted to arouse a passion for justice among whites, and for property among Negroes. It remained to discover an appropriate idiom for the pursuit of these social objectives.

Literary Ancestors

The Negro novelist arrived on the scene at a time when the Romantic tradition was rapidly being undermined by literary realism. Yet of this ferment, these glimmerings of a new century, he was oblivious. Like his housing, he inherited his literary forms at second hand, after the white folks had moved out. Not only did the early novelist write exclusively within the Romantic tradition, but he chose melodrama—the very caricature of that tradition—as his principal literary vehicle.

One generation from slavery, he had attained neither the cultural level nor the intellectual scope for anything else. He was not influenced by the incipient social realism of Howells and Garland; or by the regionalism of Harte, Twain, and Sarah Orne Jewett; or by the naturalism of Dreiser and Norris; certainly not by the stylistic subtlety and urbane cosmopolitanism of James. For all of these idioms his experience was too limited and his own cause too compelling. To discover his literary ancestors we must examine first what whites had previously written about Negroes, and secondly, the deluge of "popular" fiction which flooded the paperback market of the day.

When the early novelist took pen in hand to oppose the post-Reconstruction repression, he wrote not only as a participant in a desperate social struggle, but as a belligerent in a long series of literary wars over the status of the Negro in the United States. The historical sequence of these wars runs roughly as follows: an attack on slavery by the Abolitionists; a counterattack by writers of the so-called plantation tradition, reinforced by other less genteel advocates of white supremacy; then a spirited defense by Negro writers themselves, which began on a large scale during the 1890's and has continued to the present day. The attack on caste by white authors is a relatively recent phenomenon, appearing first in the 1920's, under the influence of the "primitive" movement in modern art. With the social realism of the 1930's the pro-Negro forces can be said to have won the day; during the last two decades literary attacks on the Negro have been obliged to assume a somewhat subtle and disingenuous form.

In tracing the literary ancestry of the early Negro novel, the first two phases of this running skirmish are directly relevant. Abolitionist literature, and especially *Uncle Tom's Cabin* (1852), left a deep imprint on early Negro fiction, for propaganda methods which had proved so effective against slavery might reasonably be expected to yield good results in the struggle against caste. The unreconstructed Southerners who later swept Abolitionism from the field provided the Negro novelist with what might be termed "negative models" for his own fiction. The exemplary characterization of the early Negro novel, for instance, must be understood in terms of the uncomplimentary, if not slanderous, stereotypes which it was designed to refute.

The post-Reconstruction repression had its literary reflex in the writings of such authors as Thomas Nelson Page and Thomas Dixon. Page was a leading spokesman of the plantation school, which devoted its talents to preserving untarnished the Golden Legend of the South. In such volumes as *In Ole Virginia, or Marse Chan and Other Stories* (1887), *The Old South: Essays Social and Political* (1892), and *Red Rock* (a novel, 1898), Page painted an idyllic picture of plantation life, peopling his works with piously devoted mammies and frolicking slaves who possessed the happy mentality of puppies. In contrast to this pat-on-the-head school, Thomas Dixon's lurid novels, *The Leopard's Spots* (1902) and *The Clansman* (1905), portrayed the Negro as a primitive savage, capable of any crime or violence, unless "kept in his place" by the civilizing influence of the Ku Klux Klan. Understandably enough, though with disastrous consequences for his art, the early Negro novelist traded blow for blow with his traducers, answering stereotype with counterstereotype in an effort to stem the rising tide of anti-Negro propaganda.

Literary wars aside, the early Negro novelist inherited another stock figure from his white predecessors in the person of the tragic mulatto. Such novels as George W. Cable's *The Grandissimes* (1880), William Dean Howells' *An Imperative Duty* (1892), and Mark Twain's *The Tragedy of Pudd'nhead Wilson* (1894) contain mulatto characters for whom the reader's sympathies are aroused less because they are colored than because they are nearly white. The novelists of the Talented Tenth were quick to incorporate this device into their own novels, for it was ideally suited to their current racial strategy. Through the figure of the tragic mulatto they could stress the "irrational" nature of caste, with the implication that the color bar should be lowered, at least for descendants of the dominant race.

The racial attitudes of contemporary white authors inevitably affected the content of the early Negro novel. Its form, however, was derived from the popular fiction of the day. Of available models there was no dearth in the Gilded Age, for as Charles Beard has observed: "For every copy of Howells' *Traveller from Altruria* or Henry James' *Portrait of a Lady* that was sold in the marts of trade, doubtless a thousand copies of Buffalo Bill's desperate deeds, Diamond Dick's frantic exploits, and Beadle's bloodcurdling jeopardies were consumed." [11] The dime novel, not to mention the flood of "success" literature which poured from the pens of writers like Horatio Alger, Jr., played a major role in determining the early novelist's idiom, by introducing him to the potentialities of melodrama. Hardly a novel of the period is untouched by this influence. In order to appreciate the advantages which melodrama offered to the early Negro novelist, we must examine its origins as an art form.

A student of the subject has described the principal ingredients of melodrama as follows:

> The freshness of this new art form . . . was due to clear-cut characters, embodying simple vices and virtues; terse and economical dialogue which, though inflated, never allowed itself to wander from the action for merely literary purposes; startling contrasts both in character and action; and above all, thrilling situations in which the physical played the major part. . . . The frank directness with which it produced its effects made its utter unreality seem real for the time being, and its excessive artificiality seem simple.[12]

11. *The Rise of American Civilization* (New York, Macmillan, 1930), 2, 445.
12. Ernest B. Watson, *Sheridan to Robertson; A Study of the Nineteenth Century Stage* (Cambridge, Harvard University Press, 1926), p. 354.

Such a form offered major advantages to the early Negro novelist. To begin with, melodrama deals with the conflict between Right and Wrong. Its moral extremes make it a natural vehicle for racial protest. Conventional melodrama assumes the existence of a stable moral universe, made manifest through the perennial triangle of hero, heroine, and villain. The early novelist gave this triad a racial twist: his hero was a handsome black man; his heroine, a beautiful mulatto girl; and his villain, a white scoundrel. The moral absolutism of melodrama thus served the strategic needs of the period, which called for colored heroes and heroines of exaggerated virtue, and white villains of bottomless perfidy.

Ordinarily in melodrama, the most improbable situations are created to balk the hero, who is then extricated from his difficulties by the creaking plot machinery. Such a medium provided the early novelist with a comfortable margin of error. If he momentarily lost control of his plot, he could intervene at will to set things right. In allowing him this latitude, melodrama did not overtax the talent of the early novelist, who was still acquiring the elementary skills of narrative fiction.

By emphasizing action, melodrama avoids the problem of characterization. A multiplicity of characters, roughly sketched and inadequately motivated, is typical of the genre. Since the moral natures of hero and villain are fixed and immutable, as characters they are without possibility of complexity or development. Once again the limitations of melodrama proved to be an asset. The early novelist had his own reasons for refusing to venture beyond the plot level into characterization. Caught between anti-Negro stereotypes and his own counterstereotypes, he was never able to achieve a rounded treatment of his Negro characters. In the end he avoided the problem by seeking refuge in the flat, static characters of conventional melodrama.

In lieu of characterization, melodrama relies on extrinsic devices to hold the reader's interest. As a substitute for inner conflict, thrilling episodes are introduced which are dramatic in themselves. Since such episodes quickly cloy, a constant quest for new and more exotic material must be undertaken. The early novelist possessed some distinct advantages in this respect. In constructing his plots he could draw upon exotic material from "slavery times," depending for his effect upon mysteries of birth, lost inheritances, and the like. Moreover, he was free to use plot material which the whites preferred to ignore, such as miscegenation, passing-for-white, and racial violence.

But above all else, melodrama is a literature of social aspiration. It has appealed traditionally to the white-collar classes—the socially thwarted whose present existence is dull by comparison with their vision of better things to come. Melodrama is essentially a romantic projection of their future in the upper class. It invariably deals with upper-class life, but so unrealistically as to expose its source in wish fulfillment. There is something servant-like in its view of upper-class life, captured in the phrase "backstairs melodrama."

One generation from slavery, the rising Negro middle class entered the white-collar zone where melodrama was a congenial medium. At this level of culture the crudities of the form were no obstacle. Yet if melodrama reflects the uncultivated sensibilities of the early Negro novelist, it reflects no less his determination to rise to greater cultural heights. Thwarted by caste and insecure in his middle-class status, he turned naturally to a futuristic art form. Melodrama expressed in unequivocal terms his ultimate social aspirations and his firm allegiance to the American success ideology.

The inherent limitations of melodrama may in themselves account for the aesthetic failure of the early Negro novel. A broader interpretation suggests itself, however, based on the theoretical concepts of assimilationism and Negro nationalism. The special world of American letters confronts the Negro author with special problems of acculturation, and in meeting them he becomes impaled on the horns of a familiar dilemma. Just as in real life the Negro is forced to assume an ambivalent attitude toward the dominant culture, so in the world of letters the Negro writer may adopt an ambivalent attitude toward the dominant literary tradition.

The early novelist, to be specific, did not approach the problem of characterization in a vacuum, for the prevailing literary tradition contained stylized caricatures of the Negro which deprived him of all human dignity. These stereotypes were part and parcel of the apparatus of white supremacy; they reflected a strain of racial chauvinism firmly embedded in American letters, and for that matter, in Western civilization itself.[13] They exercised a strong coercive influence on the early novelist, and hampered him in the free pursuit of artistic ends. His solution to this problem was characteristically ambivalent: he simultaneously accommodated to the stereotype (assimilationism), and attempted to refute it (Negro nationalism).

The tendency toward accommodation is surprisingly common. Minor characters who would be quite at home in a minstrel show are by no means rare in the early novels, starting with William Wells Brown's Sam, who pulls the wrong tooth by mistake, and Frank Webb's Kinch, who falls downstairs into a pan of batter. Pauline Hopkins describes a stout laundress who "outsings the Church organ," while Dunbar, in *The Fanatics,* portrays a colored character with "a picturesque knack for lying." Even Chesnutt and Griggs succumb, with Sandy "the very comical darkey," and Uncle Jack, the ignorant and superstitious narrator of plantation tales. These characterizations have in common that lack of dignity which is traditionally associated with burnt cork.

The essence of minstrelsy is the exploitation of folk material for Massa's entertainment. The early novelists do not ignore the folk; they simply view them in a comic perspective, whenever they turn momentarily from their aspiring middle-class heroes and heroines. Lest we miss the point, dialect distinguishes the comic (folk) characters from the serious (middle-class) characters, who of course speak only the white man's English.

Notwithstanding his comic caricatures of the folk, the early novelist is not devoid of race pride. He attempts to refute uncomplimentary stereotypes by creating exemplary middle-class characters, hoping thus to "prove" that Negroes, or at least some Negroes, are capable of honesty, courage, morality, and other virtues. Like the Player Queen, he protests too much, conveying an impression not of dignity but of insecurity.

13. For a comprehensive survey of racial stereotypes in American literature see Sterling Brown, *The Negro in American Fiction,* Washington, D.C., 1937.

The central artistic problem of the early novelist was the creation of rounded Negro characters, in the face of degrading stereotypes inherited from the whites. The proper solution was literary realism, not counterstereotype. Whatever the psychological or political justification for counterstereotype, it cannot possibly result in art. Characters created by race pride alone resemble nothing so much as figures in a wax museum. A Black Apollo may gratify the ego, but as a human being he is a bore.

The early novel was an aesthetic failure largely because it never solved this problem of rounded characterization. Most of the early novelists fell between the stools of buffoonery and counterstereotype. Writing for a double audience, they attempted to conciliate both white and colored, by including clown and Apollo in the same novel. Dunbar deliberately avoided the issue by making most of his serious characters white. Only James Weldon Johnson discovered a solution consistent with artistic integrity. His protagonist possessed human dignity but was not inhumanly virtuous. *The Autobiography of an Ex-Colored Man* (1912) was the first Negro novel to contain a complex, fully motivated Negro character.

The stylistic failure of the early novel was likewise the result of an unsolved problem in literary acculturation. From the Genteel Tradition the Negro novelist appropriated an ornate and stilted style: "See the flock of long-winged lake birds, laving their breasts anew in nature's baptismal fount!" [14] By no means exceptional for the period, this florid diction was adopted without regard for its compatibility with a militant literature of protest. Gentility of style may be appropriate enough in a sheltered Victorian world of swooning ladies and gallant gentlemen, but for the purpose of describing a lynching it has its limitations.

The Genteel Tradition complacently ignored the unpleasant aspects of human experience. The white middle class could afford this luxury, since it had in fact achieved a certain immunity from hardship. The Negro middle class, however, could not completely eliminate strife and suffering from its literature. In the face of the post-Reconstruction repression, a combative mood was inevitable. Negro nationalism found its logical literary ve-

14. J. McHenry Jones, *Hearts of Gold,* p. 4.

hicle in the protest novel. But at the same time the assimilationist tendency produced *stylistic* imitation of the Genteel Tradition. The resulting juxtaposition of gentility and protest is utterly incongruous.

The early Negro novel contained contradictions which could not be resolved within the framework of 19th-century Romanticism. The advent of literary realism was necessary before Negro characters could be fully emancipated from the stereotype, and before the theme of racial protest could find a suitable stylistic medium. Unfortunately, the Negro novelist did not break with Romanticism until the 1920's. Meanwhile, the early novel foundered on the rocks of characterization and style.

2. *Novels of the Talented Tenth*

THE novels of the Talented Tenth constitute a fairly uniform response to a well-defined social situation, and with few exceptions they possess little artistic individuality. A selection seems indicated, and perhaps it calls for a brief justification. For reasons not strictly aesthetic, five novelists of the period deserve more than passing notice: Sutton Griggs, because of current misconceptions regarding his ideology; Charles Chesnutt and Paul Laurence Dunbar, because they were the first Negro novelists to attain national prominence; W. E. B. DuBois and James Weldon Johnson, because they were harbingers of the 20th century. Between them these five authors wrote exactly half of the novels (fourteen out of twenty-eight) published between 1890 and 1920.

Before discussing these five early novelists, it is necessary to define the period itself more precisely. Strictly speaking, the history of the Negro novel begins in 1853, with the publication of *Clotel,* by William Wells Brown. Only three full-length novels were published before 1890, however, while twenty-eight appeared between 1890 and 1920. This shift from scattered to sustained production, which took place about 1890, corresponds roughly to a shift in theme from attacks upon slavery to attacks upon caste.

Abolitionist Novels

Clotel, or the President's Daughter (London, 1853) is the first novel written by an American Negro. The author, William Wells Brown, was a fugitive slave who was trained by Abolitionists as a writer and lecturer. Born "William," he acquired the rest of his name from the Quaker family which aided his escape from slavery. For the duration of the Fugitive Slave Law, Brown lived in England, where he made his living from writing and lecturing. His publications include a travel book, several historical works, and a play.

Clotel was written to arouse sympathy for the Abolitionist cause among English readers. Its structure is simple enough. The novel opens with the sale of a mother and her two daughters, traces their subsequent fate, and thereby provides a catalogue of the evils of slavery. It ends melodramatically as the heroine eludes a group of slave-chasers by throwing herself into the Potomac, within sight of the White House. The intended irony depends upon Brown's allegation that Clotel was the illegitimate daughter of Thomas Jefferson.[1]

A second Abolitionist novel, which survives only in fragmentary form, is Martin Delany's "Blake, or the Huts of America" (1859).[2] Delany departs radically from the Abolitionist formula of broken families and violated octoroons, by treating slavery primarily as an exploitative labor system. It is a remarkable novel, closer in spirit to Karl Marx than to the New England Abolitionists. The hero, who attempts to organize a general slave insur-

1. In the American edition, published by a Boston house in 1867, an anonymous senator is substituted for Jefferson, and the plot is altered accordingly.

2. This appeared serially in *The Anglo-African Magazine,* Jan.–July, 1859. We have twenty-six chapters out of a known eighty. Technically, therefore, the novel is excluded from this study, since it does not survive as a "full-length" novel. A passing comment, however, may help to round out the period.

rection throughout the South, declares to a slave audience: "Every blow you receive from the oppressor impresses the organization on your mind. . . . Punishment and misery are made the instruments of its propagation." [3] Oriented toward the "quarters" and the darker field hands rather than the "big house" and its mulatto servants, "Blake" may be thought of as representing the "proletarian" wing of the Abolitionist movement.

The Garies and Their Friends (1857), by Frank Webb, has more in common with the protest novels of the 1890's than with the contemporary Abolitionist novels of Brown and Delany. Webb was a member of Philadelphia's free colored population, and he therefore experienced the essential conditions of middle-class life far in advance of the emancipated freedman.[4] Among these conditions, the freedom to rise is basic. It is reflected in the dominant tone of Webb's novel, which is that of the conventional success story: "The boy that learns to sell matches soon learns to sell other things; he learns to make bargains; he becomes a small trader, then a merchant, then a millionaire." Although he wrote some years before Emancipation, Webb was stalking other game than Simon Legree. He is concerned not with slavery but with caste, with the artificial barriers to success which confront the free Negro. He makes a frontal assault on various sectors of the color line, attacking most directly the problems of mixed marriage, and discrimination in employment.

It was thirty-five years before another novel touching on caste relations appeared. *Iola Leroy* (1892), by Frances E. W. Harper,

3. "Blake," *Anglo-African Magazine* (April 1859), p. 108.

4. According to Hugh Gloster, Webb's racial identity is a matter of conjecture (*Negro Voices in American Fiction*, Chapel Hill, University of North Carolina Press, 1948, p. 260 n.). There is decisive evidence, however, both external and internal, that Webb was a colored man. We have first the word of Harriet Beecher Stowe, who refers to Webb in a preface to the second edition of his novel as "a young colored man, born and reared in Philadelphia . . . of the better class of colored citizens." Secondly, in the Howard University Library there are two serial stories written by Webb in a colored newspaper: "Two Wolves and a Lamb," *The New Era* (Jan.–Feb. 1870), pp. 1–4, and "Marvin Hoyle," ibid. (March–April 1870), pp. 12–15. Finally there is strong internal evidence, especially in the author's antiwhite sentiments, to indicate that he is colored. One of his characters remarks, for example, "I shall begin to have some faith in white folks after all" (p. 135). Again in the riot scenes, the author's marked antipathy for whites breaks through.

is a transitional work which combines elements of Abolitionism with incipient attacks on caste. With its setting in the Civil War and Reconstruction periods, *Iola Leroy* lacks the urgency of the other protest novels of the 1890's. The explanation is not far to seek: Mrs. Harper was one of the foremost Abolitionist poets of the 1850's, but she was sixty-seven years old when *Iola Leroy* was published. She was separated from the other novelists of this period by a full generation; her social consciousness, formed during the Abolitionist struggle, did not encompass the post-Reconstruction repression.

As the younger novelists of the 1890's grew to maturity in the shadow of the caste system, their mood became increasingly belligerent. Gradually the violence of the period filters into their works. *Appointed* (1894), by Walter Stowers and William H. Anderson, is the first novel to treat peonage, convict labor, lynching, disfranchisement, and segregation as aspects of a systematic repression. The trend continues with *Hearts of Gold* (1896), by J. McHenry Jones, in which the author characterizes this repression as "the reign of the poor whites." But the most militant note of the period is struck in 1899, with the publication of Sutton Griggs' *Imperium in Imperio.*

Sutton Griggs

Griggs was a prominent Baptist minister and a popular lecturer on the race problem. Having written five novels in the space of ten years (1899 to 1908), he organized his own publishing company in Nashville, Tenn., to promote their sale and distribution. The novels are badly written and tractarian in the extreme, but Griggs' very militancy represents something of a culmination. This militancy deserves closer examination, however, if only because of current misconceptions regarding it. Hugh Gloster has written extensively of Griggs, both in an article in *Phylon* [5] and in *Negro Voices in American Fiction.* He has treated Griggs as a political thinker of some stature whose views on the race question compare well with those of James Weldon Johnson.[6] He has found in

5. "Sutton Griggs, Novelist of the New Negro," *Phylon* (fourth quarter 1943), pp. 335–45.
6. *Negro Voices in American Fiction,* p. 62.

Griggs not a forerunner of the New Negro but "the novelist of the New Negro" incarnate.

The term "New Negro" was coined by Alain Locke during the 1920's, to express the new spirit of dignity and manhood which animated the postwar generation of Negro youth. The New Negro was distinguished by his refusal to accept subordinate status; he had decisively rejected the slavemindedness which taught the Old Negro to know his place. But freedom in the psychological sense is a process of becoming. At what point in this process is Sutton Griggs? On occasion he is militant and challenging, as Dr. Gloster avers. At other times he is conciliatory to the point of servility. His militancy has its source in a fanatical Negro nationalism; his servility, in a political outlook which is essentially feudal. The former mood is well illustrated by *Imperium in Imperio* (1899); the latter, by *Pointing the Way* (1908).

In his first novel, Griggs displays the classic attitudes of Negro nationalism. He is almost pathologically antiwhite and scarcely less antimulatto.[7] He toys with a solution to the race problem which is both revolutionary and separatist. His hero, described throughout as a "race patriot," leads a secret student society in revolt under a black flag; later he joins a revolutionary underground government which plans to seize Texas as a base for a separate Negro nation. To be sure, the hero of the novel repudiates these excesses in the end. But the symbolic drama which is being enacted is clear enough. Griggs' blind impulse toward retaliation and revenge is striving for mastery with a more moderate, and more realistic approach.

The author's next three novels,[8] while not as blatantly black-nationalist as *Imperium in Imperio,* are essentially cut from the same cloth. *Pointing the Way* (1908), however, far from being "militant and challenging," is conciliatory and accommodationist. In the words of a minor character: "Good white people kin lead de cullud folks ef dey will jes' 'gree ter do so." [9] The heroine of the novel, in attempting "to bring the better elements of white and colored people together," seeks the assistance of Seth Molair,

7. See the crude mutilation fantasies involving whites in *Imperium in Imperio,* pp. 13, 35, and 152. Note also the characterization of Bernard throughout the novel, and Viola's refusal to marry a mulatto, pp. 173 ff.

8. *Overshadowed* (1901), *Unfettered* (1902), *The Hindered Hand* (1905).

9. *Pointing the Way,* p. 99.

a young white man whose family is described in the following terms: "The Molairs had never ceased under freedom to exercise a paternal care over all those who had belonged to the family in the days of slavery" (p. 111). Illustrative of the kind of "equality" which Griggs espouses is Molair's campaign for mayor of a small Southern town, undertaken with the support of the colored community. After winning the election, he courageously makes a Negro college graduate captain of the municipal fire department! (A place for everyone, and everyone in his place.)

At one point in the novel Griggs gives the game away: "just as the Negroes had great faith in *their* white folks, the whites, as a rule, had great faith in *their* Negroes" (italics in original). Here, in an unguarded moment, Griggs reveals the paternalistic relationship which lies at the heart of his feudal psychology. In spite of his rhetoric about Negro rights, in the last analysis Sutton Griggs is an old-fashioned Southerner who relies on the "Quality white folks" to provide a solution to the race problem. He must therefore be willing to make certain compromises and opportunistic arguments. This approach to Southern politics can of course be argued on its merits, but it is certainly not the approach of the New Negro.

Sutton Griggs' vacillation between one pole which is militant and fantastic and another pole which is realistic and accommodationist faithfully reflects the political dilemma of the Negro intellectual prior to World War I. The ideological contradictions which plagued Griggs were not personal but historical. He and others of his generation were caught in an iron vise which precluded political action that was at once militant and realistic. DuBois' Niagara Movement and the subsequent founding of the NAACP marked a decisive change in the strategy of the Negro leadership, from a perspective of manipulating Southern paternalism to one of independent struggle. But before this strategy could be implemented, a vast population shift from South to North and from farm to city was necessary. The urban migration, which only made itself felt after World War I, gave the Negro leadership a mass base capable of supporting an independent struggle.

Militancy is one thing; translating it into effective political action is another. Too often Negro nationalism, for all its militancy, is politically Utopian. The most militant of the early novelists, insofar as they were realistic, were obliged to be more or less accommodationist. Conversely, insofar as they remained militant and uncompromising, their political strategy was bound to have a certain Utopian ring. *Pointing the Way* by Sutton Griggs and *The Colonel's Dream* (1905) by Charles Chesnutt represent one horn of this dilemma; *The Quest of the Silver Fleece* (1911) by DuBois and *The Immediate Jewel of His Soul* (1919) by Herman Dreer, with their Utopian agrarian communities, represent the other. All of these novelists were forerunners of the New Negro, but scholars should resist a tendency to date the New Negro movement too early in order to gloss over the long period of accommodationist politics which preceded it.

Charles Chesnutt

Charles Chesnutt and Paul Laurence Dunbar were the first Negro novelists to attract the attention of the white literary world. Both had already won distinction in other fields, Chesnutt as a short-story writer and Dunbar primarily as a poet. Both had launched their literary careers by exploiting the plantation tradition; both brought them to fruition with the help of white patrons.[10] Dunbar, however, continued to write in the plantation tradition, or avoided controversy by making his main characters white. Chesnutt, on the other hand, pioneered in his "problem" novels, pressing his publishers for freedom to treat the color line from the Negro point of view. His novels are therefore of considerable historical if not literary importance.

Charles Waddell Chesnutt (1858–1932) was born in Cleveland, Ohio. His father, a substantial farmer, moved the family to Fayetteville, N.C., when Chesnutt was eight years old. Educated only through grade school, Chesnutt was a self-made man who read voraciously and taught himself stenography, then law. He was a school teacher in Fayetteville for nine years, had a brief encounter with journalism in New York City, and finally settled in Cleveland, where he took up the profession of court stenogra-

10. Walter Hines Page in the case of Chesnutt; William Dean Howells in the case of Dunbar.

pher. After studying law in the office of a Cleveland judge, he was admitted to the Ohio bar in 1887. In addition to three novels, he published two collections of short stories and a biography of Frederick Douglass.

Chesnutt's first story, "The Goophered Grapevine," was accepted by the *Atlantic Monthly* in 1887. Thereafter he appeared sporadically in the pages of the *Monthly* until Houghton Mifflin published two collections of his stories, *The Conjure Woman* (1899) and *The Wife of His Youth* (1899). Before these stories were accepted, Chesnutt had submitted the first draft of a novel dealing with the subject of passing, but Walter Hines Page rejected this manuscript in favor of the more conventional "conjure" tales. Even then, the publishers concealed Chesnutt's racial identity from the public for almost a year. In all fairness, however, it must be added that after the success of Chesnutt's stories, Houghton Mifflin not only brought out his novel of passing (*The House behind the Cedars*) but actually invited him to submit "a strong race problem novel" published as *The Marrow of Tradition.*[11]

The House behind the Cedars (1900) is the story of a girl who crosses the color line in search of wider opportunity. Rena Walden has been brought up "behind the cedars," in a house established by her white father for his colored mistress and their children. Having reached a marriageable age, Rena is filled with misgivings concerning her future as a Negro. Encouraged by her brother, who is already established as a white person in another community, she decides to "pass." For a time all goes well, but on the eve of her marriage to a white man of good family, her deception is discovered. Appropriately heartbroken, Rena turns for consolation to schoolteaching and racial uplift. When her chastity is simultaneously besieged by her former fiancé and by an unscrupulous colored principal, for reasons somewhat obscure to the modern reader she dies.

In all important respects, *The House behind the Cedars* conforms to the prototype of the early Negro novel. Structurally speaking, Rena's social aspirations are played off against the constraining effects of caste, in a manner calculated to arouse the

11. Cf. Helen M. Chesnutt, *Charles Waddell Chesnutt* (Chapel Hill, University of North Carolina Press, 1952), p. 154.

reader's indignation. The stereotype of the tragic mulatto is employed, with all of its moral and aesthetic limitations. Nor is *The House behind the Cedars* immune from the literary infirmities of the period. The novel is incredibly overwritten in spots: "Rena, my darlin', why did you forsake yo'r pore old mother?" The dramatic conflict never transcends the plot level; there is no characterization worthy of the name; and in the end, Chesnutt avoids his artistic responsibilities by arbitrarily putting his heroine to death.

In *The Marrow of Tradition* (1901), Chesnutt comes to grips with the violence of the post-Reconstruction repression. The riot scenes in the novel are based on actual events which occurred in Wilmington, N.C., during the elections of 1898, when Negro voters were driven from the polls after a bloody battle.

Fundamentally the novel raises the issue of retaliation in the face of direct provocation from the whites. Chesnutt's protagonist, Dr. Miller, holds a moderate position on racial matters until the accidental death of his small son during the rioting. For the remainder of the novel he is torn between Christian charity and a desire for revenge. Shortly after the death of his son, he is called upon to save the life of a white child, by means of a delicate throat operation. At first he rejects the frantic appeals of the boy's mother: "He had been deeply moved, but he had been more deeply injured." Eventually, however, his wife intercedes on behalf of the white woman, and he agrees to perform the operation. Counterposed to Dr. Miller's "responsible" behavior is the attitude of a minor character, Josh Green: "I expec's ter die a vi'lent death in a quarrel wid a w'ite man . . . an' fu'thermo', he's gwine ter die at the same time, er a little befo'!" [12] Once again, as in Griggs' *Imperium in Imperio,* the Negro's natural impulse toward retaliation is projected fictionally, only to be abandoned in favor of more moderate views, but always with a warning to the whites that provocation to violence must cease.

The novel is heavily overplotted; the maze of characters precludes adequate motivation; the style is excessively formal and unsuited to the highly emotional quality of the theme, and an element of melodrama pervades the whole novel. To a large ex-

12. *The Marrow of Tradition,* p. 110.

tent the fiction is merely a scaffolding through which Chesnutt can present his views on contemporary race relations. In the theme of retaliation he has the makings of a good novel, but he fails to cast his theme in an appropriate dramatic mold.

Chesnutt's third novel, *The Colonel's Dream* (1905), can best be described as the work of a pamphleteer. As Helen Chesnutt candidly remarks in her biography, "This was an avowed purpose novel written to expose peonage and the convict-lease system." [13] Yet it is conciliatory and ingratiating in tone, for it represents that phase in Chestnutt's development in which he means to talk business with the Southern whites. The novel depicts the struggle of Colonel French, a progressive white Southerner, against Bill Fetters, a former poor white who represents the survival of the spirit of slavery. Perhaps nowhere in the early Negro novel is the bourgeois spirit so manifest. The Colonel's dream consists of a plan to build cotton mills throughout the South, where "in the absence of labor agitation . . . the trinity of peace, prosperity, and progress would reign supreme."

An appraisal of Chesnutt's novels is hardly a fair measure of his talent. On the strength of his short stories alone, he raised the standards of Negro fiction to a new and higher plane. These short stories—especially the conjure tales—can be judged on their own merits, and in this department Chesnutt's reputation seems secure. In his novels, however, he became an overt propagandist, to the detriment of his art. Furthermore, he never succeeded in mastering the aesthetic requirements of the longer genre. Of this fatal deficiency Walter Hines Page once remarked to him: "You had so long and so successfully accustomed yourself to the construction of short stories that you have not yet, so to speak, got away from the short story measurement and the short story habit." [14] It is a shrewd insight into Chesnutt's failure as a novelist, and a fairly accurate summary of his contribution to American letters.

Paul Laurence Dunbar

While most of the early novelists were concerned in one way or another with racial protest, Paul Laurence Dunbar went his

13. *Charles Waddell Chesnutt,* p. 211.
14. Quoted ibid., p. 109.

own way, seeking to amuse rather than arouse his white audience. Viewing Dunbar's literary career as a whole, it is impossible to avoid the conclusion that his chief aim was to achieve popular success by imitating the plantation tradition. Most of his poems and short stories, as well as one of his novels, fall safely within the broad tradition established by Thomas Nelson Page. Whenever Dunbar had something to say which transcended the boundaries of the plantation tradition, he resorted to the subterfuge of employing white characters, rather than attempting a serious literary portrait of the Negro. The net effect of his work, therefore, was simply to postpone the main problem confronting the Negro novelist.

Dunbar (1872–1906) was born and raised in Dayton, Ohio, by parents who were illiterate ex-slaves. His literary talents were developed in public high school, where he became editor-in-chief of the school paper, president of the literary society, and class poet. After rejecting a career in the ministry, he worked as an elevator boy, until Robert Ingersoll and William Dean Howells introduced him to the reading public in the pages of *Harper's Weekly.* Thereafter he earned his living as a professional writer, with occasional supplements from other sources. In the field of fiction he published four collections of short stories and four novels. He is perhaps better known as a writer of dialect verse, which appeared in numerous small volumes from 1893 to his early death from tuberculosis in 1906.

Dunbar's first and most successful novel, *The Uncalled* (1898), is widely regarded as his spiritual autobiography. It is the story of a young white man who rebels against his Puritan heritage, and against his guardian's grim determination to make him a minister. Freddie Brent, the protagonist, is the child of a broken marriage, who is reared from boyhood by his maiden aunt. Stern, undemonstrative, and duty-bound, Hester Prime represses every natural impulse of her ward. Freddie's only relief from the stifling atmosphere of his boyhood is his friendship with Hodges, a genial bachelor who is broadly tolerant of human frailty.

The tension between Freddie and Hester culminates inevitably in rebellion. Carefully groomed for the ministry, Freddie asserts his independence by disappointing his guardian's hopes. When he fails to appear at his ordination dinner, Hester is forced to accept defeat. Meanwhile, Freddie wins a more important spiritual victory by refusing to preach against a "fallen girl" at the behest of a self-righteous and unforgiving congregation. Having found a God of love to replace the avenging God of his youth, Freddie leaves home for Cincinnati, where his new concept of religion is soon put to the test. There he meets his father, whose recklessness and irresponsibility have almost ruined his life. Behind the eventual reconciliation of father and son looms the figure of Hodges, symbolic of all that is charitable in human nature.

Perhaps by virtue of its autobiographical content, *The Uncalled* ranks a notch above most of the early novels. It is relatively free of melodrama, and not without some attempt at characterization. Conflict and resolution take place on a psychological plane, rather than at the elementary level of plot. The principal setting of the novel is the small Ohio town of "Dexter," before the advent of industrialism. Dunbar's realistic description of these transplanted Yankees, with their narrow religion, their small-town gossip, and their frontier humor, adds a local-color dimension to the book. In short, the characters, setting, and theme of *The Uncalled* are well within range of Dunbar's provincial consciousness.

Most of this writer's important themes are foreshadowed in his first novel. The conflict between the Natural (Freddie) and the Artificial (Hester) is basic to Dunbar's agrarian values, in which nature plays a vital part. In Freddie's experiences in Cincinnati there is a hint of the provincial's distrust of the "wicked city." A sense of fate, of forces beyond human control, pervades the novel: "When Fate is fighting with all her might against a human soul, the greatest victory that the soul can win is to reconcile itself to the unpleasant, which is never quite so unpleasant afterwards." [15] This note of fatalistic surrender, which appears frequently in Dunbar's novels, may be traceable to his illness, and perhaps it accounts for his supine response to Negro life in America.

The Love of Landry (1900) is by far the worst of Dunbar's novels. It hinges on the romantic separation of two lovers by a class barrier, resulting from the fact—so unpalatable to Victorian sensibilities—that the hero works with his hands. But Landry, as

15. *The Uncalled,* p. 124.

it turns out, has been a gentleman all along, for at the propitious moment he produces an old Virginia grand-daddy and thereby wins his bride. Insofar as the novel can be said to have a theme, it opposes the freedom of the Western plains to the stuffiness of the Eastern seaboard: "What does [civilization] mean after all, except to lie gracefully, to cheat legally, and to live as far away from God and Nature as the world will let?" [16] Landry's romantic retreat from civilization to his ranch in Colorado has its parallel in Dunbar's spiritual retreat from the conditions of modern life to the old plantation.

Dunbar's third novel, *The Fanatics* (1901), is a well-disguised attempt at racial protest, so carefully veiled that only the subtlest of readers will grasp the point. The novel has an historical setting in an Ohio town during the Civil War. Two white families, one Yankee, the other Copperhead, provide a focus for the action. The plot concerns two lovers who are separated by the "fanaticism" of their fathers. The Yankee patriarch eventually overcomes his blind prejudices as a result of his son's death in battle, and the lovers are united.

The Fanatics is ostensibly an attack upon sectional chauvinism, as well as an abstract plea for toleration of differences and recognition of individual worth. The closing paragraph of the novel reveals the brand of fanaticism that Dunbar actually has in mind. A minor character, Nigger Ed, comes home in glory from the wars: "And so they gave him a place for life and everything he wanted, and from being despised he was much petted and spoiled, for they were all fanatics." [17] North and South, Dunbar is saying, may have reconciled their differences, but both sections are united and fanatical in their determination to keep the Negro in his place.

This oblique protest is self-defeating, however, because the medium is corrupted in advance. Pandering to the prejudices of his white audience in order to gain a hearing, Dunbar resorts to caricature in his treatment of minor Negro characters. In order to flatter Southern pride, he singles out Bradford Waters' "New England fanaticism" for special condemnation. In contrast, his

16. *The Love of Landry*, p. 73.
17. *The Fanatics*, p. 312.

old-fashioned Southerner, Stephen Van Doren, is presented sympathetically: "'Come boys,' he said, addressing the negroes, and they grinned broadly and hopefully at the familiar conduct and manner of address of the South which they knew and loved" (p. 171). Such a passage is its own best commentary. Far from altering the attitudes of prejudiced whites, Dunbar merely reinforces them.

The Sport of the Gods (1902) is the only Dunbar novel whose main characters are colored. Like several of Dunbar's short stories, the novel reiterates the plantation-school thesis that the rural Negro becomes demoralized in the urban North. The first five chapters develop, not altogether credibly, the trial and imprisonment of Berry Hamilton, a loyal servant who is falsely accused of theft. The remainder of the novel traces the effects of this disgrace on the Hamilton family. Forced by the hostility of a small Southern community to migrate to New York City, the family soon disintegrates in that sinful metropolis. By the time Berry is released, he finds his son in jail, his daughter (worse than dead) on the stage, and his wife married to another man.

Dunbar's ulterior motives are revealed in a long didactic passage, which begins by warning of "the pernicious influence of the city on the untrained Negro." To be sure, Dunbar concedes, "The South has its faults—no one condones them," but in spite of the most flagrant injustice (like Berry's), it is preferable to the sidewalks of New York: "Good agriculture is better than bad art . . . brown-jeaned simplicity is infinitely better than broad-clothed degradation . . . better and nobler for them to sing to God across the Southern fields than to dance for rowdies in the Northern halls." [18] Thus at the height of the post-Reconstruction repression, with the Great Migration already under way, Dunbar was urging Negroes to remain in the South, where they could provide a disciplined labor force for the new plantation economy. His only fear was that the stream of young Negro life would continue to flow Northward, a sacrifice to "false ideals and unreal ambitions."

Before dismissing Dunbar as an Uncle Tom, it is well to recall that he was the first Negro author in America who tried seriously to earn a living from his writings. Dependent for his income on the

18. *The Sport of the Gods,* pp. 212–13.

vagaries of the market, he was not overly disposed to challenge the prejudices of his white audience. On a deeper level, his midwestern agrarian values coincided at many points with the anti-industrial bias of the plantation tradition. His horizon was the village. A provincial and a romantic, he was a stranger to the pressing problems of the rising Negro middle class. Escape from industrial civilization is the dominant motif in his writings. Through his dialect verse and his plantation tales, even more than his novels, he sought refuge in the Golden Legend of the South. Nevertheless, despite his narrow social horizons, Dunbar produced one novel, *The Uncalled,* which is superior to the political tracts of his more sophisticated Negro contemporaries.

W. E. B. DuBois

W. E. B. DuBois (1868-1963) was born in Great Barrington, Mass. He was educated at Fisk and Harvard, followed by two years abroad in German universities. Soon after his return to America, DuBois assumed a position of leadership among those who opposed the conciliatory policies of Booker T. Washington. In 1905 he organized the militant Niagara Movement, a forerunner of the National Association for the Advancement of Colored People. DuBois' long career has been divided about evenly between college teaching and the staff of the NAACP. His major publications include three collections of essays, two historical works, a doctoral dissertation in sociology, an autobiography, and two novels, *The Quest of the Silver Fleece* (1911) and *Dark Princess* (1928).

DuBois borrowed the germinal idea for his first novel from Frank Norris. Just as Norris had structured *The Octopus* (1901) and *The Pit* (1903) around the production of wheat, so DuBois employed cotton as a unifying device in *The Quest of the Silver Fleece.* But while Norris used the wheat as a symbol of the vast, impersonal forces which determine the destiny of man, DuBois invaded the cotton belt in order to expose the economic roots of the American caste system. He was an active member of the Socialist party when he wrote *The Quest of the Silver Fleece,*[19] and unlike most of the early novelists, he understood the connection

19. Cf. DuBois' autobiography, *Dusk of Dawn,* p. 235.

between racial oppression and the cotton crop. Unfortunately, his social and economic insights far surpassed his artistic powers.

The structure of the novel is pedagogical rather than truly fictional. It falls naturally into three parts, corresponding to the level of political development of the central characters. In Part I, Bles and Zora labor innocently in a kind of economic Eden, unstained by property relations. In order to provide money for Zora's education, they plant cotton in an unused swamp. Their cotton will be raised in love: "We'll love it into life." Unknown forces are at work, however, which eventually deprive them of the fruits of their labor. When a Southern landowner, under pressure from Northern financiers, robs them of their crop, they begin to comprehend the harsh realities of the plantation economy.

In Part II the scene shifts from the deep South to Washington, D.C. Here the protagonists acquire a sudden sophistication, rising rapidly if unconvincingly to the heights of political power. In the end, however, they despair of finding a remedy for the evils of the plantation system at the level of pressure-group politics in the nation's capital. In Part III, after resuming their burden in the South, Bles and Zora recognize their antagonist in the cotton trust, and in the plantation system which it controls. They try to break its power over the black man by organizing colored sharecroppers into a cooperative settlement. The author's ultimate solution, voiced by a poor-white farmer, is Marxist: "Durned if I don't think these white slaves and black slaves had ought ter git together."

So much for political allegory. The secondary theme of Zora's redemption provides an illuminating insight into the later DuBois of the 1920's. Unlike most early heroines, Zora is dark, almost black in color. A primitive and sensual figure, as the novel opens she dances half naked to a "wondrous, savage music." In contrast to Bles, she hates school and has an easy morality with regard to lying or stealing. Above all, while still a child Zora was forced by Elspeth, her slave mother, to submit to the sexual pleasures of her former master. In a word, Zora represents the moral degradation of the Negro under slavery. After the symbolic death of Elspeth, she is released from the past, and with the help of Bles and a Yankee schoolmistress she makes "a desperate resolve to find some way up toward the light."

If for a moment we imagine the young DuBois as he stepped off the boat after two years of university education abroad, we can begin to appreciate the significance of Zora. Arna Bontemps has described him as a fastidious young man of aristocratic bearing, carrying gloves and a cane, wearing a goatee, and looking for all the world like a white gentleman.[20] What sort of empathy could this young intellectual feel for the black masses who, like Zora, are cursed with the heritage of slavery? Is it not clear, when Bles struggles with his ambivalent feelings for Zora, that DuBois is striving symbolically to embrace the race? Yet DuBois, as we shall see, has important reservations, which are faithfully reproduced in his protagonist: Bles will embrace only a redeemed Zora—a Zora made eminently respectable. The novel thus anticipates DuBois' violent attacks upon the writers of the Harlem School, when they take the unregenerate masses to their bosom.

DuBois' first novel is a literary hybrid. The author has one foot firmly anchored in the Romantic tradition, while with the other he is testing the swirling ideological currents of the early 20th century. Veblen and Norris, Spencer and Darwin, Marx and the muckrakers have all left their mark on the novel. But in spite of its 20th-century intellectual veneer, *The Quest of the Silver Fleece* is written in 19th-century idiom. This schizophrenia is strikingly revealed by a clashing diction, in which such lines as "Bles, almost thou persuadest me" are followed in a few pages by "Hell, I thought you was a man . . . is this a new gag?" It is as if the novelist's new meanings cannot be contained by the old idiom; they strain against it, but it will not yield. The result of this bizarre union is something of a literary monstrosity.

James Weldon Johnson

James Weldon Johnson (1871–1938) was born and raised in Jacksonville, Fla., and educated at Atlanta University. His career reveals a man of remarkable scope and versatility. While still the principal of a public school in Jacksonville, he was admitted to the Florida bar, only to abandon both professions for the bright lights of Broadway. Then, partly in order to have leisure for his literary interests, he accepted political appointments as U.S. Con-

20. Cf. Arna Bontemps, "The Talented Tenth," *Negro Digest,* Dec. 1947.

sul in Venezuela and Nicaragua. From 1916 to 1930 he was a member of the staff of the NAACP, and thereafter was Professor of Creative Literature at Fisk University. In addition to editing an anthology of Negro verse and two collections of spirituals, he is the author of some eight volumes of poems and essays, an autobiography (*Along This Way*, 1933), and a novel, *The Autobiography of an Ex-Colored Man* (1912).

Johnson is the only true artist among the early Negro novelists. His superior craftsmanship is undoubtedly due to his early training in the musical comedy field. As a young man, Johnson formed a very successful partnership with his brother Rosamond, in which he wrote lyrics and librettos for his brother's music. While the two brothers strove primarily to turn their combined talents into popular Broadway hits, they also thought seriously of the implications of their work: "I now began to grope toward a realization of the importance of the American Negro's cultural background and his creative folk-art, and to speculate on the superstructure of conscious art that might be reared upon them."[21] Johnson's seven years as a "conscious artist" in musical comedy proved to be an invaluable apprenticeship. He acquired a skill with words in this exacting medium, and entered a sophisticated world which helped him to attain a cosmopolitan outlook.

The Autobiography of an Ex-Colored Man, simply by virtue of its form, demanded a discipline and restraint hitherto unknown in the Negro novel. It is written in the first person, and as the title indicates it purports to be an autobiography. Johnson, let it be noted, deliberately fostered this illusion by publishing the book anonymously. So well did he succeed in his deception that most of the early reviewers accepted the book at face value. Even after Johnson revealed his identity, he was so beset by readers who thought it was the story of his life that he was forced to write a real autobiography in self-defense.[22]

The narrative structure of the novel consists of a series of episodes which runs the gamut of Negro life in America. The first episode covers the boyhood of the protagonist, in which he learns

21. *Along This Way* (New York, Viking Press, 1933), p. 152.

22. The authorship of the novel was not acknowledged until 1927, when it was re-issued by Knopf.

through a traumatic experience that he is a Negro. After the death of his mother he sets out for Atlanta University, but never reaches his destination because his "inheritance" is stolen. The third episode finds him in a cigar factory in Jacksonville; the fourth, in New York's Negro Bohemia; and the fifth, traveling with a white patron in Europe. Having returned to the rural South, he witnesses a lynching and is driven by shame and fear into the white race. The final episode describes his financial success and his marriage to a white woman.

The theme that runs persistently through this narrative is the moral cowardice of the protagonist. A dramatic tension develops between his boyhood resolve "to be a great colored man" and the tragic flaw which prevents him from realizing this ambition. At every crisis in his life he takes the line of least resistance, allowing circumstance to determine his fate. Rather than confess the loss of his savings to university officials, he abandons college altogether. Just as he is about to marry and establish himself in the trade of cigar-making, the factory in Jacksonville shuts down, and he drifts into New York. Here he slips into an aimless existence, from which he is extricated by a patron who admires his musical talent. In Europe, for the first time in his life he makes a decision of his own, resolving in a remorseful mood to become a great Negro composer. He returns to the South in order to collect folk songs as a basis for his art, but his ambitions in this direction do not survive the sight of a lynching.

In spite of his ironical success as a white businessman, the protagonist is a failure on his own terms. Overpowered by life, he becomes a symbol of man's universal failure to fulfill his highest destiny:

> My love for my children makes me glad that I am what I am and keeps me from desiring to be otherwise; and yet, when I sometimes open a little box in which I still keep my fast yellowing manuscripts, the only tangible remnants of a vanished dream, a dead ambition, a sacrificed talent, I cannot repress the thought that, after all, I have chosen the lesser part, that I have sold my birthright for a mess of pottage.[23]

23. *The Autobiography of an Ex-Colored Man,* p. 142.

Much of the novel's meaning is conveyed by its tone, which is a subtle blend of tragedy and irony. This tone flows naturally from the life of the protagonist, which has both tragic and ironic aspects. When the protagonist plays Beethoven's "Sonata Pathetique" at the end of the first episode, he is summing up the emotional quality of his boyhood. By emphasizing "the two sacred sorrows of [his] life" (the deaths of his mother and wife), he provides a tragic framework for his adult years. He avoids self-pity, however, through an attitude of ironic detachment. At the moment of writing, he can look back upon his life as a wry joke: "And back of it all, I think I find a sort of savage and diabolical desire to gather up all the little tragedies of my life and turn them into a practical joke on society" (p. 9).

Because of his sympathetic portrayal of Bohemian life, Johnson has been widely regarded as a precursor of the Harlem School. It is certainly true that he is the first Negro novelist to show overt sympathy for this aspect of racial life. He champions ragtime music and the cakewalk, for example, as accomplishments of which the race should be proud rather than ashamed. Nevertheless, in terms of the structure of the novel, the Bohemian episode is presented as an evasion of the protagonist's higher responsibility. A transitional figure, Johnson is no Claude McKay; the low-life milieu of the Harlem School is hardly his natural habitat.

Johnson indisputably anticipates the Harlem School by subordinating racial protest to artistic considerations. For the most part, the racial overtones of the novel form an organic part of its aesthetic structure. While in one sense the racial identity of the protagonist is the central fact of his existence, in another, it is almost irrelevant. The protagonist faces a series of situations from which he flees; his flight into the white race is merely the crowning instance of his cowardice. To be sure, his tragedy is heightened because there are good objective reasons for his final flight, but these reasons in no sense constitute a justification. The focus of the novel is not on the objective situation but on the subjective human tragedy.

Compared to the typical propaganda tract of the period, *The Autobiography of an Ex-Colored Man* is a model of artistic detachment. Yet even Johnson cannot wholly repress a desire to educate the white folks. Artificially contrived discussions of the race problem mar the novel, and at times the author is needlessly defensive. But despite an occasional lapse, he retains a basic respect for his function as an artist. He once wrote of Bob Cole, the famous colored vaudeville performer: "In everything he did he strove for the fine artistic effect, regardless of whether it had any direct relation to the Negro or not. Nevertheless, there was an element of pro-Negro propaganda in all his efforts."[24] It is an apt summary of his own career.

The End of an Era

Whatever the shortcomings of the early Negro novelist, at least he displayed a certain vitality in confronting the realities of caste. Toward the end of this period, however, a group of novelists appeared who treat the color line as nonexistent or unimportant. Oscar Micheaux in *The Conquest* (1913) and *The Forged Note* (1915), Henry Downing in *The American Cavalryman* (1917), and Mary Etta Spencer in *The Resentment* (1921) stoutly maintain that there is no barrier to success which diligence and perseverance cannot hurdle. Rather than face the hard facts of caste, these novelists prefer to indulge in crude success-fantasies. They "play white" in their novels in much the same sense as children "play house." Their Negro protagonists are invariably modeled upon white culture-heroes: the Western Pioneer (Micheaux), the Empire Builder (Downing), and the Hog King (Spencer). Their antagonists are not prejudiced whites but rather those "lazy" or "indifferent" members of the race who, in their view, willfully refuse to succeed.

The sudden appearance of these assimilationist authors, who have lost all contact with Negro life and culture, is symptomatic of a broader crisis in the development of the Negro novel. By the beginning of World War I the creative force of the Talented Tenth had been spent. The Victorian tradition, within which the early Negro novel moved and had its being, was disintegrating under the shattering impact of the war. New stirrings were in the air; a new generation was steeling its talent in the crucible

24. *Along This Way,* p. 173.

of war; forces were at work beneath the surface of Negro society which would soon result in a new literary awakening. Meanwhile the Negro novel entered a period of decline, characterized by a sterile tendency toward assimilationism.

In the shadow of the Negro Renaissance let us pause to take stock. On the strictly literary side, the achievement of the early novelist is meager enough. Only two novels—Dunbar's *The Uncalled* and Johnson's *The Autobiography of an Ex-Colored Man*—are worthy of honorable mention. The next generation of Negro novelists found that their literary heritage from the early period was largely negative. It taught them only what pitfalls to avoid. There was a substantial legacy from the early period, however, without which the Negro Renaissance could not have occurred. This legacy was a firm economic base from which a true Negro intelligentsia could evolve. The level of culture which the race had attained by the 1920's was not attained without a struggle. That struggle was the burden and the triumph of the rising Negro middle class.

PART II. *The Discovery of the Folk: 1920–1930*

GETTING down to our native roots and building up from our own people is not savagery. It is culture.

CLAUDE MCKAY

3. *The Background of the Negro Renaissance*

The Great Migration

ALAIN LOCKE has described the Negro Renaissance as "the mass movement of the urban immigration of Negroes, projected on the plane of an increasingly articulate elite." [1] The Great Migration to which Locke refers was the most important event in the history of the American Negro since his emancipation from slavery. In the course of this migration, centuries of historical development were traversed in a few decades. It was not merely a movement of the colored population from South to North, or from country to city; it was the sudden transplanting of a debased feudal folk from medieval to modern America.

From 1890 to 1920, while the business and professional class was fighting for the right to rise, the base of the Negro social pyramid was shifting from a peasantry to an urban proletariat. In these decades more than 2,000,000 Negroes left the farm for the

1. "The Negro's Contribution to American Culture," *Journal of Negro Education,* 8 (1939), 521–29.

factory.[2] As growing numbers of Negro sharecroppers were pushed off the land by erosion and drought, by an exhausted soil, and by the mechanical cotton-picker, they were drawn to the cities by the demands of American industry for cheap labor. Competition from the European immigrant was conveniently eliminated by World War I and by the immigration laws of 1924. At the same time, the war encouraged a vast expansion of American industry, creating a labor market for thousands of black workers. Under these circumstances, the urbanization of the American Negro took place at an unprecedented rate.

The Great Migration brought the Negro masses into contact with the quickened pulse of the modern city. There they were faced with a mass of strange experiences which forced them to revise their traditional ways of thinking. The crowded ghetto, unlike the isolated farm, provided a basis for a vigorous group life. A rising standard of living and better educational opportunities fostered new attitudes of self-respect and independence. In a word, the Negro's urban environment lifted him to a new plane of consciousness. Such a profound transformation could hardly occur among the masses without reverberations in the world of letters. The new group experience called for a new literary movement to interpret it.

It was a foregone conclusion that Harlem should become the center of the new movement. The largest Negro community in the world, Harlem was itself a product of the Great Migration. Doubling its population from 1900 to 1920, it was wrested from the whites by sheer weight of numbers. As it grew to metropolitan proportions, it gradually acquired the character of a race capital. Negroes from Africa and the West Indies, from North and South, and from all classes and backgrounds poured into the crucible of dark Manhattan. Harlem thus provided the Negro artist with an infinite variety of human subjects, as well as an opportunity to observe urban life at its maximum intensity.

Moreover, this black metropolis evolved within the womb of a city which was the literary, musical, and theatrical capital of America. Harlem meant proximity to Broadway, to the little magazines and the big publishing houses, to Greenwich Village and

2. Myrdal, *An American Dilemma,* pp. 191–96.

its white intellectuals, to avant-garde literary groups and successful, established writers. It offered a unique, cosmopolitan milieu, where artists and intellectuals of all kinds could find mutual stimulation. Under the circumstances, it is hardly surprising that Harlem became the cultural center of Negro America.

Rise of an Intelligentsia

Before any group can prosper artistically, as Arthur Koestler notes, it must produce an intelligentsia.[3] This social layer arises in bourgeois society, according to Koestler, when enough gifted individuals have broken with their middle-class background to form a community of emancipated intellectuals. Shortly after World War I just such an intellectual community began to form in Harlem. Young men and women of introspective leanings came to Harlem from every corner of the nation, drawn by the changing kaleidoscope of metropolitan life.

These young intellectuals were a different breed from the Negro writers of the prewar period. Like their contemporaries of the Lost Generation, they reached maturity in a world of crumbling values. "I had no reason to think," wrote Claude McKay, "that the world I lived in was permanent, solid, and unshakable." [4] Lacking the comforting assurance of an integrated moral universe, they were forced to cope as best they could with what Henry Adams called 20th-century multiplicity. Unsure of their positive goals, they began by sweeping aside the moral debris of the previous era. At one stroke they cut through the taboos of the Victorian Age, demolished its shallow optimism, repudiated its value system, and entered the mainstream of contemporary intellectual life.

The significance of the Negro intelligentsia, which emerged for the first time in the 1920's, lay precisely in this realm of values. The middle-class writer, as Koestler suggests, is inclined not toward new hierarchies of values but toward climbing to the top of the existing hierarchy. The intelligentsia, more independent in outlook, debunks existing values and attempts to replace them

3. *The Yogi and the Commissar* (New York, 1945), pp. 61–76.
4. *A Long Way from Home* (New York, Lee Furman, 1937), p. 69.

with values of its own. Koestler's theoretical point may thus serve to sharpen the contrast between the early Negro novelist and his Renaissance successor. The early novelists were loyal members of the middle class who desired only equal rights within the status quo. The younger writers of the 1920's were the second generation of educated Negroes; they were the wayward sons of the rising middle class.[5] In psychological terms, they were rebelling against their fathers and their fathers' way of life.

This pattern of rebellion appears in the lives of many Renaissance authors. Langston Hughes, for example, observes in his autobiography, "My father was what the Mexicans call *muy americano,* a typical American. . . . He was interested only in making money." [6] Hughes' most vivid memory of his father was his constant injunction to hurry up. His father tried to hurry him through a course in bookkeeping and then through Columbia University, but Hughes left college to ship out, taking his Grand Tour on a tramp steamer. Claude McKay's rebellion carried him from Greenwich Village to the Left Bank, and from militant Negro nationalism to the early Communist party. Jean Toomer abandoned a law career for literature and the Gurdjieff Institute. Countee Cullen, whose father was a minister, has recorded his rebellion against religious formalism in his novel *One Way to Heaven.*

The rebellious mood of the emerging Negro intelligentsia is revealed by the little magazines they founded. *The Messenger,* for example, displayed as its credo:

> I am an Iconoclast
> I break the limbs of idols
> And smash the traditions of men.

Fire, according to one of its founders, was intended "to burn up a lot of the old, dead, conventional Negro ideas of the past." In their rebelliousness and defiance the Negro writers of the 1920's were no different from their white contemporaries, who were engaged in a similar labor of destruction in such little magazines as

5. The *parents* of the Renaissance novelists were 55 per cent professionals and 45 per cent white collar (compare 13 per cent and 20 per cent in the early period).

6. *The Big Sea* (New York and London, Knopf, 1940), p. 39.

Broom, *transition*, and *Secession*. The younger Negro intellectuals, whose consciousness was formed during the war years, were members of an uprooted generation. Critical, skeptical, iconoclastic, they raised the banner of the New Negro against the stubborn guardians of the Victorian tradition.

The New Negro Movement

The term "New Negro" presents certain difficulties, for it has been used to describe both a racial attitude and a literary movement. The extension of the term from its original meaning was the work of Alain Locke, who in 1925 published an anthology of younger writers entitled *The New Negro*. The title struck a responsive chord, and it soon became the accepted designation of the new literary movement. From the standpoint of literary history this was unfortunate. "New Negro" is not a descriptive term in any literary sense; basically it indicates a rejection of racial conservatism on the part of those who employ it. It is nonetheless of considerable subjective importance that Renaissance writers should think of themselves as "New Negroes." To establish the primary meaning of the term may therefore cast additional light on the period.

The New Negro, with his uncompromising demand for equal rights, was the end product of a long historical process which began when the Negro middle class emerged from slavery and entered upon a new kind of social relations. As the patriarchal relations of slavery were replaced by the contractual relations of bourgeois society, a corresponding psychological transformation took place. Feudal attitudes of servility and dependence were abandoned in favor of the sturdy bourgeois virtues of initiative and self-reliance. This psychological transformation crystallized politically when DuBois challenged the "accommodating" leadership of Booker T. Washington in the name of universal manhood suffrage. Manhood suffrage, the basic aim of DuBois' Niagara Movement, became a symbol of the new spirit which animated the Negro middle class. This sense of manhood, greatly enhanced by the Negro's participation in World War I, was passed on to the Renaissance generation as part of its spiritual heritage.

There is a direct line from the Niagara Movement of the early 1900's to the New Negro Movement of the 1920's. The descent may be traced through Negro defense organizations such as the NAACP and the National Urban League, and more precisely through their house organs, *Crisis* and *Opportunity*. These two periodicals and their editors, Jessie Fauset and Charles S. Johnson, did yeoman's work for the Negro Renaissance. They encouraged new talent, opened their pages to young writers, and offered cash prizes for outstanding literary achievement. In this manner, as well as through overt patronage, the Negro middle class made a substantial contribution to the birth of the New Negro Movement. Whether they were prepared to acknowledge the lusty and sometimes ungrateful infant which they sired is another matter.

As the Negro Renaissance gained momentum and its break with the tradition of Chesnutt and Dunbar became apparent, the term "New Negro" began to take on an additional connotation of modernism. As a result, it became intellectually fashionable to declare oneself a member of the New Negro coterie. Yet if the New Negro slogan created something of a vogue, it also provided the literary movement of the 1920's with a unifying idea. "New Negro" literary societies sprang up in several large cities; [7] New Negro magazines were founded by avant-garde writers; and one novelist playfully christened his first-born "the New Negro"! This self-consciousness, this sense of belonging to a movement, made for a high group morale, and for an atmosphere which encouraged literary effort. Moreover, in its own way the New Negro Movement expressed that determination to ring out the old and ring in the new which was the central theme of the decade.

Cultural Collaboration in the Jazz Age

The years following World War I were marked by a sudden upsurge of interest in Negro life and culture among the white intelligentsia. Manifestations of this interest were numerous and

7. The Writers' Guild, New York; Black Opals, Philadelphia; The Saturday Evening Quill Club, Boston; The Ink-Slingers, Los Angeles; Book and Bench, Topeka, Kansas, etc.

varied. Throughout the 1920's books on the Negro by white authors appeared in ever-increasing numbers. *Survey Graphic* came out with an issue devoted entirely to Harlem, while Albert and Charles Boni offered a prize of $1,000 for the best novel written by an American Negro. Musical reviews which featured Negro performers broke downtown box-office records, and nightly throngs of white "tourists" invaded Harlem, drawn to night club and cabaret by colored celebrities of musical and theatrical fame. By the mid-1920's the Negro had become a national pastime.

What had happened to change the intellectual climate from hostility and indifference to sympathetic, if often misguided, interest? For one thing the Jazz Age, which derived its very character from the Negro's music, was in full swing. With "flaming youth" leading the way, a popular uprising was in progress against the stuffiness and artificial restraint of the Victorian era. These were the years of postwar catharsis—of Freud and the sexual revolution, of heavy drinking in defiance of authority, of a wild dance called the Charleston, and of a wilder music which made its way from the bordellos of New Orleans to the night clubs of Chicago and New York. Somewhat to his surprise and not entirely to his liking, the Negro suddenly found himself called upon to uphold a new stereotype: he became a symbol of that freedom from restraint for which the white intellectual longed so ardently.

In the sophisticated art centers of Europe and America, interest in the Negro focused around the cult of the primitive. Insofar as it idealizes simpler cultures, primitivism is a romantic retreat from the complexities of modern life. Reflecting the writings of Sigmund Freud, it exalts instinct over intellect, Id over Super-Ego, and is thus a revolt against the Puritan spirit. For such an artistic movement the Negro had obvious uses: he represented the unspoiled child of nature, the noble savage—carefree, spontaneous, and sexually uninhibited. The discovery of primitive African sculpture and the ascendancy of jazz reinforced the development of this new stereotype.

Like all previous stereotypes, that of the primitive Negro exercised a coercive effect on the Negro novelist. As in the past, the degree of accommodation was astonishing; with few exceptions the Negro intelligentsia accepted this exotic image of themselves. Perhaps they found in primitivism a useful support for the cultural dualism which they espoused during the Renaissance period. In any event, the younger Negro writers were quite carried away. Langston Hughes wrote ecstatically of jazz as "the tom-tom of revolt," while Countee Cullen discovered "elemental" religion in a Harlem revival meeting. Claude McKay glorified the instinctive Negro in all of his novels, and proudly proclaimed the "primitive sexuality" of the Negro race. Jean Toomer, perhaps the most authentic exponent of Renaissance primitivism, wrote in a sophisticated vein of "the zoo-restrictions and keeper-taboos" of modern civilization.

Whatever its excesses, primitivism provided the common ground for a fruitful period of cultural collaboration. Works like Eugene O'Neill's *The Emperor Jones* (1920) and *All God's Chillun Got Wings* (1924), Waldo Frank's *Holiday* (1923), Sherwood Anderson's *Dark Laughter* (1925), Dubose Heyward's *Porgy* (1925) and *Mamba's Daughters* (1927), and Carl Van Vechten's *Nigger Heaven* (1926), acted as a spur to Negro writers and created a sympathetic audience for the serious treatment of Negro subjects. Personal association with white authors meant an end of cultural isolation and provincialism, and an immense gain in technical maturity for the Negro writer. In economic terms alone, considerable patronage and sponsorship occurred, while publishing forts and editorial desks capitulated in the face of a growing market for novels of Negro life. In the forefront of these developments, consciously promoting this cultural exchange, was a white *littérateur* named Carl Van Vechten.

Van Vechten's role in furthering the Negro Renaissance was unique. His literary salons provided a warm atmosphere in which artists and intellectuals of both races could break down their taboos against personal association. His one-man "know the Negro" campaign was eminently successful in overcoming prejudice and awkwardness among his white contemporaries. His efforts on behalf of individual Negro writers and artists were indefatigable, and were amply rewarded in later years when many of his former protégés entrusted their literary effects to his care.[8]

8. Most of this material is presently housed in the James Weldon Johnson Collection of Negro Arts and Letters at Yale University.

A more questionable contribution, at least in the eyes of some Negro critics, was Van Vechten's *Nigger Heaven,* a novel which appeared in 1926 and quickly ran through several editions. Emphasizing the bawdy and exotic aspects of Harlem life, and heavily influenced by primitivistic conceptions, *Nigger Heaven* shattered the complacency of the Negro intelligentsia by threatening to steal their literary thunder. For most of the Negro middle class the title of the novel was enough. Bitterly attacked in some quarters as a slander against the race, *Nigger Heaven* has been ably defended by James Weldon Johnson,[9] and requires no apologia here. It is sufficient to acknowledge its role in creating an audience for the exotic novel of Harlem life, and its influence on certain members of the so-called Harlem School.

The influence of white intellectuals on the Negro Renaissance ought not to be overestimated. Some Negro critics have charged the New Negro Movement with white domination, but a sober appraisal leaves no doubt of its indigenous character. The New Negro Movement was not a "vogue" initiated by white "literary faddists," [10] but a serious attempt by the Negro artist to interpret his own group life. There were excesses, to be sure, for which the whites must bear their share of responsibility. Insofar as the Negro novelist adopted a pose in response to the "primitive" effusions of the white intellectual, it produced a certain shallowness in his work, and a legitimate suspicion that his novels, like his cabarets, were designed to entertain the white folks. In the long run, however, the Negro novelist outgrew his primitive phase; meanwhile it helped him to discover unsuspected values in his own folk culture.

The Essence of the Negro Renaissance

There is a phase in the growth of a derivative literature which corresponds to the adolescent rebellion in an individual—a time when it must cut loose from the parent literature and establish an independent existence. This phase occurred in American litera-

9. See *Along This Way,* pp. 381–82.

10. See Hugh Gloster, "The Van Vechten Vogue," *Negro Voices in American Fiction,* pp. 157–73.

ture during the flowering of New England; it was highlighted by Emerson's famous Phi Beta Kappa address, in which he protests, "We have listened too long to the courtly Muses of Europe." The Negro Renaissance represents a similar impulse toward cultural autonomy on the part of the American Negro.

The Negro Renaissance was essentially a period of self-discovery, marked by a sudden growth of interest in things Negro. The Renaissance thus reversed the assimilationist trend of the prewar period, with its conscious imitation of white norms and its deliberate suppression of "racial" elements. The motivation for this sudden reversal was not primarily literary but sociological. The Negro Renaissance, as E. Franklin Frazier has observed, reflects a pattern of adjustment common to all ethnic minorities in America: "At first the group attempts to lose itself in the majority group, disdaining its own characteristics. When this is not possible, there is a new valuation placed upon these very same characteristics, and they are glorified in the eyes of the group."[11]

The discovery of autonomous "racial" values by the Renaissance generation was prompted by a wave of Negro nationalism which swept over the colored community in the wake of World War I. As a direct result of his war experience the American Negro became bitterly disillusioned with the promises of the white majority. Discrimination in the armed forces, brutal attacks on returning veterans, and the bloody riots of the summer of 1919 convinced the Negro that his sacrifices for the nation would be acknowledged only by renewed oppression. With every avenue of assimilation apparently closed, a strongly nationalistic reflex occurred on all levels of Negro society.

Among the Negro masses this reflex took the form of recruitment to Marcus Garvey's "Back to Africa" movement. Garvey's program, in spite of its utterly Utopian content, deserves the closest scrutiny, for it stirred the imagination of the Negro masses as never before or since.[12] Garvey held that the Negro must re-

11. "Racial Self-Expression," *Ebony and Topaz* (1927), pp. 119–21 (special supplement to *Opportunity*).

12. The numerical strength of the Garvey movement has been estimated at one to four million.

nounce all hope of assistance or understanding from American whites, leave the country, and build a new civilization in Africa. His secessionist movement preyed upon a dissatisfaction so deep that it amounted to despair of ever achieving a full life in America. His immense popularity stands as a sober warning to all who would underestimate the nationalism of the Negro masses.

Meanwhile the logic of events forced the Negro middle class to adopt what might be called a tactical nationalism. As the fluid patterns of the post-Reconstruction period hardened into a rigid and unyielding color line, it became increasingly clear to the Talented Tenth that they could never hope to breach this caste barrier as a special class of "white" Negroes. The war years in particular convinced them that they could not succeed short of an all-out assault on Jim Crow. Abandoning their former strategy, they turned to the Negro masses for support in the coming struggle.

This *rapprochement* with the black masses could not be consummated without great psychological effort. The habit of emphatically differentiating themselves from the "lower classes" was not easily relinquished by the Talented Tenth. Race leaders perceived at once that they would have to cultivate a mild nationalism in order to achieve a decent show of racial solidarity. One of their number, Jessie Fauset, has preserved this insight for posterity in her novel *Plum Bun:*

> Those of us who have forged forward are not able as yet to go our separate ways apart from the unwashed, untutored herd. We must still look back and render service to our less fortunate, weaker brethren. And the first step toward making this a workable attitude is the acquisition not so much of a racial love as a racial pride. A pride that enables us to find our own beautiful and praiseworthy, an intense chauvinism that is content with its own types, that finds completeness within its own group, that loves its own as the French love their country.[13]

The nationalist reflex of the Negro intelligentsia consisted of a withdrawal of allegiance from the values of the dominant cul-

13. *Plum Bun* (1928), p. 218.

ture, and a search for alternative values within their own tradition. Unlike the nationalism of the masses or of the middle class, that of the intelligentsia was not based on racial considerations alone. It was motivated by factors larger than, but including, race—factors related to the universal revolt of the modern artist from bourgeois civilization. The Negro intellectual of the 1920's shared fully in the spiritual alienation of the Lost Generation. Like the white expatriate, he rejected the chromium plate of American culture. His alienation as an artist caused him in turn to alter his goals as a Negro. Instead of advocating blind assimilation into a hopelessly materialistic culture, he began to think in terms of preserving his racial individuality.

The search for a distinctive tradition led in many directions. The alienated Negro intellectual fell back predominantly on the folk culture, with its antecedents in slavery, its roots in the rural South, and its final flowering on the city pavements. Where the folk culture seemed inadequate to his needs, he turned to the cult of African origins, and to primitivism. At the same time, a new concept of the Negro's manifest destiny arose, to replace the old faith in race progress. Along with a sophisticated critique of (white) European civilization, the thesis was advanced that certain enduring qualities in the racial temperament would redeem the decadent and enervated West. The sum and substance of these explorations was an unequivocal cultural dualism—a conscious attempt to endow Negro literature with a life of its own, apart from the dominant literary tradition.

The frank espousal of cultural dualism by the Negro intelligentsia was viewed with great alarm by the Negro middle class, whose long-range strategy called for eradicating cultural differences. Even at the peak of Renaissance nationalism the middle-class writer could never muster more than token enthusiasm for a distinctive Negro culture. The issues posed by cultural dualism therefore divided the novelists of the period into two schools. The Harlem School, pursuing the nationalist impulse to its logical conclusion, turned to the black masses for literary material. The Old Guard, still intent upon portraying "respectable" Negroes, remained prisoners of the Genteel Tradition.

4. *The Harlem School*

THOSE Negro writers of the 1920's who did not shrink from the implications of cultural dualism found that it altered their art in several important respects. To begin with, whatever is distinctively Negro is likely to be of folk, if not of slave, origin. The Harlem School therefore turned to the folk for their major characters and a low-life milieu for their principal setting. Langston Hughes has preserved the flavor of this development: "But then there are the lowdown folks, and they are the majority—may the Lord be praised! The people who have their nip of gin on Saturday nights and are not too important to themselves or the community. Their religion soars to a shout. Work maybe a little today, rest a little tomorrow. Play awhile. Sing awhile. O, let's dance!" [1]

In the second place, whatever is culturally distinctive has been exaggerated to the point of caricature by ignorant and prejudiced whites. Cultural dualism therefore involves characterizations

1. "The Negro Artist and the Racial Mountain," *Nation, 122* (1926), 692–94.

which run dangerously close to the stereotype. The Harlem School faced this issue squarely, by insisting on their artistic prerogatives. It was up to a mature audience, in their view, to distinguish between a dialect farce by Octavus Roy Cohen and a dialect interpretation by a serious writer, designed to achieve a greater literary realism. The Harlem School had simply outgrown what Alain Locke has called "the pathetic over-compensations of a group inferiority complex." Their bold defiance of the stereotype was a refreshing change from the lifeless, "exemplary" characterization of the prewar novel.

Thirdly, the corollary of a distinctive culture is a distinctive language. Beginning with the Harlem School, the linguistic texture of the Negro novel has been greatly influenced by the rhythms and inflections of Negro speech, and especially by jive, the colorful argot of the urban Negro. The certain mark of the Harlem School, for example, are the terms "ofay" (white man) and "dickty" (high-toned Negro). In the early Negro novel a "professor" was a school teacher (inflated achievement); in the Harlem School novel a "professor" is strictly the third party to a rickety piano and a precarious glass of beer. Even in the 1920's jive had developed to a point where one novelist felt compelled to add a "Glossary of Contemporary Harlemese" to his work, in order to make himself intelligible to a mixed audience.

Finally, the Harlem School was more interested in interpreting Negro culture than in pleading the cause of racial justice. Having affirmed the existence of a distinctive Negro culture, they chose to write novels of Negro life rather than novels dealing with relations between the races. Racial tension, though present, is a muted note in the Renaissance novel. Renaissance Harlem is a place of love and laughter, not of struggle and oppression. By insisting that the novel is an art form and not primarily an instrument of racial protest the Harlem School broke cleanly with a long tradition of overt propaganda and moral appeal. This conscious abandonment of "protest" literature freed the Negro novelist from a false conception of racial loyalty which has constantly threatened to strangle his art.

In the last analysis it was a distinctly "racial" atmosphere which gave the Harlem School its revolutionary character. It was not so much that these writers formed a literary coterie in Harlem, nor even that Harlem was a favorite setting for their novels, but rather that a Harlemesque *quality* permeated their work. In the best instances this quality was more than an exotic veneer; it expressed a unique and partially non-Western way of life. The Harlem School, in a word, discovered the advantages of straddling two worlds. These advantages may seem more tangible after a concrete discussion of the novels.

Claude McKay

Claude McKay has been called *l'enfant terrible* of the Negro Renaissance. Proud of his identification with the black masses and contemptuous of all things middle class, he led a successful revolt against the sanctimonious literary treatment of the Negro. "There was never any presentation more ludicrous," he maintained. McKay writes mockingly of "educated Negroes, ashamed of their race's intuitive love of color, wrapping themselves up in respectable gray." In his own work he exalts all that is colorful and distinctive in the Negro's cultural heritage. His insistence on legitimate differences is typical of the Renaissance generation.

McKay (1889–1948) was born in Jamaica, of prosperous peasant stock. He received his early education from a "freethinking" elder brother, and came to the United States in 1912 to complete his schooling at Tuskegee Institute and the University of Kansas. After two years of college, however, he kicked over the traces: "The spirit of the vagabond, the daemon of some poets, had got hold of me." Thereafter McKay spent his working life among the masses, and his intellectual life in Bohemian and radical circles. Harlem, London, Berlin, Paris, Marseilles, Morocco, and Moscow were his haunts. His intellectual interests, which were equally transient, carried him from the Irish Renaissance to the Russian Revolution, and from the writings of Tolstoy and Gandhi to Roman Catholicism. With the appearance of *Harlem Shadows* (1922), a book of verse, McKay became a major figure in the Negro Renaissance. His publications include three volumes of poems, a collection of short stories, a book on Harlem, an autobiography (*A Long Way from Home*), and three novels.

McKay's first novel, *Home to Harlem* (1928), was an immediate popular success. Like many novels of the 1920's, it opens with a farewell to arms. Jake, the central character, goes AWOL from the white folks' war and comes "home to Harlem." He picks up a "tantalizing brown" for $50, but she returns his money as a gift, after leaving him during the night. The plot, which is little more than a device, concerns his attempt to find her again. The narrative structure is loose and vagrant, tracing Jake's movements from cabaret to "rent party," from poolroom to gin mill, from the docks to the dining car. McKay depends upon atmosphere to carry the book. The style is appropriately impressionistic, full of hyphenated adjectives aimed at vivid impressions of Harlem life.

The beginnings of a dramatic structure may be seen, however, in the characters of Jake and Ray. Jake represents pure instinct. Physical well-being—whether from good food, good liquor, or a good woman—is his prime value. Work when you feel like it. Loaf when the mood strikes you. Take life easy. Joy is the key word in understanding Jake; lust is a sign of repression: "Gambling did not have a strangle-hold upon him any more than dope or desire did. Jake took what he wanted of whatever he fancied and . . . kept on going."[2] Through Jake, McKay strikes at the heart of the Protestant ethic. Jake's very existence is an act of affirmation, an injunction to enjoy life!

Ray is a young Haitian, consumed with a desire to write, whom Jake befriends on his railroad run. Ray embodies the dilemma of the inhibited, overcivilized intellectual. A misfit in the white man's civilization, he refuses to be penned in "like bank clerks in steel-wire cages." Yet he is unable, like Jake, to entrust himself wholly to instinct. For Ray, "Thought is suffering"—the opposite of joy. He is depressed by the state of contemporary society, which he describes as "the vast international cemetery of this century." His is that profound disgust which modern life sometimes evokes in men of artistic sensibilities.

Through a faulty denouement, the symbolic import of Jake and Ray is imperfectly conveyed. Ray, disgusted with all that is sordid and ugly in the lives of the dining-car waiters, ships out on a freighter bound for Europe. Jake, in the closing pages of

2. *Home to Harlem,* p. 269.

the novel, finds his lost Felice, whose name signifies joy. By contrasting Jake's happiness with Ray's restless wandering, McKay attempts to convey the superiority of instinct over reason. But at bottom, Jake and Ray represent different ways of rebelling against Western civilization. Jake rebels instinctively, while Ray's rebellion occurs on an intellectual plane. Both characters acquire a broader significance only through their negative relationship to contemporary society. McKay's failure to develop this relationship is the failure of the novel.

Jake is the typical McKay protagonist—the primitive Negro, untouched by the decay of Occidental civilization. The validity of this symbol, however, depends upon McKay's view of contemporary life. Since the author cannot take this view for granted, he introduces himself into the novel as Ray, in order to expound it. But Ray hardly helps matters; in *Home to Harlem* he does little more than state his prejudices. As a result, the novel is left without a suitable antagonist. Jake and Ray are vivid enough, but what they would deny is not always clear. The novel, unable to develop its primary conflict, bogs down in the secondary contrast between Jake and Ray.

In *Banjo* (1929), the sequel of *Home to Harlem*, McKay comes closer to realizing his central theme. He is moving slowly toward the finished form which he finally achieves in *Banana Bottom*. The setting of *Banjo* has shifted from Harlem to the waterfront at Marseilles, but the main symbols are the same. Jake's role is played by Banjo, an irrepressible, joy-loving vagabond, while Ray is present once more to act as interpreter.

Part I presents the milieu and introduces the main character. The Ditch, familiar name for Marseilles' waterfront section, makes the setting of *Home to Harlem* seem like a Victorian drawing room. Hoboes, panhandlers, pimps, prostitutes, sailors on shore leave, syphilitics, and beachcombers are its chief inhabitants. In the midst of this international flophouse lives Banjo with his "beach boys," from whom he hopes to fashion a jazz band. Part II witnesses the fulfillment of this ambition, as Banjo and his boys play "Stay, Carolina, Stay!" in a local bistro: "It was perhaps the nearest that Banjo, quite unconscious of it, ever came to an aesthetic realization of his orchestra." After a description of the breakup of the band and the subsequent troubles of the beach boys, Part III moves rapidly toward a denouement when Ray decides to cast his lot with "the Jakes and Banjoes of this world."

Ray editorializes freely throughout the novel, and from his lengthy discourses we can reconstruct McKay's indictment of European civilization. To begin with, Western society harbors against the colored man a not-so-blind prejudice, which is "controlled by the exigencies of the white man's business." Commercialism is the canker which is destroying the soul of the West. Hypocrisy is its handmaiden—a pious pose of patriotism, Christianity, and sexual purity which cloaks colonialism, economic rapacity, and bawdiness. An unwholesome attitude toward sex is warping the personality of "civilized" man: "Terrible is their world that creates disasters and catastrophes from simple natural incidents." Finally, a sterile trend toward standardization and conformity threatens to destroy the rich cultural diversity exemplified by such minorities as the Jews, the Irish, and the American Negro.

In dramatizing his indictment of Western civilization, McKay relies too heavily on Ray's rhetoric, but he also gropes toward a fictional presentation. The American steamship company named the Dollar Line, the brutality of the French police toward the beach boys, and a pornographic film of the "Blue Cinema" variety, help him to make his point. The French chauffeur, who intends to buy a suburban lot from his proceeds as a pimp, is a symbol of bourgeois respectability founded on sordid commercialism. The setting of the novel is likewise symbolic. Marseilles is the chief port of Mediterranean commerce and the crossroads of Europe and Africa. Its waterfront district provides a worm's-eye view of European civilization. But these scattered symbols can never replace successful characterization. Even in *Banjo,* McKay's antagonist remains an abstraction.

The protagonist of the novel, however, succeeds as both character and symbol. Convincing as a person, Banjo takes on additional depth, until in the end he comes to stand for a way of life. McKay expects us to see beyond the Ditch to the positive values which Banjo embodies. A careless attitude toward money is central to these values. "Them's all sous-crazy, these folkses," Banjo says of the French. He plays jazz for fun, not for the commercial motives of the white musicians. He knows how to laugh, how to love, how to enjoy life in the carefree manner of the vagabond. Above all, he is a folk artist—a symbol of the Negro's inventiveness and creativity. His nickname and his instrument link him to the world of jazz, with all its connotations of impudence, freedom from restraint, spontaneous improvisation, and defiance of everything drab and respectable.

In seeking values to oppose to those of bourgeois society, McKay falls back upon a separate Negro culture. Banjo's devotion to "nigger music," the beach boys' gift of language, which Ray calls "their rich reservoir of niggerisms," and Ray's more sophisticated interest in African folk tales and primitive African sculpture are obvious manifestations of McKay's Negro nationalism. It follows from McKay's position that he must resist assimilation into the dominant culture. In all of his novels he bitterly attacks the mulatto middle class for its "imitativeness." The lower-class Negro's stubborn resistance to assimilation is the true theme of *Banjo:*

> "That this primitive child, this kinky-headed, big-laughing black boy of the world, did not go down and disappear under the serried crush of trampling white feet; that he managed to remain on the scene, not worldly wise, not "getting there," yet not machine-made nor poor-in-spirit like the regimented creatures of civilization was baffling to civilized understanding. . . . He was a challenge to civilization itself." [3]

McKay poses the central conflict in these terms: black vagabond vs. white civilization. At this point, however, the novel breaks down. Although the author intends a decisive rejection of "civilization" in favor of "Banjo," he cannot dramatize it successfully through the character of Ray. At the end of the novel Ray joins Banjo in the vagabond life. But Ray, who is more the child of modern civilization than he would care to admit, can never be a Banjo. His intellect is too great a barrier. For Ray no decisive choice is possible, but only a more or less unsatisfactory compromise: "Ray wanted to hold on to his intellectual acquire-

3. *Banjo,* p. 314.

ments without losing his instinctive gifts. The black gifts of laughter and melody and simple sensuous feelings and responses" (pp. 322–23). The novel thus slips out of a clear-cut dualism into a fuzzy dialectical structure—*thesis,* white civilization; *antithesis,* Banjo; *synthesis,* Ray.

Banana Bottom (1933) represents the culmination of McKay's search for a form. Cultural dualism is his central theme, and for its most successful expression he turns to his native Jamaica. Here the folk culture is more developed, and the clash between "native" and European values sharper. McKay has dispensed with Ray and achieved a proper distance between himself and his novel. The Craigs, a white missionary couple, are his first successful personification of Anglo-Saxon civilization. In Bita, their protégé, McKay has at last found his protagonist. Jake and Banjo, while they embodied McKay's values, were static characters. Ray, being an intellectual, was limited in his powers of renunciation. But Bita is a peasant girl, educated by white missionaries. Caught between two cultures, she is yet free to return to the folk.

The novel opens with the story of Bita's seduction by an idiot boy, at age twelve. Two different responses to this "tragedy" immediately set the stage for the deep cultural cleavage with which the novel deals. The Craigs adopt Bita and help her to overcome her "shame"; but Sister Phibby expresses an opposing view: "Although she thought it was a sad thing as a good Christian should, her wide brown face betrayed a kind of primitive satisfaction in a good thing done early." [4]

After being educated in England by her benefactors, Bita returns to assist them with their missionary work. She soon becomes restless under the regimen of the Mission, and a struggle ensues between the gentle domination of the Craigs and Bita's desire to be herself. On the one side is the Christ God, the Calvinist austerity, and the naive ethnocentrism of the Mission. On the other is the Obeah God, the primitive sexuality, and the simple values of the folk culture. Bita's choice is in the best Renaissance spirit: "I thank God that although I was brought up and educated among white people, I have never wanted to be anything but myself. I take pride in being coloured and different.

4. *Banana Bottom,* p. 15.

. . . I can't imagine anything more tragic than people torturing themselves to be different from their natural unchangeable selves" (p. 169).

McKay uses sex as the chief means of dramatizing his theme. He understands that the major conflicts in a woman's life will be sexual, and that Bita's struggle with the Craigs will naturally assume this form. Bita rebels against her guardians by forming an attachment to a fun-loving, irresponsible scamp named Hopping Dick. In order to prevent her from backsliding, the Craigs try to arrange a marriage with a respectable young divinity student. Much to their consternation, the prospective bridegroom puts himself out of the running by defiling himself with a goat. Encouraged by her moral victory, Bita goes her own way, and the novel reaches a climax when she participates in an atavistic dance ritual. Since Hopping Dick is not a marrying man, Bita eventually settles down with Jubban, a sturdy black peasant, whose child she conceives during their engagement.

Sterling Brown has described *Banana Bottom* as a quiet story, quietly told. The novel moves at the leisurely pace of the life which it portrays. Its tone is tranquil, in contrast to the tumultuous quality of McKay's earlier novels. Ray's tirades are gone, along with the hyphenated adjectives which McKay formerly employed to present a panorama of urban life. He strives instead for a simplicity of style suited to his pastoral setting. Much of the novel is devoted to exotic descriptions of Jamaican peasant life. Partly ornamental, these scenes are also functional in revealing the beauty of the life which Bita embraces.

Although much of the tension in McKay's work derives from his Negro nationalism, it would be a mistake to conclude that his rejection of bourgeois society is based solely, or even primarily, on his experience as a Negro. McKay drew freely on his broader cultural heritage, and participated widely in the intellectual currents of his day.[5] His social realism comes from the Dickens-Tolstoy-Zola tradition, his sense of satire from Shaw, Ibsen, and Anatole France. His emphasis on sex reflects his reading of Sherwood Anderson and D. H. Lawrence. Strongly influenced by

5. For acknowledged influences on Ray's intellectual development see *Home to Harlem*, pp. 225 ff.

Marxism, for a time he was associate editor of the *Liberator* under Max Eastman. In Paris he mingled freely with the cosmopolitan expatriates, from whom he discovered his basic affinity for Expressionism. Expressionism exerted a strong influence on most of the Parisian art colony of the early 20th century. At the core of the movement was a deep sense of alienation from modern society: to renew its waning vitality, art must turn from a decadent sophistication to the unspoiled outpourings of primitive man. Influenced by Freud and the new psychology, the movement exalted emotion over intellect, and in its extreme form (Dada) advocated the uninhibited expression of personal emotion, even at the sacrifice of intelligibility. As a result of this sudden enthusiasm for primitivism, the Negro—or rather an imaginary facsimile thereof—became an object of the white man's admiration and envy. Picasso discovered primitive African sculpture; Hugues Panassié introduced Europe to jazz; and authors like Gertrude Stein and E. E. Cummings made literary history with their characterizations of primitive Negroes.

None of this glorification of things Negro was lost upon a young writer of Claude McKay's temperament. It is a short step from Gertrude Stein's *Melanctha* with its central conflict between instinct and reason, to the characters of Jake and Ray. It is an even shorter step from Cummings' Jean le Nègre to McKay's Banjo. *The Enormous Room* (1922) and *Banjo* (1929) contain striking parallels, in both theme and situation. There is the same sordid environment with its "delectable (human) mountains"; the same senseless bureaucratic oppression by the French government; and the same uncorrupted primitives who resist integration into a degenerate society. Nor is it a matter of proving "influence"—these authors simply shared the same myth.

In the last analysis Expressionism is a form of escape. McKay anticipates his own spiritual flight when he writes of Ray: "Some day he would escape from the clutches of that magnificent monster of civilization and retire behind the natural defenses of his island, where the steam-roller of progress could not reach him." [6] *Banana Bottom* is McKay's romantic escape from the machine age, and his symbolic link with the Expressionists. Like Gauguin,

6. *Home to Harlem,* p. 155.

the founder of French Expressionism who sought inspiration in the South Seas, McKay found artistic fulfillment in his novel of West Indian peasant life. If McKay's spiritual journey carried him "a long way from home," in the end he returned to his native island.

Langston Hughes

In the summer of 1926, the *Nation* carried an article which was widely acclaimed as the literary manifesto of the New Negro. The main burden of the article was an attack on assimilationism. The writer urged the Negro artist to make full use of the colorful, distinctive material at his disposal, and to avoid the example of a Negro society woman who enthusiastically attended recitals of Andalusian folk songs but wouldn't be seen dead at a Bessie Smith recital of the blues. After calling upon the Negro artist to interpret the beauty of his own people, the article closed with a ringing declaration of independence: "We younger Negro artists who create now intend to express our individual dark-skinned selves without fear or shame. If white people are pleased, we are glad. If they are not, it doesn't matter. . . . If colored people are pleased, we are glad. If they are not, their displeasure doesn't matter either." The author of this manifesto was a young writer named Langston Hughes.[7]

The importance of Hughes as a literary figure far transcends that of his only novel, *Not without Laughter* (1930). Primarily a poet, his verse was influenced thematically by the social realism of Lindsay, Masters, and Sandburg, and technically by the rhythms of jazz. His first two volumes of poems, *The Weary Blues* (1926) and *Fine Clothes to the Jew* (1927), provoked a fierce controversy because of their forthright and sympathetic treatment of lower-class Negro life. Hughes, perhaps more than any other author, knows and loves the Negro masses. His newspaper sketches of Jess B. Semple,[8] an unlettered but philosophical Harlemite (just be simple), are among his finest literary creations. A

7. "The Negro Artist and the Racial Mountain," *Nation*, pp. 692–94.

8. Appearing originally in the *Chicago Defender*, these sketches were collected and published as *Simple Speaks His Mind*, Simon and Schuster, 1950.

prolific author, Hughes has published some seven volumes of verse, two collections of short stories, an autobiography, a book for children, and several plays, librettos, translations, radio skits, and magazine articles.

Not without Laughter deals with the childhood of a colored youth in a small midwestern town. The plot consists of Sandy's early experiences with school and work, with sex and race, and with his family, the major formative influence in his life. His grandmother, Aunt Hager, is a humble religious woman who has raised three daughters by taking in washing. Harriet, the youngest, is pleasure-seeking, rebellious, and bitterly resentful of racial injustice. Her secular values clash sharply with the religious zeal of her mother. Tempy, who has married well, is a social climber and a refugee from everything "niggerish." Anjee, Sandy's mother, lives from day to day between visits from her wandering husband, the guitar-plucking, blues-singing Jimboy.

Laughter is the central symbol of the novel—the complex, ironic laughter which is the Negro's saving response to racial oppression. The characters cluster around the poles of laughter and not-laughter. Jimboy and Harriet, with their low-down blues and comical dances, are the hub of laughter in Aunt Hager's household. Anjee, too, must be near laughter (Jimboy), at whatever cost. Hager and Tempy, for different reasons, represent the forces of sobriety. Hager's religion requires her to regard laughter as sinful, while for Tempy, laughter is an inexcusable digression from the serious business of accumulating property. Unfortunately, Sandy disrupts the symbolic unity of the novel. Presumably torn by the conflicting forces which divide the family, his inner struggle fails to materialize. There is no laughter in his life, but only an altogether commendable determination to be a credit to the race. At this point, the novel bogs down in hopeless ideological confusion.

The author sets out to make a defense of laughter. To those like Tempy who claim that Negroes remain poor because of their dancing and singing and easy laughter, Hughes replies: "The other way 'round would be better; dancers because of their poverty; singers because they suffered; laughing all the time because they must forget." [9] Such a view of laughter rests on the assumption that "achievement," at least for the Negro masses, is largely illusory, and that some form of compensatory self-expression is therefore necessary. But it is precisely on this point that Hughes is most ambivalent. If he defends laughter, he also defends achievement: "I wants you to be a great man, son." "I won't disappoint you, Aunt Hager." At the end of the novel, Sandy returns to school to fulfill his grandmother's dream.

In short, Hughes tried to reject the Protestant ethic (joy is wrong), while retaining the success drive on which it is based. It is an untenable halfway house, which Claude McKay and Jessie Fauset would equally scorn to occupy. In any event, Hughes' ideological ambivalence has disastrous aesthetic consequences. The novel and its main character simply part company. Instead of supporting the defense-of-laughter theme, Sandy emerges as a symbol of racial advancement, which is hardly a laughing matter. Given his main theme of suffering and self-expression, Hughes might better have written the novel around Harriet, who emerges from a life of prostitution to become "Princess of the Blues."

Not without Laughter has been compared in some quarters to the first book of the *Studs Lonigan* trilogy. No service is rendered either to American literature or to Hughes by this exaggerated claim. A mediocre novel, *Not without Laughter* was undertaken before its author was prepared to meet the rigorous requirements of the genre. Ideologically confused and structurally defective, the novel gives a final impression of sprawling formlessness. The author, to his credit, is fully aware of these shortcomings, if some of his frendly critics are not. In his autobiography, *The Big Sea* (1940), Hughes makes a courageous apology to the characters of his early novel: "I went to Far Rockaway that summer and felt bad, because I had wanted their novel to be better than the published one I had given them; I hated to let them down." [10]

9. *Not without Laughter,* p. 313.
10. *The Big Sea,* p. 306.

Countee Cullen

Among the poets of the Negro Renaissance there was none more talented than Countee Cullen (1903–46). While still an undergraduate at New York University, he had already placed poems in a dozen of the best literary magazines. Soundly educated at NYU and Harvard and thoroughly familiar with his literary past, Cullen was more sophisticated in technique and choice of subject than most Negro poets of the period. A Keatsian idiom, a biblical emphasis on moral paradox, and a somewhat self-conscious espousal of African primitivism are the distinguishing characteristics of his verse. His publications include seven books of poems, three plays, an anthology, and a novel, *One Way to Heaven* (1932).

Countee Cullen has often been described as one of the more "respectable" Renaissance novelists, with the implication that he avoided the "sordid" subject matter of the Harlem School. Nothing could be farther from the truth. Cullen neither exploited low-life material for its own sake nor avoided it when it served his artistic ends. Though distinctly not of a Bohemian temperament, neither did he value respectability above art. His mischievous sense of humor and his penchant for satire differentiated him from those Renaissance novelists who were forever defending the race before the bar of white opinion. Countee Cullen had a lighter and truer touch, which speaks for itself in *One Way to Heaven.*

Sam Lucas, the protagonist of the novel, is as typical a Harlem-School creation as Banjo or Jimboy. With the help of a missing arm, he makes his living as a professional convert. Traveling from one revival meeting to the next, he comes forward to the mourner's bench when the testimonials are nearly over and dramatically throws a deck of cards and a gleaming razor to the floor. Electrified by this eleventh-hour conversion, and moved to pity by his empty sleeve, the congregation can usually be relied upon to press a few dollars into Sam's good hand.

The narrative interest of *One Way to Heaven* centers upon Sam's relationship with Mattie Johnson, an attractive, hard-working dark girl. As the novel opens, Sam decides to try his luck in a large Harlem church, where a famous singing evangelist is preaching. Mattie, who is present in the audience, has stubbornly resisted the call of the evangelist, but where Heaven fails, Sam Lucas and the Devil succeed. Sam's cards and razor become the instruments of Mattie's conversion, and the glittering illusion on which she builds her faith. Subsequently Sam and Mattie marry, but Sam is a travelin' man, with none of the makings of a steady husband. Having left Mattie for another woman, he returns in the fullness of time with a fatal case of pneumonia, contracted during a drunken spree. The stage is thus set for the crowning irony of the novel. As Sam lies dying, he decides to simulate a death-bed conversion for Mattie's sake. Since his final act of deception is, so to speak, a benefit performance, Sam unwittingly accomplishes his own salvation.

The aesthetic design of the novel consists of variations on a theme. The moral ambiguity of Sam's life and death is echoed in the lives of the other characters. Both the evangelist and the Reverend Drummond are sincere men of God, but neither is above a little showmanship for the Lord's sake. The devout but worldly wise Aunt Mandy takes a practical view of Mattie's marital difficulties: "Sometimes when the angels is too busy to help you, you have to fight the devil with his own tools." Even Mattie, "the gentle servitor of the gentlest of all the gods," abandons her Jesus for a conjure-woman and nearly murders her husband's mistress. The author's point is clear: he that is without sin among you, let him cast the first stone at Sam Lucas.

Sam's cards and razor provide an appropriate symbol for Cullen's theme. Like people, the cards and razor contain potentialities for either good or evil. In Sam's hands, they are the tools of deceit, yet they are no less the instruments of Mattie's salvation. In Mattie's possession, they are the sacred tokens of her conversion, but in her extremity she uses them as a voodoo charm. When Sam asks Aunt Mandy, "Don't you think that cards is evil?" she replies, "It all depends on the kind of cards you have and what you do with them." In Cullen's view the moral universe is infinitely complex. Form is unimportant; there is more than one way to heaven.

Attached to the main body of the novel by the thinnest of threads is a subplot which deals satirically with Harlem's intelligentsia. By the simple expedient of hiring Mattie out to Harlem's most popular hostess, Cullen creates a vantage point from which to launch his barbs. Constancia Brandon's *soirées* are attended by Harlem socialites, New Negro poets, inquisitive white intellectuals, Garveyites, and even a Southern Bourbon. Cullen deflates them all indiscriminately, exposing their foibles while respecting their essential humanity. Yet it is difficult to see how these satirical episodes are related to the rest of the novel. Clever but shallow sketches, they do not approach the depth of moral insight which Cullen achieves through Sam and Mattie.

In spite of its faults, *One Way to Heaven* overshadows the average Renaissance novel. Countee Cullen has a poet's way with words, for which much can be overlooked. He also has a sure instinct for drama, which at times invests the novel with surprising power. He manages symbols skillfully, and for the most part achieves convincing characterization. Yet in making a final appraisal, it is difficult to disagree with Blyden Jackson, one of the younger Negro critics, who speaks of Countee Cullen's *two* novels: the one "with the charm of a fairy tale," the other "too stilted and self-conscious for good satire." [11]

Jean Toomer

The writers of the Lost Generation, as John Aldridge has observed, "were engaged in a revolution designed to purge language of the old restraints of the previous century and to fit it to the demands of a younger, more realistic time." [12] Stein and Hemingway in prose, Pound and Eliot in poetry, were threshing and winnowing, testing and experimenting with words, stretching them and refocusing them, until they became the pliant instruments of a new idiom. The only Negro writer of the 1920's who participated on equal terms in the creation of the modern idiom was a young poet-novelist named Jean Toomer.

11. "An Essay in Criticism," *Phylon* (fourth quarter 1950), pp. 338–43.

12. *After the Lost Generation*, New York and London, McGraw–Hill, 1951, p. 88.

Jean Toomer's *Cane* (1923) is an important American novel. By far the most impressive product of the Negro Renaissance, it ranks with Richard Wright's *Native Son* and Ralph Ellison's *Invisible Man* as a measure of the Negro novelist's highest achievement. Jean Toomer belongs to that first rank of writers who use words almost as a plastic medium, shaping new meanings from an original and highly personal style. Since stylistic innovation requires great technical dexterity, Toomer displays a concern for technique which is fully two decades in advance of the period. While his contemporaries of the Harlem School were still experimenting with a crude literary realism, Toomer had progressed beyond the naturalistic novel to "the higher realism of the emotions," to symbol, and to myth.

Jean Toomer (1894–) was born in Washington, D.C., where his parents, who were cultivated Negroes of Creole stock, had moved in order to educate their children. Toomer's maternal grandfather, P. B. S. Pinchback, had been acting governor of Louisiana during Reconstruction days, so that tales of slavery and Reconstruction were a household tradition. Toomer was educated for the law at the University of Wisconsin and at the City College of New York, but literature soon became his first love. An avant-garde poet and short-story writer, he contributed regularly to such little magazines as *Broom, Secession, Double Dealer, Dial,* and *Little Review.* After a brief literary apprenticeship in cosmopolitan New York, he visited rural Georgia as a country schoolteacher—an experience which directly inspired the production of *Cane.*

During his formative period Toomer was a member of a semi-mystical literary group which included Hart Crane, Waldo Frank, Gorham Munson, and Kenneth Burke. Influenced philosophically by Ouspensky's *Tertium Organum,* they formed a bloc called Art as Vision—some of their catchwords being "the new slope of consciousness," "the superior logic of metaphor," and "noumenal knowledge." The group eventually split over the writings of Gurdjieff, the Russian mystic. So far did Toomer succumb to Gurdjieff's spell that he spent the summer of 1926 at the Gurdjieff Institute in Fontainebleau, France, returning to America to proselytize actively for his mystical philosophy.

In spite of his wide and perhaps primary association with

white intellectuals, as an artist Toomer never underestimated the importance of his Negro identity. He attained a universal vision not by ignoring race as a local truth, but by coming face to face with his particular tradition. His pilgrimage to Georgia was a conscious attempt to make contact with his hereditary roots in the Southland. Of Georgia, Toomer wrote: "There one finds soil in the sense that the Russians know it—the soil every art and literature that is to live must be embedded in." [13] This sense of soil is central to *Cane* and to Toomer's artistic vision. "When one is on the soil of one's ancestors," his narrator remarks, "most anything can come to one."

What comes to Toomer, in the first section of *Cane,* is a vision of the parting soul of slavery:

> . . . for though the sun is setting on
> A song-lit race of slaves, it has not set;
> Though late, O soil, it is not too late yet
> To catch thy plaintive soul, leaving, soon gone.[14]

The soul of slavery persists in the "supper-getting-ready songs" of the black women who live on the Dixie Pike—a road which "has grown from a goat path in Africa." It persists in "the soft, listless cadence of Georgia's South," in the hovering spirit of a comforting Jesus, and in the sudden violence of the Georgia moon. It persists above all in the people, white and black, who have become Andersonian "grotesques" by virtue of their slave inheritance. Part I of *Cane* is in fact a kind of Southern *Winesburg, Ohio.* It consists of the portraits of six women—all primitives—in which an Andersonian narrator mediates between the reader and the author's vision of life on the Dixie Pike.

There is Karintha, "she who carries beauty" like a pregnancy, until her perfect beauty and the impatience of young men beget a fatherless child. Burying her child in a sawdust pile, she takes her revenge by becoming a prostitute; "the soul of her was a growing thing ripened too soon."

In "Becky" Toomer dramatizes the South's conspiracy to ignore

13. Quoted in Alain Locke, "Negro Youth Speaks," *The New Negro* (New York, Boni, 1925), p. 51.

14. *Cane,* p. 21 ("The Song of the Son").

miscegenation. Becky is a white woman with two Negro sons. After the birth of the first, she symbolically disappears from sight into a cabin constructed by community guilt. After the birth of the second, she is simply regarded as dead, and no one is surprised when the chimney of her cabin falls in and buries her. Toward Becky there is no charity from white or black, but only furtive attempts to conceal her existence.

Carma's tale, "which is the crudest melodrama," hinges not so much on marital infidelity as on a childish deception. Accused by her husband of having other men ("No one blames her for that") she becomes hysterical, and running into a canebrake, pretends to shoot herself. "Twice deceived, and the one deception proved the other." Her husband goes berserk, slashes a neighbor, and is sent to the chain gang. The tone of the episode is set by the ironic contrast between Carma's apparent strength ("strong as any man") and her childish behavior.

Fern, whose full name is Fernie May Rosen, combines the suffering of her Jewish father and her Negro mother: "at first sight of her I felt as if I heard a Jewish cantor sing. . . . As if his singing rose above the unheard chorus of a folksong." Unable to find fulfillment, left vacant by the bestowal of men's bodies, Fern sits listlessly on her porch near the Dixie Pike. Her eyes desire nothing that man can give her; the Georgia countryside flows into them, along with something that Toomer's narrator calls God.

"Esther" is a study in sexual repression. The protagonist is a near-white girl whose father is the richest colored man in town. Deprived of normal outlets by her social position, she develops a neurotic life of fantasy which centers upon a virile, black-skinned, itinerant preacher named King Barlo. At sixteen she imagines herself the mother of his immaculately conceived child. At twenty-seven she tries to translate fantasy into reality by offering herself to Barlo. Rebuffed and humiliated, she retreats into lassitude and frigidity.

Louisa, of "Blood-Burning Moon," has two lovers, one white and the other colored. Inflamed by a sexual rivalry deeper than race, they quarrel. One is slashed and the other is lynched. Unlike most Negro writers who have grappled with the subject of lynching, Toomer achieves both form and perspective. He is not primarily concerned with antilynching propaganda, but in capturing a certain atavistic quality in Southern life which defies the restraints of civilized society.

Part II of *Cane* is counterpoint. The scene shifts to Washington, where Seventh Street thrusts a wedge of vitality, brilliance, and movement into the stale, soggy, whitewashed wood of the city. This contrast is an aspect of Toomer's primitivism. The blacks, in his color scheme, represent a full life; the whites, a denial of it. Washington's Negroes have preserved their vitality because of their roots in the rural South, yet whiteness presses in on them from all sides. The "dickty" Negro, and especially the near-white, who are most nearly assimilated to white civilization, bear the brunt of repression and denial, vacillating constantly between two identities. Out of this general frame of reference grow the central symbols of the novel.

Toomer's symbols reflect the profound humanism which forms the base of his philosophical position. Man's essential goodness, he would contend, his sense of brotherhood, and his creative instincts have been crushed and buried by modern industrial society. Toomer's positive values, therefore, are associated with the soil, the cane, and the harvest; with Christian charity, and with giving oneself in love. On the other side of the equation is a series of burial or confinement symbols (houses, alleys, machines, theaters, nightclubs, newspapers) which limit man's growth and act as barriers to his soul. Words are useless in piercing this barrier; Toomer's intellectualizing males are tragic figures because they value talking above feeling. Songs, dreams, dancing, and love itself (being instinctive in nature) may afford access to "the simple beauty of another's soul." The eyes, in particular, are avenues through which we can discover "the truth that people bury in their hearts."

In the second section of *Cane,* Toomer weaves these symbols into a magnificent design, so that his meaning, elusive in any particular episode, emerges with great impact from the whole. "Rhobert" is an attack on the crucial bourgeois value of home ownership: "Rhobert wears a house, like a monstrous diver's helmet, on his head." Like Thoreau's farmer, who traveled through life pushing a barn and a hundred acres before him, Rhobert is a victim of his own property instinct. As he struggles with the weight of the house, he sinks deeper and deeper into the mud:

> Brother, Rhobert is sinking
> Let's open our throats, brother
> Let's sing Deep River when he goes down.

The basic metaphor in "Avey" compares a young girl to the trees planted in boxes along V Street, "the young trees that whinnied like colts impatient to be free." Avey's family wants her to become a school teacher, but her bovine nature causes her to prefer a somewhat older profession. Yet, ironically, it is not she but the narrator who is a failure, who is utterly inadequate in the face of Avey's womanhood.

In "Theatre" Toomer develops his "dickty" theme, through an incident involving a chorus girl and a theater-manager's brother. As John watches a rehearsal, he is impressed by Dorris' spontaneity, in contrast to the contrived movements of the other girls. He momentarily contemplates an affair, but reservations born of social distance prevent him from consummating his desire, except in a dream. Dorris, who hopes fleetingly for home and children from such a man, is left at the end of the episode with only the sordid reality of the theater.

"Calling Jesus" plays a more important role than its length would indicate in unifying the symbolism of the novel. It concerns a woman, urbanized and spiritually intimidated, whose "soul is like a little thrust-tailed dog that follows her, whimpering." At night, when she goes to sleep in her big house, the little dog is left to shiver in the vestibule. "Some one . . . eoho Jesus . . . soft as the bare feet of Christ moving across bales of Southern cotton, will steal in and cover it that it need not shiver, and carry it to her where she sleeps, cradled in dream-fluted cane."

In "Box Seat" Toomer comes closest to realizing his central theme. The episode opens with an invocation: "Houses are shy girls whose eyes shine reticently upon the dusk body of the street. Upon the gleaming limbs and asphalt torso of a dreaming nigger. Shake your curled wool-blossoms, nigger. Open your liver-lips to the lean white spring. Stir the root-life of a withered people. Call them from their houses and teach them to dream" (p. 104).

The thought is that of a young man, whose symbolic role is developed at once: "I am Dan Moore. I was born in a canefield. The hands of Jesus touched me. I am come to a sick world to heal it." Dan, moreover, comes as a representative of "powerful underground races": "The next world-savior is coming up that way. Coming up. A continent sinks down. The new-world Christ will need consummate skill to walk upon the waters where huge bubbles burst." The redemption motif is echoed in Dan's communion with the old slave: "I asked him if he knew what that rumbling is that comes up from the ground." It is picked up again through the portly Negro woman who sits beside Dan in the theater: "A soil-soaked fragrance comes from her. Through the cement floor her strong roots sink down . . . and disappear in blood-lines that waver south."

The feminine lead is played by Muriel, a school teacher inclined toward conventionality. Her landlady, Mrs. Pribby, is constantly with her, being in essence a projection of Muriel's social fears. The box seat which she occupies at the theater, where her every movement is under observation, renders her relationship to society perfectly. Her values are revealed in her query to Dan, "Why don't you get a good job and settle down?" On these terms only can she love him; meanwhile she avoids his company by going to a vaudeville performance with a girl friend.

Dan, a slave to "her still unconquered animalism," follows and watches her from the audience. The main attraction consists of a prize fight between two dwarfs for the "heavy-weight championship"; it symbolizes the ultimate degradation of which a false and shoddy culture is capable. Sparring grotesquely, pounding and bruising each other, the dwarfs suggest the traditional clown symbol of modern art. At the climax of the episode the winner presents a blood-spattered rose to Muriel, who recoils, hesitates, and finally submits. The dwarf's eyes are pleading: "Do not shrink. Do not be afraid of me." Overcome with disgust for Muriel's hypocrisy, Dan completes the dwarf's thought from the audience, rising to shout: "JESUS WAS ONCE A LEPER!" Rushing from the theater, he is free at last of his love for Muriel—free, but at the same time sterile: "He is as cool as a green stem that has just shed its flower."

Coming as an anticlimax after "Box Seat," "Bona and Paul" describes an abortive love affair between two Southern students at the University of Chicago—a white girl and a mulatto boy who is "passing." The main tension, reminiscent of Gertrude Stein's *Melanctha,* is between knowing and loving, set in the framework of Paul's double identity. It is not his race consciousness which terminates the relationship, as one critic has suggested, but precisely his "whiteness," his desire for knowledge, his philosophical bent. If he had been able to assert his Negro self—that which attracted Bona to him in the first place—he might have held her love.

In "Kabnis" rural Georgia once more provides a setting. This is the long episode which comprises the concluding section of *Cane.* By now the symbolic values of Toomer's main characters can be readily assessed. Ralph Kabnis, the protagonist, is a school teacher from the North who cringes in the face of his tradition. A spiritual coward, he cannot contain "the pain and beauty of the South"; cannot embrace the suffering of the past, symbolized by slavery; cannot come to terms with his own bastardy; cannot master his pathological fear of being lynched. Consumed with self-hatred and cut off from any organic connection with the past, he resembles nothing so much as a scarecrow: "Kabnis, a promise of soil-soaked beauty; uprooted, thinning out. Suspended a few feet above the soil whose touch would resurrect him."

Lewis, by way of contrast, is a Christ figure, an extension of Dan Moore. Almost a T. S. Eliot creation ("I'm on a sort of contract with myself"), his function is to shock others into moral awareness. It is Lewis who confronts Kabnis with his moral cowardice: "Can't hold them, can you? Master; slave. Soil; and the overarching heavens. Dusk; dawn. They fight and bastardize you. The sun tint of your cheeks, flame of the great season's multi-colored leaves, tarnished, burned. Split, shredded, easily burned" (p. 218).

Halsey, unlike Kabnis, has not been crushed by Southern life, but absorbed into it. Nevertheless, his spiritual degradation is equally thorough. An artisan and small shopkeeper like his father before him, he "belongs" in a sense that Kabnis does not. Yet in order to maintain his place in the community, he must submit to the indignities of Negro life in the South. Like Booker T. Washington, whose point of view he represents, Halsey has settled for something less than manhood. Restless, groping tentatively toward Lewis, he escapes from himself through his craft, and through an occasional debauch with the town prostitute, whom he loved as a youth.

Father John, the old man who lives beneath Halsey's shop, represents a link with the Negro's ancestral past. Concealed by the present generation as an unpleasant memory, the old man is thrust into a cellar which resembles the hold of a slave ship. There he sits, "A mute John the Baptist of a new religion, or a tongue-tied shadow of an old." When he finally speaks, it is to rebuke the white folks for the sin of slavery. The contrast between Lewis and Kabnis is sharpened by their respective reactions to Father John. Through the old slave, Lewis is able to "merge with his source," but Kabnis can only deny: "An' besides, he aint my past. My ancestors were Southern blue-bloods."

In terms of its dramatic movement "Kabnis" is a steep slope downward,[15] approximating the progressive deterioration of the protagonist. Early in the episode Kabnis is reduced to a scarecrow replica of himself by his irrational fears. His failure to stand up to Hanby, an authoritarian school principal, marks a decisive loss in his power of self-direction. Gradually he slips into a childlike dependence, first on Halsey, then on the two prostitutes, and finally on Halsey's little sister, Carrie Kate. In the course of the drunken debauch with which the novel ends, Kabnis becomes a clown, without dignity or manhood, wallowing in the mire of his own self-hatred. The stark tragedy of "Kabnis" is relieved only by the figure of Carrie Kate, the unspoiled child of a new generation, who may yet be redeemed through her ties with Father John.

A critical analysis of *Cane* is a frustrating task, for Toomer's art, in which "outlines are reduced to essences," is largely destroyed in the process of restoration. No paraphrase can properly convey the aesthetic pleasure derived from a sensitive reading of *Cane*. Yet in spite of Toomer's successful experiment with the modern idiom—or perhaps because of it—*Cane* met with a cold reception from the public, hardly selling 500 copies during its

15. See Gorham B. Munson, *Destinations* (New York, 1928), pp. 178–96.

first year. This poor showing must have been a great disappointment to Toomer, and undoubtedly it was a chief cause of his virtual retirement from literature. Perhaps in his heart of hearts Jean Toomer found it singularly appropriate that the modern world should bury *Cane*. Let us in any event delay the exhumation no longer.

The Satirists

During the 1920's when the advance guard of American letters fled overseas into exile, a strong detachment remained at home to fight a rear-guard action with the Philistines. Using satire as their weapon, such authors as H. L. Mencken, Sinclair Lewis, and James Branch Cabell maintained a running skirmish with those elements of the American population who were proud of their own ignorance. Echoes of this conflict could soon be heard in the Negro intellectual world, and the embattled novelists of the Harlem School quickly availed themselves of the striking power of satire. At the same time—and this is typical of the Negro's cultural history—specifically racial factors were at work behind this sudden penchant for satire.

Satire as a literary attitude was out of the question for the early Negro novelist. The social struggle in which he was engaged was too compelling, and humor too keen a blade for his blunt needs. Self-satire, moreover, could hardly be expected of those whose first impulse was to defend their race against the slanderous attacks of white authors. It was not until the freer atmosphere of the 1920's that satire came into its own. The novels of Countee Cullen and Rudolph Fisher contain nascent satirical elements,[16] but Renaissance satire reaches its highest development in George Schuyler's *Black No More* (1931) and Wallace Thurman's *Infants of the Spring* (1932).

George Schuyler (1895–) was educated in the public schools of Syracuse, followed by eight years in the U. S. Army. Primarily a journalist, he began his career on an Army magazine called the *Service*. From 1922 to 1928 he was on the staff of the *Messenger*, a

16. *The Walls of Jericho* (1928), by Rudolph Fisher, contains a devastating portrait of Miss Agatha Cramp, a well-meaning white philanthropist.

radical weekly founded by two Negro Socialists, A. Philip Randolph and Chandler Owen. From there he moved to a more lucrative position as a regular columnist for the *Pittsburgh Courier.*

Those who know George Schuyler only as the Westbrook Pegler of Negro journalism will be pleasantly surprised by *Black No More.* In his younger, more intellectual days, Schuyler possessed a ready wit and an authentic gift for satire. A disciple of H. L. Mencken, he regarded mirth as the proper antidote to folly. In *Black No More* he accords the same treatment to American racism which Mencken was currently administering to the American "booboisie."

The imaginary situation on which the novel turns is the discovery by a colored doctor of a glandular treatment which will transform Negroes into full-fledged Caucasians. As more and more Negroes vanish into the white population, panic seizes the nation. Race leaders tremble, for their profitable business and uplift organizations are faced with ruin. In the South the social structure completely disintegrates. Jim Crow facilities lie in idleness; ostensible white couples have colored babies; the Knights of Nordica (KKK) is taken over by former Negroes; and the party of white supremacy loses its *raison d'être.* The national balance of power is upset, and Black-No-More becomes the chief issue of a presidential campaign. In the end, life returns to "normal" when someone discovers that the ersatz Caucasians are a shade lighter than the garden variety. Segregation is promptly restored, based this time on the desideratum of a dark skin!

A satirist must have a consistent vantage point from which to rebuke his fellow mortals. It is not difficult to trace Schuyler's satire to its source. An occasional article in the *American Mercury,* founded by H. L. Mencken in 1924, emphasizes his debt to Mencken and to the tendency in American letters which he represents. During the 1920's Schuyler was active in the Socialist party, where he acquired an ideological basis for the satire of *Black No More.* Journalism also contributed to the development of his satirical powers. Schuyler's cutting edge was sharpened on his column in the *Messenger,* significantly titled "Shafts and Darts." Yet none of these explanations is sufficient in itself. It seems more likely, in view of the evident relish with which Schuyler lampoons the race, that assimilationism is the key to his satirical bent.

George Schuyler's writings provide, in fact, a classic study in assimilationism. In one of his early columns he vehemently attacks " the lie that Negroes wish to be white"; [17] yet he based *Black No More* on this very conception. His attacks on Negro nationalism, whether of the Garvey or DuBois variety, run true to form.[18] So, too, does his growing alienation from the realities of race. In his early days Schuyler was content to deny the existence of a distinctive Negro art; [19] today he does not shrink from denying the existence of a Negro problem! [20]

Perhaps more suggestive, from a theoretical point of view, is Schuyler's "red assimilationist" phase in the Socialist party. Beyond a doubt, one of the advantages which left-wing politics offers to the Negro is an opportunity to submerge his racial identity in a broader historical movement.[21] His reference group is no longer ethnic but ideological; instead of striving exclusively for racial advancement, he participates in the struggle for social justice on a universal plane. It thus becomes possible for a Negro of Schuyler's temperament to move from a bourgeois to a socialist ideology—and back again—without relinquishing his basic assimilationist impulse. Schuyler's ideological vacillation assumes a certain consistency, if we look beneath the purely ideational level to the bedrock of social psychology.

Such an analysis of the roots of Schuyler's satire would be of limited interest if it merely cast light on the idiosyncrasies of a minor Renaissance novelist. As it happens, however, a similar pattern can be found in the work of Wallace Thurman. This literary parallel is not surprising in view of the close personal

17. "Shafts and Darts," *Messenger,* Nov. 1923.

18. *Black No More,* pp. 86 ff., 102 ff.

19. "The Negro Art Hokum," *Nation, 122* (1926), 622–23.

20. "What's Wrong with the NAACP?" *Negro Digest,* Sept. 1947; "What's Wrong with Negro Authors?" ibid., May 1950; and "The Van Vechten Revolution," *Phylon,* fourth quarter 1950.

21. In the Communist party, to be sure, this advantage is largely offset by the party's cynical exploitation of Negro nationalism. It is no accident that Schuyler joined the Socialist party, which has traditionally held naive assimilationist views on the Negro question.

ties between Schuyler and Thurman. For a time they were colleagues on the staff of the *Messenger*, and Thurman apparently helped Schuyler to publish on more than one occasion. In turn, he was influenced by Schuyler's satirical bent, and in all likelihood by his assimilationist outlook.

Wallace Thurman (1902–34) came directly to Harlem from the University of Southern California. Employed as a reader at Macaulay's, he devoted his main energies to his first love, the Negro Renaissance. His home was a rendezvous for the New Negro coterie, and he himself became actively involved in the avant-garde Renaissance magazines, *Fire* and *Harlem*. Thurman first attracted attention as the co-author of a successful Broadway play entitled *Harlem* (1929). He wrote two novels, *The Blacker the Berry* (1929) and *Infants of the Spring* (1932).

"The blacker the berry, the sweeter the juice"—so runs the Negro folk saying. In a mood of bitter irony, Thurman borrows this phrase for the title of his novel about a dark girl who is the victim of intraracial prejudice. From the moment that Emma Lou enters the world—a black child rejected by her own parents—her pigmentation is a constant source of pain. It results in an unhappy adolescence, in social ostracism at a large California university, and in relentless discrimination when she seeks white-collar employment in Harlem. It leads to her sexual exploitation by a light-skinned lover and finally forces her to reconsider the whole pattern of her life.

Emma Lou's real tragedy is that she accepts the values of the system which torments her. Her use of bleaching agents, for example, betrays her unconscious belief in the magical power of a fair complexion. As the novel unfolds, she outgrows this crippling frame of reference and comes to recognize that her main enemy is within: "What she needed now was to accept her black skin as being real and unchangeable." This theme of self-acceptance is typically Renaissance: to be one's dark-skinned self and not a bleached-out imitation is the essence of emancipation. But Thurman's hard-won victory (the conflict he is acting out, through Emma Lou, is clear enough) does not prove to be decisive. His second novel shows him to be incapable of holding his feelings toward the race in stable equilibrium.

Infants of the Spring is a neurotic novel, in which Thurman broods introspectively on the "failure" of the Negro Renaissance. The novel opens with Laertes' advice to Ophelia, from which it derives both title and theme:

> The canker galls the infants of the spring
> Too oft before their buttons be disclosed,
> And in the morn and liquid dew of youth
> Contagious blastments are most imminent.

It was the canker of Bohemianism, in Thurman's eyes, which threatened to nip the New Negro Movement in the bud. The symbolic setting of his novel is Niggeratti Manor, where colored artists, writers, and musicians live in various stages of decadence and sterility. The central characters are Paul, a symbol of dissipated genius, and Ray, a young writer who struggles to free himself from an obsessive race-consciousness. Much of the "action" consists merely of dialogue, which serves to convey the author's impressions of the Negro Renaissance.

After a series of satirical sketches of leading Renaissance personalities, the novel draws to a depressing close. Paul commits suicide in such a manner that his masterpiece is destroyed. A drawing on the title page of the ruined manuscript pictures Niggeratti Manor with a foundation of crumbling stone: "At first glance it could be ascertained that the sky-scraper would soon crumble and fall, leaving the dominating white lights in full possession of the sky." [22] The dream of the Negro Renaissance was, for Thurman, to end thus in disillusion and despair. The tone of the novel is too bitter, however, and Thurman's sense of personal failure too acute, to accept his critique of the Renaissance at face value.

It was appropriate enough that Thurman should seek to become the undertaker of the Negro Renaissance; at the time, he was busy digging his own grave with bad gin. His self-hatred, and the suicidal impulses which it engendered, were the central facts of his later years. No one who has read *The Blacker the Berry* will doubt that the source of this self-hatred was his dark complexion. The old struggle for self-acceptance, which Thurman had

22. *Infants of the Spring,* p. 284.

apparently won through Emma Lou, is reopened and finally abandoned through the character of Ray. "Eventually," Ray remarks, "I'm going to renounce Harlem and all it stands for." This mood of renunciation pervades *Infants of the Spring*. In his wholesale indictment of the Renaissance generation, Thurman was simply working out his self-destructive impulses on the level of a literary movement. The most self-conscious of the New Negroes, he ultimately turned his critical insight against himself and the wider movement with which he identified.

The satire of the Harlem School, though often directed against whites, is predominantly self-satire. As such it represents a gain in maturity, and a conscious rebellion against the "defensive" attitudes of the early Negro novelist. Nevertheless, the novels of George Schuyler and Wallace Thurman strongly suggest that Renaissance satire had its psychological roots in assimilationism. Since humor is often a form of veiled aggression, may not self-satire be a permissible form of self-aggression? Perhaps in a period which was predominantly nationalistic in tone, satire was the only available outlet for the assimilationist impulses of the more sophisticated Negro novelists.

5. *The Rear Guard*

IN a society which has traditionally viewed its artists with suspicion, it would have been surprising indeed if the Negro novelist had gone unscathed. It was not long before the Harlem School was engaged in a pitched battle with the spokesmen of Negro Philistia. The dispute centered around the right of the Negro novelist to use low-life material. It was thus a recapitulation of an earlier contest between American naturalism and the guardians of the Genteel Tradition. As Dreiser, Crane, and Norris had shocked Victorian sensibilities, so the Harlem School offended those members of the Negro middle class who believed that "unassimilable" elements in the race should be hidden, and not exposed to public view in sordid novels.

A conservative faction arose, led by W. E. B. DuBois, Benjamin Brawley, and William Stanley Braithwaite, which accused the Harlem School of glorifying the lowest strata of Negro life, pandering to sensationalism, and succumbing to the influence of white Bohemia. A few random phrases will capture the flavor of their criticism:

> *Home to Harlem* for the most part nauseates me, and after the dirtier parts of its filth I feel distinctly like taking a bath [DuBois].[1]

> A perverted form of music originating in the Negro slums, and known as jazz. . . . A style that attacks the very foundations of grammar [Brawley].[2]

> The pity of it! *Walls of Jericho* and *Home to Harlem* perched upon our bookshelves with *Plum Bun* and *Passing* nowhere to be seen. Doctors, lawyers, men of affairs, their wives and daughters are neither less valuable nor less richly human members of society than jazz boys and girls, roustabouts, and drunks [Mary Fleming Labaree].[3]

The Harlem School and its defenders replied vigorously to these attacks. Some novelists, like Langston Hughes and Wallace Thurman, wrote articles in their own defense, contending that an inability to differentiate between art and propaganda lay at the bottom of the controversy. Sophisticated critics like Sterling Brown and Alain Locke were quick to point out that virtually all of the major authors in modern literature made use of lower-class subjects. James Weldon Johnson, whose instinct was always sound in such mattters, vigorously defended the lower-class Negro as "higher" literary material. "It takes nothing less than supreme genius," he once remarked, "to make middle-class society, black or white, interesting—to say nothing of making it dramatic."

The storm of controversy which greeted the Harlem School in the mid-1920's marks the beginning of a growing breach between the Negro writer and the Negro middle class. The early Negro novelist, insulated from the impact of modern literature by a culture lag, was firmly integrated into the social class which produced him. With the advent of the Harlem School, however, the Negro novelist begins to develop that sense of alienation from bourgeois society which is the mark of the modern artist. Before

1. Review of *Home to Harlem*, in *Crisis*, 35 (1928), 202, 211.

2. "The Negro Literary Renaissance," *Southern Workman*, 56 (1927), pp. 177–84.

3. Review of *Passing*, in *Opportunity*, 7 (1929), 255.

tracing this process of alienation through the 1930's, a group of Renaissance novelists must be considered who sought to perpetuate the traditions of the early Negro novel.

Literary history is no tidier than any other history. In addition to those writers who give a period its distinctive character, there are those who are ahead of their time, and those who lag behind. Among the latter, during the Negro Renaissance of the 1920's, was a group of novelists who sought a middle ground between the established traditions of the Negro novel and the radical innovations of the Harlem School. Two of these novelists, Walter White and W. E. B. DuBois, were staff members of the NAACP who devoted their lives to the fight for Negro rights. A third, Jessie Fauset, was a high school teacher of prominent family, who worked under DuBois on the editorial staff of *Crisis.* Nella Larsen, the only successful novelist among them, was born in the Virgin Islands of a Danish mother and a Negro father. Her first novel, *Quicksand* (1928), is perhaps the best of the period, with the exception of Jean Toomer's *Cane.*

Fundamentally these novelists still wished to orient Negro art toward white opinion. They wished to apprise educated whites of the existence of respectable Negroes, and to call their attention—now politely, now indignantly—to the facts of racial injustice. From these nonliterary motives certain familiar consequences flowed. Where the Harlem School turned to the folk for literary material, these novelists continued to draw their characters from the Negro middle class. Where the characterization of the Harlem School often defied the stereotype, that of the Rear Guard remained exemplary. Where the Harlem School emphasized "racial" differences, these authors suppressed them. Where writers of the Harlem School explored broad facets of Negro life, these novelists specialized in racial protest. In most essentials, therefore, the work of the Rear Guard conformed to the canons of the early Negro novel.

In spite of their allegiance to an earlier tradition, the Rear Guard could not wholly escape the influence of the Renaissance *Zeitgeist;* while striving valiantly to preserve the genteel character of Negro fiction, they made minor concessions to the boisterous spirit of the Jazz Age. Without embracing cultural dualism, they allowed a diluted version of Negro nationalism to influence their work. From too fervent a racialism they were of course protected by their traditional social distance from the Negro masses. Jessie Fauset expresses their fundamental attitude in all its ambivalence when she writes of "that oneness which colored people feel in a colored crowd, even though so many of its members are people whom one does not want ever to know." This is the essence of bourgeois nationalism: to hold these conflicting ethnic and social-class attitudes in a delicate and unstable equilibrium.

A distinguishing characteristic of this school is its fondness for the novel of "passing." Walter White's *Flight* (1926), Jessie Fauset's *Plum Bun* (1928), and Nella Larsen's *Passing* (1929), all deal in a similar vein with this exotic theme. Emphasis is placed on the problems which confront the person who passes: the fear of discovery, the anxious prospect of marriage, with its fear of throwback, and so forth. The invariable outcome, in fiction if not in fact, is disillusionment with life on the other side of the line, a new appreciation of racial values, and an irresistible longing to return to the Negro community.

This concerted attack upon passing by the novelists of the Rear Guard is a good index to their central values. It represents, in the first place, an affirmation of racial loyalty. If the act of passing is an expression of assimilationism carried to its logical conclusion, then surely a novel which condemns passing must have nationalist implications. Such a novel represents, in psychological terms, a symbolic rejection of the author's unconscious desire to be white. He projects this desire fictionally, only to repudiate it, thus fortifying his racial loyalty against the threat from within. Since the moral of these novels is to accept one's racial identity, they represent an important manifestation of Renaissance nationalism.

At the same time, the novel of passing is part of a growing body of literature which serves to adjust Americans to the realities of a society which perennially promises more than it can deliver. To be content with what you are, after all, is only the Negro version of familiar injunctions in the mass media to be content with what you've got. In the last fifty years, our popular "success" literature has been radically altered from the formula that every newsboy can become a millionaire to the theme that millionaires (read: white people) are not as happy as we think. Prior to World War I, the Talented Tenth dreamed of becoming "white"—that is, of attaining speedy access to all the prizes which the nation holds forth. When the Negro's experience during and after the war revealed the implacable nature of caste, a "sour grapes" adjustment was clearly indicated. The result was a renewed attack upon passing by the novelists of the Negro middle class.

The literary revolution known as the Negro Renaissance may be thought of as occurring in two distinct phases: one phase which was anti-assimilationist, and a subsequent phase which was anti-bourgeois. The more conservative novelists of the period stopped short in the midst of the revolution. They accepted, at least in part, the nationalist implications of the Renaissance, but they clung tenaciously to their middle-class values. As a result, they remained strangers to that profound crisis in belief which motivates the modern novel. While the Harlem School understood perfectly well that Western civilization had been shaken to its foundations by the war, the Rear Guard continued to write as if the Victorian world were still intact.

Walter White and W. E. B. DuBois

At the present time it is no longer required of a Negro author that he enter political life, nor of a Negro political leader that he write novels. There was a time, however, before the present age of specialization, when a Negro intellectual of national stature was expected to double in brass. Only a few men of rare versatility such as James Weldon Johnson were equal to the challenge. Others, like Walter White and W. E. B. DuBois, were sometimes tempted into waters beyond their depth. Able political leaders and competent writers of expository prose, these men lacked the creative imagination which is the *sine qua non* of good fiction.

Walter White's first novel, *The Fire in the Flint* (1924), is an antilynching tract of melodramatic proportions. It was written in twelve days, according to White, and the novel itself provides no grounds for doubting his word. It is essentially a series of essays, strung on an unconvincing plot, involving the misfortunes of a colored doctor and his family in a small Southern town. White's second novel, *Flight* (1926), is an undistinguished treatment of passing, perhaps more susceptible to the influence of the Harlem School than most novels of the Rear Guard. Taken together, Walter White's novels comprise an object lesson in what Blyden Jackson has called "Faith without Works in Negro Literature."

W. E. B. DuBois provides a personal link between the early Negro novel and the conservative wing of the Negro Renaissance. His first novel, *The Quest of the Silver Fleece* (1911), was intellectually in advance of its time, but by 1928, when *Dark Princess* appeared, times had changed, though DuBois had not. It may seem strange to speak of DuBois, with his militant Negro nationalism and his fellow-traveling politics, as a conservative. Nevertheless, his emotional tirades against the Harlem School, when he was editor of *Crisis*, plainly reveal the strength of his attachment to the Victorian tradition. It is well to remember that DuBois was already in his mid-fifties at the beginning of the Negro Renaissance.

Dark Princess, though a poor novel, is an important social document, for it heralds the Negro intellectual's growing interest in the national independence movements of Asia and Africa. DuBois first became interested in the colonial problem through participation in the Pan-African Congresses of 1911 and 1919. He has subsequently performed a valuable service by placing the American race problem in its proper historical perspective. Throughout his political and historical writings, he views the slave trade and its consequences as an aspect of white European colonialism—a useful corrective for those who approach the American race problem in isolation.

The plot of *Dark Princess* concerns a cosmopolitan group of Asian and African revolutionaries, who plan to liberate the darker peoples of the earth from white rule. Ideologically, the novel represents an extension of the principle of Negro nationalism into world politics. In effect, the propaganda slogan of the novel is "Non-whites of the world, unite!" With its conspiratorial, romantic politics, its aristocratic revolutionaries, its ultranationalism, and its unconvincing rejection of revenge, *Dark Princess* is strongly reminiscent of Sutton Griggs' *Imperium in Imperio* (1899).

Jessie Fauset

Viewing the Negro Renaissance in retrospect, Richard Wright has written caustically of "the prim and decorous ambassadors who went a-begging to white America, dressed in the knee-pants of servility, curtsying to show that the Negro was not inferior, that he was human, and that he had a life comparable to that of other people." Without a doubt, one of the prime offenders whom Wright had in mind was Jessie Fauset. Yet with all her primness, Miss Fauset presents something of a paradox, for in her editorial work on the *Crisis* she often championed the young rebels of the Harlem School. Unlike DuBois, who was a Philistine and objected to the Harlem School on moral grounds, she showed a genuine interest in the development of Negro art even when its main current ran counter to her own social prejudices.

Claude McKay writes of Jessie Fauset in his autobiography, "All the radicals liked her, although in her social viewpoint she was away over on the other side of the fence." But if Miss Fauset won personal acceptance among Harlem's colorful Bohemians, in her novels she maintained an irreproachable decorum. Her literary career was inspired, as a matter of fact, by the publication of T. S. Stribling's *Birthright* (1922), a "respectable" novel of middle-class Negro life. "Nella Larsen and Walter White," Miss Fauset remarks, "were affected just as I was. . . . We could do it better." From the first, therefore, her literary aspirations were circumscribed by her desire to convey a flattering image of respectable Negro society.

Jessie Fauset was the most prolific of the Renaissance novelists, publishing four novels during a ten-year period from 1924 to 1933. But in spite of an admirable persistence, her novels are uniformly sophomoric, trivial, and dull. *There Is Confusion* (1924) is nothing if not well titled, for it is burdened with a plethora of characters whose complex genealogy leaves the most conscientious reader exhausted. *Plum Bun* (1928) is a typical novel of passing, structured around the nursery rhyme

> To market, to market, to buy a plum bun;
> Home again, home again, market is done.

The Chinaberry Tree (1931) seems to be a novel about the first colored woman in New Jersey to wear lounging pajamas. *Comedy American Style* (1933) is an account of a colored woman's obsessive desire to be white, not unlike the novels which condemn passing in its nationalist implications.

Undoubtedly the most important formative influence on Miss Fauset's work was her family background. An authentic old Philadelphian (known as "O.P.'s" in the colored society of that day), she was never able to transcend the narrow limits of this sheltered world. It accounts for her gentility, her emphasis on heredity and genealogy, and her attitude toward race. Miss Fauset's characters are bred to "rise above" racial discrimination, to regard it merely as "an extra complication of living." Yet "the artificial dilemma," as she calls it, is always present as an obstacle to gracious living, and is the real antagonist of her novels. Racial protest, be it ever so genteel, is an irrepressible feature of bourgeois nationalism.

Nella Larsen

Drawing upon much the same material as Jessie Fauset, Nella Larsen was more successful in infusing it with dramatic form. Even her less important novel, *Passing* (1929), is probably the best treatment of the subject in Negro fiction. The novel contrasts the lives of two colored women, both fair enough to pass. The one, desiring safety and security, marries a Negro professional man; the other, crossing the line, "lives on the edge of danger." Unfortunately, a false and shoddy denouement prevents the novel from rising above mediocrity. *Quicksand* (1928), on the other hand, is tightly written; its subtleties become fully apparent only after a second reading. The narrative structure of the novel is derived from a central, unifying metaphor; its characterization is psychologically sound; and its main dramatic tension is developed unobtrusively but with great power.

The protagonist of *Quicksand* is Helga Crane, a neurotic young woman of mixed parentage, who is unable to make a satisfactory adjustment in either race. Educated by a white uncle after the death of her parents, she embarks on a teaching career at Naxos, a Southern Negro college. Quickly disillusioned by the realities of

Negro education in the South, and disappointed by a loveless romance with a smug instructor, she leaves the campus for points north. Harlem provides a temporary refuge, but a growing resentment with her lot as a Negro drives her to Denmark and her mother's people. In Copenhagen, a romantic involvement with a famous portrait painter poses the problem of mixed marriage—a prospect which she is unwilling to contemplate because of the tragic effect of miscegenation on her own life.

Helga returns to America with the problem of her identity still unsolved. Back in Harlem, she learns of the marriage of her best friend to Dr. Anderson, a former Naxos administrator of exceptional self-confidence and maturity. Strongly attracted to Dr. Anderson, she prepares herself for an extramarital affair, but the object of her passion refuses to cooperate. More insecure than ever, she takes refuge from a rainstorm in a revival meeting and impulsively submits to the pastor, who has comforted her in a helpless moment. Subsequently, she marries the Reverend Green, accompanying him to a small town in Alabama, where she sinks inexorably into a morass of child-bearing and domestic drudgery.

The key to the narrative structure of *Quicksand* is contained in a passage toward the end of the novel in which Helga Crane rebels against her lot as a brood mare: "For she had to admit it wasn't new, this feeling of dissatisfaction, of asphyxiation. Something like it she had experienced before. In Naxos. In New York. In Copenhagen. This differed only in degree." [4] Helga's quest for happiness has led her, floundering, through a succession of minor bogs, until she is finally engulfed by a quagmire of her own making. The basic metaphor of the novel, contained in its title, is supported throughout by concrete images of suffocation, asphyxiation, and claustrophobia. Associated always with Helga's restlessness and dissatisfaction, these symbols of a loathsome, hostile environment are at bottom projections of Negro self-hatred: "It was as if she were shut up, boxed up with hundreds of her race, closed up with that something in the racial character which had always been, to her, inexplicable, alien. Why, she demanded in fierce rebellion, should she be yoked to these despised black folk?" (p. 120).

4. *Quicksand*, pp. 298–99.

On one level, *Quicksand* is an authentic case study which yields readily to psychoanalytic interpretation. Each of the major episodes in Helga's life is a recapitulation of the same psychological pattern: temporary enthusiasm; boredom, followed by disgust; and finally a stifling sense of entrapment. Then escape into a new situation, until escape is no longer possible. Race is functional in this pattern, for it has to do with Helga's initial rejection and therefore with her neurotic withdrawal pattern. Her tendency to withdraw from any situation which threatens to become permanent indicates that she is basically incapable of love or happiness. No matter how often she alters her situation, she carries her problems with her.

Deserted by her colored father and rejected by her white stepfather, Helga's quest may be viewed as the search for a father's love. The qualities of balance and security which she finds so appealing in Danish society; her attraction for Dr. Anderson, an older married man; her desire for "nice things" as a substitute for the security of parental love; and her belated return to religion can all be understood in these terms. Her degrading marriage to a jackleg preacher who "fathers" her in a helpless moment plainly has its basis in the Oedipal triangle. Her unconscious need to be debased is in reality the need to replace her mother by marrying a "no-account" colored man not unlike her gambler father. Such an interpretation can never be a substitute for aesthetic criticism, but it is useful as verification of Larsen's psychological depth and skillful characterization.

The dramatic tension of the novel can be stated in terms of a conflict between Helga's sexuality and her love for "nice things." Her desire for material comfort is static; it is the value premise on which the novel is based: "Always she had wanted . . . the things which money could give, leisure, attention, beautiful surroundings. Things. Things. Things" (p. 147). Helga's sexuality, on the other hand, is dynamic; its strength increases until she is overwhelmed and deprived of the accouterments of gracious living forever.

At Naxos, during the period of her frigid romance with James Vayle, Helga's inner conflict is as yet only dimly perceived (p. 23):

> The uneasy sense of being engaged with some formidable antagonist, nameless and un-understood, startled her. It wasn't, she was suddenly aware, merely the school and its ways and its decorous and stupid people that oppressed her. There was something else, some other more ruthless force, a quality within herself which was frustrating her, had always frustrated her, kept her from getting the things she had wanted.

As the novel proceeds, the nature of this "ruthless force" becomes increasingly apparent to the reader, if not to Helga herself. After a visit to a Harlem cabaret, she discovers "a shameful certainty that not only had she been in the jungle, but that she had enjoyed it." In Copenhagen, when Axel Olsen paints a sensual portrait of Helga, she denies the likeness, only to be told: "You have the warm, impulsive nature of the women of Africa, but the soul of a prostitute."

Olsen's insight is fully justified by Helga's subsequent behavior. Disappointed by her chosen lover, she sells herself in marriage to the Reverend Green. The meaning of the marriage, as far as Helga is concerned, is plain enough: "And night came at the end of every day. Emotional, palpitating, amorous, all that was living in her sprang like rank weeds at the tingling thought of night, with a vitality so strong that it devoured all the shoots of reason" (p. 273). Lest the thematic significance of Helga's sexuality be lost upon the reader, Larsen poses the alternatives once more at the end of the novel: "It was so easy and so pleasant to think about freedom and cities, about clothes and books, about the sweet, mingled smell of Houbigant and cigarettes in softly lighted rooms filled with inconsequential chatter and laughter and sophisticated timeless music. It was so hard to think out a feasible way of retrieving all these agreeable, desired things. Later. When she got up. By and by" (p. 301).

At this point the tone of the novel, which arises from the author's attitude toward her material, becomes decisive. Helga's tragedy, in Larsen's eyes, is that she allows herself to be declassed by her own sexuality. The tone of reproach is unmistakable. It is this underlying moralism which differentiates *Quicksand* from the novels of the Harlem School. It is manifested not in Helga's behavior, which is "naturalistic" and well motivated, even inevitable, but in the symbols of luxury which are counterposed to the bog, in the author's prudish attitude toward sex, and in her simple equation of "nice things" with the pursuit of beauty.

A comparison of Larsen's best novel with the best work of Claude McKay may help to sharpen the contrast. Objectively, Helga Crane's fate is not much different from that of Bita in *Banana Bottom*. Bita, too, having been educated for something "higher," returns to a folk existence in the end. That one author interprets this event as a tragedy and the other as a natural expression of cultural dualism is a measure of their respective attitudes toward bourgeois society. Two normative judgments are involved: an evaluation of "nice things" and an evaluation of the folk culture. Nella Larsen sees beauty only in "gracious living," and to her the folk culture is a threatening swamp. Yet within the limits of her values she has organized one aspect of Negro life into a complex aesthetic design. *Quicksand*, for this reason, is a better novel than *Banana Bottom*, although its structure is reared on a narrower ideological base.

The novelists of the Rear Guard made the last serious attempt to orient Negro fiction toward bourgeois ideals. As the "normalcy" of the 1920's gave way to depression and then to war, the shallowness of this approach became apparent. The sensibilities of the modern artist have on the whole prevented him from developing an affirmative attitude toward contemporary society; he has responded to the modern situation with an appropriate sense of catastrophe. This sense of catastrophe, this awareness of the destructive impulses of our time, first entered Negro fiction through the better authors of the Harlem School. It is hardly surprising, in view of the insularity of Negro life, that a significant number of Negro authors remained temporarily untouched by the crisis in values of Western society. In the long run, however, the Rear Guard was doomed to extinction. There were stranger things in the new century than were dreamed of in their philosophy.

The Morning After

On a dismal morning in the fall of 1929 the nation woke up with an aching head and an empty pocketbook. The Great Hangover had begun. Ten years of pleasant memories were quickly obliterated by the sobering impact of the stock-market crash. In literary circles, the reverberation was immediate. Negro and white author alike, to paraphrase Langston Hughes, slid downhill toward the WPA. Negro literature, in particular, experienced a slump year in 1930. In his annual review in *Opportunity,* Alain Locke wrote, "The much exploited Negro Renaissance was after all a product of the expansive period we are now willing to call a period of inflation and overproduction." An inevitable reaction had set in; the carefree abandon of the Harlem School was soon to be challenged by a grimmer view of Negro life in the "proletarian" fiction of the 1930's. Meanwhile the Negro Renaissance suffered an unspectacular demise.

In the afterglow of the Renaissance, what final assessment should be made? The Rear Guard, to begin with, represents the force of inertia; an evaluation of the Renaissance is essentially an evaluation of the Harlem School. That the latter was guilty of excesses is certainly beyond dispute. If mediocrity dominated the period, it was largely because of the Harlem School's exoticism, and its consequent emphasis on "atmosphere" rather than form. Yet even mediocrity was a gain over the hopeless incompetence of the early Negro novel. The Harlem School writers found Negro literature in the grip of narrow class prejudice and moral melodrama; they liberated it by a combination of literary realism and local color. However unscrupulously they may have exploited a fad, they established the Negro novelist's right to distinctive cultural material, and they provided Negro literature with an indispensable transition to the modern age.

PART III. *The Search for a Tradition: 1930–1940*

THEME for Negro writers will emerge when they have begun to feel the meaning of their history as a race as though they in one lifetime had lived it themselves throughout all the long centuries.

RICHARD WRIGHT

6. *The Great Depression*

AFTER twenty-five years of war-borne prosperity, it is difficult for most Americans to recapture the mood of the lean and hungry thirties. Yet if the well-fed sixties are to establish contact with the sensibilities of the earlier decade, an effort must be made to reconstruct the era before Pearl Harbor when the American economy found itself in a state of virtual collapse. Between 1929 and 1933, it is necessary to recall, the gross national product was reduced by approximately one-half. Banks closed their doors, farms and factories lay idle, unemployment soared, bread lines grew, relief rolls burgeoned, and hoboes roamed the land. While large sections of the urban population suffered from malnutrition, the countryside was busy dumping thousands of gallons of milk into nearby rivers; cotton was ploughed under; sheep were slaughtered; and kerosene was poured over pyramids of Florida and California oranges.

The collapse of the economic system wrought profound changes in the climate of American intellectual life. The reckless mood of the 1920's vanished under a rubble of avalanching stock quotations. In the course of time, the gay, party mood of the flapper era was replaced by a new social consciousness, which emanated from vast stirrings beneath the surface of American society. These were the years of organized hunger marches, of mass demonstrations for an increase in relief payments, of tenant leagues to fight evictions, of spontaneous sit-down strikes, of the rise of industrial unionism, and of a sharp leftward turn in American politics. By and large, the American intelligentsia of the 1930's allied itself with these popular movements, articulated their grievances, and expressed their aspirations for social justice. The Depression, which ought to have shattered whatever values the war had left intact, paradoxically gave the Lost Generation something to believe in.

The Negro intelligentsia was no exception to the general trend. If anything, Negro intellectuals were even more responsive to the social crisis of the 1930's than were the whites, in direct proportion to the greater suffering of the Negro masses. Traditionally the last to be hired and the first to be fired, the Negro wage worker bore the brunt of the economic blow. Goaded by his knowledge of the black worker's double burden, the Negro intellectual of the 1930's was readily inclined to support the new movements of social protest.

This new militancy, however, in contrast to that of earlier periods, was social rather than racial in emphasis. It was based on the grievances of the Negro masses rather than on those of the rising middle class. In some instances, under the influence of Marxist ideology, it came to embrace the grievances of the white working class as well. During the Depression, for the first time in their history, the Negro masses made common cause with their white fellows, in the campaign of organized labor for higher wages, union recognition, and greater unemployment benefits. As a result of their trade-union experience, the Negro masses began to break through the narrow confines of their lives and enter a broader arena of social struggle. In a parallel development, the race consciousness of the Negro intelligentsia widened into class consciousness, as they emerged from the narrow stream of racial experience into the broad intellectual current of the turbulent thirties.

The Federal Writers' Project

Two institutions which arose and flourished against the Depression background greatly accelerated this development. The first of these was the Federal Writers' Project, a subdivision of the WPA which attempted to create work for unemployed writers by utilizing their literary skills in the public interest. The chief project of the agency was the compilation of an "American Guide" —a handbook of the forty-eight states which might serve as a kind of American Baedeker. According to Sterling Brown, who was the FWP's Editor of Negro Affairs, the project turned up a vast store of information about American culture which might well have formed the basis for a new regional art. The significance of the FWP for the Negro novelist, however, lay not so much in the realm of source material as in the extracurricular activities which surrounded the project.

The Federal Writers' Project was more than a job; it was a milieu. Most of the writers joined the WPA government-workers' union, an affiliation which brought them into direct organizational ties with the American labor movement. Many members of the FWP contributed regularly to *Direction,* an independent political and cultural monthly which warmly endorsed government support of creative writing. Nor was the FWP officially indifferent to the publishing needs of its members. In 1937 the directors of the project called for contributions of original work written during off-project hours. The result was an anthology called *American Stuff* (Viking Press, 1937), which contained contributions from several Negro authors, including Sterling Brown, Richard Wright, and Robert E. Hayden.[1]

The roster of Negro writers connected with the Federal Writers' Project reads like a Who's Who of contemporary Negro literature. Richard Wright, Claude McKay, Arna Bontemps, Roi Ottley, William Attaway, Margaret Walker, Ralph Ellison, Frank Yerby, and Willard Motley participated at one time or another. Working in the same office on the same job with whites, these colored writers had an unprecedented opportunity to break out of their

1. Excerpts from this collection were published separately by *Direction* in a special number called "American Stuff" (*1,* No. 3, Feb. 1938).

closed world. The white world which they entered, to be sure, was not "typically American," nor could they have entered, if it were. It was in large measure a Stalinized world, but at least it was prepared to accept Negroes on a basis of social equality.

Role of the Communist Party

The second institution which for better or worse tended to overcome the Negro writer's spiritual isolation was the ubiquitous annexation apparatus of the Communist party. During the 1930's the party was active politically in virtually every sphere of American life. In its heyday, it conducted successful propaganda work both among writers as a professional group and among Negroes as such. In an effort to win writers to its cause, it worked through such front organizations as the American Writers' Congress, the League of American Writers, the early John Reed Clubs, and countless local groups of similar character. It offered a forum for "progressive" writers in such journals as *New Masses*, and through its vast periphery was able to supply young unknowns with a captive audience. Many young writers, both white and colored, succumbed to the flattering publicity which the party was willing to bestow—for a political price.

The party also made great strides in its "Negro work" during the Depression years. It began rather ineffectually with the League of Struggle for Negro Rights (1930–34), Langston Hughes, President.[2] Far more spectacular was its share in the defense of the Scottsboro boys, undertaken by a front organization known as the International Labor Defense. By fighting the case of nine Negro youths from Alabama accused of raping two white girls of dubious morality,[3] the party was able to pose successfully as the champion of the Negro people. In the national elections of 1932 and 1936 it ran a Negro, James Ford, as its showpiece candidate

2. Most of the factual material which follows is based on Wilson Record, *The Negro and the Communist Party* (Chapel Hill, University of North Carolina Press, 1951): pp. 54–119, "The Kremlin and the Black Republic," and pp. 120–83, "Building the Negro People's United Front."

3. Convictions by the State of Alabama were twice set aside by the U.S. Supreme Court, once because the defendants were denied counsel, and once because Negroes were systematically excluded from the jury.

for vice-president. In accordance with its new popular-front policy of the mid-thirties, it helped to initiate, and eventually took over, the National Negro Congress, perhaps the most promising attempt to organize Negroes since the formation of the NAACP. As a result of these activities, the Communist party achieved a certain influence among Negro intellectuals which should not be belittled or underestimated.

More important, however, than the party's organizational tactics was the theoretical formulation on which they were based. The American Negro problem, so runs the Communist rationale, is an aspect of a broader pattern of imperialism, and its solution should follow Lenin's pronouncements on "the national question." The American Negro is not merely an ethnic minority but a separate and distinct *nation,* like any other oppressed colonial people. The American Negro "nation" should therefore be granted the right of "self-determination," on the model of the national minorities in the Soviet Union.[4] From this underlying conception flowed the party's slogan calling for the formation of a Negro Soviet Republic, embracing a hypothetical black belt in Southern United States. Only at a recent party convention (1957) was this position finally abandoned.

Taken literally, the proposal for a separate Negro nation within continental United States is adventurist enough. Most American readers will wonder how a Negro intellectual of, for example, Richard Wright's stature could have entertained it seriously, even for a moment. Yet merely to raise the question is to underestimate Negro nationalism, an error never committed by the Communist party. As a metaphor, or as a myth, the idea of a separate Negro nation expresses a separatist impulse deeply embedded in Negro psychology. The mass support which Marcus Garvey once achieved among American Negroes, not to mention the strength of the Zionist movement among American Jews, should suffice to show that separatist solutions, though extreme, are not wholly irrelevant to the American scene. They are a barometer of minority group insecurity and therefore of the partial failure of American democracy.

4. In reality, national minorities in the Soviet Union enjoy little or no autonomy but are constantly subject to the pressures of Great Russian chauvinism.

Whatever one's evaluation of the party's position, it exerted a profound influence on the Negro writers of the 1930's who accepted it in full or in part. Wherever it was put forward, it gave additional impetus to the nationalist content of Negro literature. The Communist party did not invent Negro nationalism, but it did its best to encourage it for political reasons. Wilson Record describes the party line on Negro art as follows: "It was with the struggle of this Negro nation to achieve its manhood that the Negro artists and intellectuals were to be concerned. Its trials, its tribulations, its sufferings,—these were to be the major themes of novels, of music, of other creative forms. To select other themes was tantamount to the betrayal of the race." [5] By thus enjoining the Negro author to explore his own tradition, the party inadvertently advanced the legitimate development of Negro art. It is not the first time in its history that the American Communist party has done the right thing for the wrong reasons.

The Little Magazines

The dominant tendencies of a literary period often crystallize in its little magazines. During the 1930's two periodicals appeared called *Challenge* (1934–37) and *New Challenge* (1937), which took up where *Fire, Harlem,* and the *Messenger* had left off. Like the little magazines of the Harlem School, these publications were motivated by the growing breach between the Negro artist and the Negro middle class, further aggravated in the thirties by the influence of Marxism upon the Negro intelligentsia. *Crisis* and *Opportunity* had been taken over by the Philistines, and were no longer performing the service to Negro art which they had rendered in the salad days of the Negro Renaissance. In any case, they were sponsored by organizations with wider interests and commitments and could not possibly be predominantly literary in character. A new venture which would reflect the mood of a new decade was clearly in order.

Challenge appeared in 1934 under the editorship of Dorothy West, a minor Renaissance figure who was later to write an important novel called *The Living Is Easy* (1948). Among the

5. *The Negro and the Communist Party,* p. 110.

contributors were transitional figures like Arna Bontemps, Langston Hughes, and Zora Neale Hurston, as well as newcomers like William Attaway, Owen Dodson, and Frank Yerby. The lead editorial of the first issue was addressed to the younger generation of Negro writers: "We who were the New Negroes *challenge* them to better our achievements. For we did not altogether live up to our fine promise." [6] A foreword by James Weldon Johnson which acknowledges the "flash-in-the-pan" nature of the Negro Renaissance sustains the transitional and somewhat defensive tone of the magazine. The chief concern of those involved was apparently to recapture the "spirit of '26" and to restore the former vigor of Negro art.

A clue to the future of the enterprise appears in a letter to the editor from a reader who asks why *Challenge* is so "pale pink." Miss West's reply is short and to the point: "Because the 'red' articles we did receive were not literature." Apparently Miss West's views on literature and society suffered a sea change during the next few years, for in 1937 the magazine was reorganized, appearing thereafter as *New Challenge,* with Richard Wright as associate editor.

The first issue contained an editorial manifesto, addressed to "all writers who realize the present need for the realistic depiction of life through the sharp focus of social consciousness." Combined with this emphasis on social realism were distinct echoes of the party line on Negro art: "A literary movement among Negroes, we feel, should first of all be built upon the writer's placing his material in the proper perspective with regard to the life of the Negro masses. For that reason we want to indicate . . . the great fertility of folk material as a source of creative effort." [7] The lead article by Richard Wright, called "Blueprint for Negro Writing," pleads explicitly for a "Marxist" (i.e. Stalinist) orientation, which "points the way for Negro writers to stand shoulder to shoulder with Negro workers in mood and outlook." Largely by virtue of Wright's participation and influence, *New Challenge* marks a high point in the Negro writer's excursion into "proletarian art."

6. *Challenge, 1,* No. 1, March 1934.
7. *New Challenge, 1,* No. 1, fall 1937.

The Search for a Tradition

The impact of the Depression on the Negro novel is clear enough in broad outline. There were, to begin with, fewer novels produced than during the previous decade. Output was cut in half, from twenty-five novels in the 1920's to twelve in the 1930's, undoubtedly because of the urgency of the economic struggle. The novels which did appear displayed a greater social realism, and presented a more balanced view of Negro life than the joy-centered novels of the Harlem School. Jazz exoticism, as a dominant tone, was abandoned in favor of social protest. For the first time, as Ralph Ellison has remarked, the Negro novelist came to recognize the themes and problems of Dreiser, Sinclair, and London as relevant to Negro experience.

Yet even as the Great Depression linked the Negro novelist to a broader tradition of social protest, it paradoxically encouraged a continuing interest in his Negro heritage as such. The forces set in motion by the Negro Renaissance had by no means spent themselves, and independently of all political considerations they resulted in an intensive exploitation of the materials of Negro life. The writers of the 1930's accepted "race material" as the basis for their art, and sought to expand their social consciousness in order to cope with it more effectively. The result was a gain in scope which at once embraced depth in time and breadth in understanding of contemporary society.

Perhaps this gain in perspective can best be interpreted as a phase in the Negro novelist's search for a myth—a framework in terms of which he can structure his art, as the Christian myth structures *Paradise Lost.* No myth as shallow as the early faith in race progress could survive the racial tyranny of World War I; no myth as shallow as primitivism could survive in a decade of bread lines and unemployment. In such a period, realism becomes the order of the day; myth must at least approximate historical reality. It was thus that the Negro novelists of the 1930's began to construct a framework for their art based on the race's actual experience in America.

Slavery, the folk culture of the rural South, the Great Migration, the black ghettos of the industrial North—these are the central aspects of the American Negro's tradition. Most of the important novels of the 1930's explore one phase or another of this common heritage. In a sense, therefore, the novels of the period recapitulate the very historical development which in its totality the Negro novelist of the 1930's was striving to comprehend.

7. *Aspects of the Racial Past*

Arna Bontemps

ARNA BONTEMPS is a transitional figure whose novels bear the mark both of the Negro Renaissance and of the depression years which follow. Born in Louisiana of Creole parentage, he moved to Los Angeles at an early age. He was educated at Pacific Union College and the University of Chicago; at present he is head librarian of Fisk University. A minor poet during the 1920's, Bontemps turned later to fiction, history, and books for children. He has written three novels, of which the first, *God Sends Sunday* (1931), is an unadulterated product of the Negro Renaissance. The setting of the novel is the sporting world of racetrack men and gamblers, of jazz and the shimmy, of fights and razor carvings. His historical novels, however, which deal with slavery times, reflect the mood of the Depression era. By choosing slave insurrections as a basis for his plots, Bontemps stresses an aspect of slavery which was emotionally appealing to the rebellious thirties.

Black Thunder (1936) is based on authentic court records of the State of Virginia, which describe an abortive slave rebellion near Richmond in the year 1800. The insurrection was led by Gabriel Prosser, a Negro slave who paid with his life for his love of freedom. In Bontemps' version, the uprising is touched off by the unusually cruel punishment of a mischievous slave. Winning widespread support among the slaves on nearby plantations, among free men of color in the town, and among white sympathizers in the *Amis des Noirs,* the rebellion all but succeeds in taking Richmond. Gabriel's slave army is defeated only by the intervention of a torrential rainstorm and an eleventh-hour betrayal. The uprising is suppressed by the middle of the novel, after which the plot interest shifts to the pursuit and capture of the ringleaders; the guilt, fear, and blind retribution of the whites; and the courageous death of Gabriel, the defeated romantic hero.

The narrative technique, which conveys the action by a progressive treatment of the participants, is reminiscent of the novels of Dos Passos. The plot is developed in fragments, through short chapters which open with the name of the character under consideration. From this constant shift in point of view, the reader must piece together the full panorama. It is a technique especially suited to the presentation of complex historical events, and Bontemps employs it skillfully. At its best, this technique requires deft characterization, since the action of the novel is constantly refracted through a new consciousness, which the reader must understand in its own right.

The characterization of *Black Thunder* is condensed but well rounded. The major figures emerge not merely as symbols of social strata but as credible individuals with their own motives, who have been swept momentarily onto the stage of history by the force of events. Gabriel, "who was too old for joy, too young for despair"; "that brown gal, Juba, with her petticoats on fire"; Mingo, the free artisan whose wife is still a slave; and M. Creuzot, the reluctant Jacobin who must fish or cut bait as the rebellion gains momentum—these and other portraits transform what might have been arid history or romantic extravaganza into good historical fiction.

Through the use of symbols, Bontemps achieves both economy

and scope. Bundy's whipping, for example, does duty for all injustice of master to slave, making it unnecessary to belabor the point. The novel begins and ends with Old Ben, as if to suggest that the "contented" slave provides a continuity of which Gabriel's uprising is a violation. Juba, whose flashing naked thighs astride the black colt Araby are the signal for the rebellion to begin, adds another dimension to the novel. Thorstein Veblen has noted that in primitive societies the slave status and the woman status are practically identical. A slave insurrection therefore has sexual overtones; it is above all an assertion of manhood. Bontemps dramatizes this situation successfully through Juba's challenge to the slaves: "Always big-talking about what booming bed-men you is. . . . Well, let's see what you is good for, sure 'nough. Let's see if you knows how to go free; let's see if you knows how to die" (p. 99).

A leitmotiv runs through *Black Thunder,* pointing the way to the theme: "Anything what's equal to a gray squirrel want to be free." As the novel unfolds, the idea of freedom becomes linked with the idea of death: "A wild bird what's in a cage will die anyhow, sooner or later. . . . He'll pine hisself to death. He just as well to break his neck trying to get out" (p. 82). By developing this tension between freedom and death, the author suggests that the determination to be free is itself a kind of bondage.

It is Bontemps' intention in *Black Thunder* to credit the Negro slave with an obsessive love of freedom. The extent to which this interpretation is historically valid is a moot point. That some slaves felt an overwhelming desire to "go free" and acted upon it is certainly beyond dispute. In any case, complexity of characterization, together with a tone of restraint and a tendency to underwrite, combine to save *Black Thunder* from the worst features of a propaganda novel. What remains of protest and of race pride limits the book but does not destroy it.

Arna Bontemps' second historical novel, *Drums at Dusk* (1939), is in every respect a retreat from the standards of *Black Thunder.* Deriving its plot from the Haitian slave rebellion which brought Toussaint l'Ouverture to power, the novel is unworthy of its subject. In writing of a successful rebellion, Bontemps is deprived of the dramatic power of tragedy, and he discovers no appropriate attitude to take its place. Upon a highly romantic plot he grafts a class analysis of society which is post-Marxian and flagrantly unhistorical. Frequently lapsing into crude melodrama, he embroiders his narrative with all of the sword-play, sex, and sadism of a Hollywood extravaganza.

George Wylie Henderson and Zora Neale Hurston

The literary possibilities of the canefield and the cotton patch were for the most part deliberately ignored by the novelists of the Negro Renaissance. It was perhaps predictable that the first generation of Negro cosmopolitans should desire to put as much distance as possible between themselves and the feudal South. But in the long run the Negro's ties to the South are too strong to be denied. Even without the stimulus of the new Southern realism, and of such white interpreters of the Southern scene as T. S. Stribling, Erskine Caldwell, and William Faulkner, it was inevitable that the Negro novelist should turn to the South for literary material. Any serious quest for a tradition was bound to lead "down home." During the 1930's a number of Negro novelists attempted an interpretation of the rural South, and two of them, George Wylie Henderson and Zora Neale Hurston, met with considerable success.

George Wylie Henderson (1904–) was born in Warrior's Stand, Alabama, where his grandfather owned a small farm and his father was minister of the A.M.E. Church. Educated at Tuskegee Institute, he came to New York during the early years of the Depression, where he obtained employment as a printer with the *Daily News.* While working in the shop, he wrote short stories for the *News* and for several magazines, including *Redbook.* In 1935 his first novel, *Ollie Miss,* appeared. It was followed eleven years later by a sequel, *Jule* (1946), which is so badly written that the author of *Ollie Miss* is scarcely recognizable.

Ollie Miss is a pastoral, in the classical sense of the word. By treating of unimposing events in a simple microcosm, it reduces human experience to manageable proportions. The setting of *Ollie Miss* is rural Alabama, where "the song of the sweep beneath the soil" is interrupted only by an occasional barbecue, camp meeting, or Saturday night dance. The linguistic texture of the novel reflects its peasant setting: dialogue consists of short, simple sentences; figures of speech are based on nature imagery and barnyard metaphor. In terms of plot *Ollie Miss* can be divided into three parts. As the novel opens, Ollie, the protagonist, is on her way to visit her lover, Jule. At once there is a long flashback (Part I), whose primary purpose is to establish the strength of Ollie's love. Through a detailed recounting of her recent past, the intensity of Ollie's feeling is defined.

Ollie, who left her guardian because of a dispute over Jule, has been hired as a field hand on the farm of Uncle Alex. Through her behavior toward the other field hands and domestic workers, her own personality is gradually disclosed. Three traits are stressed: her unconventionality, her maturity, and her bodily vigor. Ollie's unconventionality prepares the reader for her future visit to Jule. Set off against Nan, who is a prude and a gossip, Ollie is simply indifferent to minor conformities. Her maturity is established at the outset, when she assures Uncle Alex that she will not become a source of sexual rivalry among his men-folk: "Guess you won't hab to worry much 'bout nuthin' lak dat, Uncle Alex." This self-assurance is contrasted later with her emotional dependence upon Jule.

In a subtle adumbration of theme, the reader's attention is repeatedly drawn to Ollie's body. She is described as "full-bodied and strong," with an enormous appetite and a corresponding capacity for hard work. Her body possesses a natural sexuality which is direct and uncomplicated in its expression. In Jule's absence she is neither strictly faithful nor promiscuous. Rejecting Slaughter because he is in love with her, she provides for her physical needs through a casual affair with an immature boy: "Willie don't matter." She can take such a lover without violating her feelings for Jule. The Willie episode thus introduces the dichotomy of body and feelings which forms the main tension of *Ollie Miss*.

Part II contains most of the present action of the novel. After an absence of several months, Ollie visits Jule's cabin and finds it empty, except for traces of another woman. She promptly seeks out Della, one of Jule's jilted lovers, and inquires about his present situation. Learning that Jule plans to attend a nearby camp meeting, she precedes him there with a definite end in view. It has been Ollie's intention all along, the reader suddenly realizes, to become the mother of Jule's child. Without issue, her love is incomplete, and her fear of losing Jule makes a child all the more imperative. Finding Jule at last, she persuades him to spend the night with her, but in the morning Jule insists stubbornly upon his freedom. Ollie, crushed and despondent, returns to the camp ground, where she invites attack from her current rival and is badly slashed with a razor.

In Part III the focus of the novel shifts to Ollie's inner development. With Jule's rejection of her love, Ollie's spiritual crisis begins. Its initial phase is a sense of alienation from the rest of humanity, "as though they existed in a world apart from her, and she was no longer among them." The razor-cutting episode is the outward manifestation of this mood. As Ollie lies seriously injured at Uncle Alex's farm, she experiences a further sense of dissociation from her own body, accompanied by a painful awareness of the importance of her feelings. Her inner wound proves to be the more grievous; in comparison with Jule's desertion, the injury to her body is insignificant: "I don't feel no pains. I don't feel nuthin'. I jes feels like I is—is dead. Hit jes feels like somethin' inside of me been dyin' a long time an' all of hit is 'bout dead now, 'cept dat part dat ain't got no feelings" (p. 217). As if to show contempt for her body and its wounds, Ollie refuses to press charges against her assailant.

It is Ollie's feelings that matter, yet everyone else, including Jule, is concerned solely with the welfare of her body. Dead inside, she recovers the will to live only when she learns of her pregnancy. Jule, remorseful over the razor-cutting, is ready "to do the right thing," but this is not enough for Ollie. She has grasped a higher concept of love, and in the light of her new understanding she is prepared to renounce Jule. This new concept, achieved through suffering, includes but transcends bodily fulfillment: "Soul-loving somethin' is lak eating yo' victuals when you ain't hungry. You kin eat hit, or you kin leave hit alone, but you is full right on" (p. 273).

Ollie Miss is concerned thematically with ways of loving. There is one way of loving which insists on possession, and which may have either positive or negative consequences. It may mean life, as with Ollie's early love for Jule: "Just thinking of Jule, of the fact that she wanted to see Jule, made Ollie want to live." Or it may mean a kind of death, when possession is denied, as with Slaughter or Della. But ironically, to Ollie of the full body, a different kind of love is revealed: "Mebbe ef dere had been somethin' us could want and not hab'—somethin' us could work for an' still want—mebbe hit mought hab been different" (p. 272). It is a religious view, based on renunciation, and for Ollie it signifies escape from a deadening corporality: "Walking again, her body felt free and light and strangely at peace."

Zora Neale Hurston (1903–) was born and raised in an all-Negro town in Florida—an experience with "separate-but-equal" politics which deeply affected her outlook on racial issues, as well as her approach to the Negro novel. Her father was a tenant farmer and jackleg preacher whose colorful sermons were an important influence on Miss Hurston's style. Her mother urged her to "jump at the sun," and at the first opportunity she left home, employed as a maid in a traveling Gilbert and Sullivan company. An ambitious reader in secondary school, she set her sights on college, achieving this aim largely through her own efforts. She attended Morgan State College in Baltimore, Howard University, and Columbia University, where she studied anthropology under Franz Boas.

At Howard she joined the Stylus, an undergraduate literary society sponsored by Alain Locke. Drawn at once into the vortex of the Negro Renaissance, she published several stories in *Opportunity,* and collaborated with Langston Hughes and Wallace Thurman on the editorial board of *Fire*. In the early 1930's a prize story called "The Gilded Six-Bits" appeared in *Story* magazine, leading to an invitation from Lippincott's to do a novel. The result was *Jonah's Gourd Vine* (1934). Her second and more important novel, *Their Eyes Were Watching God,* appeared in 1937, while a third novel, *Seraph on the Suwanee,* was published in 1948. In addition to her short stories and novels, Miss Hurston has written three books of folklore, an autobiography, a one-act play, one or two librettos, and several magazine articles.

Jonah's Gourd Vine has style without structure, a rich verbal texture without dramatic form, "atmosphere" without real characterization. It is the story of John Buddy, a field hand turned preacher whose congregation accepts him as "a man amongst men," but is unprepared to find him also a man amongst women. A great preacher (the author introduces a ten-page sermon to prove it), John Buddy is no less a lover. An erratic tension arises between folk artist and philanderer, but it is not carried forward to a suitable denouement. In its emphasis on atmosphere and local color, in its exploitation of the exotic, and especially of exotic language, and in its occasional hint of primitivism, *Jonah's Gourd Vine* expresses a sensibility molded predominantly by the Negro Renaissance.

The style of the novel is impressive enough. Zora Neale Hurston, whom Langston Hughes has described as a rare *raconteuse,* draws freely on the verbal ingenuity of the folk. Her vivid, metaphorical style is based primarily on the Negro preacher's graphic ability to present abstractions to his flock. Take the opening sentence of the novel: "God was grumbling his thunder and playing the zig-zag lightning through his fingers"; or such an image as "the cloud-muddied moonlight"; or the small-town flavor of "Time is long by the courthouse clock." The danger is that these folk sayings may become the main point of the novel. Overdone, they destroy rather than support authentic characterization. In *Jonah's Gourd Vine* they are too nonfunctional, too anthropological, and in the end merely exotic. Miss Hurston has not yet mastered the form of the novel, but her style holds promise of more substantial accomplishment to come.

The genesis of a work of art may be of no moment to literary criticism but it is sometimes crucial in literary history. It may, for example, account for the rare occasion when an author outclasses himself. *Their Eyes Were Watching God* (1937) is a case in point. The novel was written in Haiti in just seven weeks, under the emotional pressure of a recent love affair. "The plot was far from the circumstances," Miss Hurston writes in her autobiography, "but I tried to embalm all the tenderness of my passion for him in *Their Eyes Were Watching God.*" Ordinarily the prognosis for such a novel would be dismal enough. One might expect immediacy and intensity, but not distance, or control, or universality. Yet oddly, or perhaps not so oddly, it is Miss Hurston's best novel, and possibly the best novel of the period, excepting *Native Son.*

The opening paragraph of *Their Eyes Were Watching God* encompasses the whole of the novel's meaning: "Ships at a distance have every man's wish on board. For some they come in with the tide. For others they sail forever on the horizon, never out of sight, never landing, until the Watcher turns his eyes away in resignation, his dreams mocked to death by Time. That is the life of man" (p. 9). For women, the author continues, the dream is the sole reality. "So the beginning of this was a woman, and she had come back from burying the dead."

Janie has been gone for almost two years as the action of the novel commences. The townspeople know only that she left home in the company of a lover much younger than herself, and that she departed in fine clothes but has returned in overalls. Heads nod; tongues wag; and the consensus is that she has played the fool. Toward the gossiping women who, from the safety of a small-town porch "pass nations through their mouths," Janie feels only contempt and irritation: "If God don't think no mo' 'bout 'em than Ah do, they's a lost ball in de high grass." To Pheoby, her kissing-friend, she tells the story of her love for Tea-Cake, which together with its antecedents comprises the main body of the novel.

Janie's dream begins during her adolescence, when she is stirred by strange wonderings as she watches a pear tree blossom. No sooner is her dream born, however, than it is desecrated by her grandmother. Nanny, who has witnessed her share of the sexual exploitation of Negro women, declares firmly: "[Neither] de menfolks white or black is makin' a spit cup outa you." Seeking to protect Janie from the vicissitudes of adolescent love, she puts her up on the auction block of marriage. To Nanny, being married is being like white folks: "You got yo' lawful husband same as Mis' Washburn or anybody else." Against her better judgment, therefore, Janie acquiesces in an early marriage with Logan Killicks, a hard-working farmer considerably older than herself.

"There are years that ask questions and years that answer: Did marriage compel love like the sun the day?" Janie soon realizes her mistake. She aspires to more than sixty acres and an organ in the parlor, and refuses to barter her fulfillment as a woman in exchange for property rights: "Ah ain't takin' dat ole land tuh heart neither. Ah could throw ten acres of it over de fence every day and never look back to see where it fell" (p. 42). Affairs reach a crisis with the appearance of Jody Starks, a younger man who offers Janie a fresh start in a neighboring county. "Janie pulled back a long time because he did not represent sun-up and pollen and blooming trees, but he spoke for far horizon." Her first dream dead, she runs off with Jody to the all-Negro town of Eatonville.

Janie's second dream scarcely fares better than the first. Although her husband becomes "a big voice," a property owner, and eventually mayor of the town, Janie remains restless, unfulfilled. Asked by Jody how she likes being "Mrs. Mayor," she replies: "It keeps us in some way we ain't natural wid one 'nother. Youse always off talkin' and fixin' things, and Ah feels lak Ah'm jus' markin' time" (p. 74). A widening rift develops in the marriage as a fundamental clash of values becomes apparent. Janie can no more reconcile herself to Jody's store than to Logan Killicks' sixty acres: "The store itself was a pleasant place if only she didn't have to sell things." On one occasion, when the townsfolk playfully take off from work for the mock funeral of a dead mule, Jody remarks, "Ah wish mah people would git mo' business in 'em and not spend so much time on foolishness." Janie's reply is caustic: "Everybody can't be lak you, Jody. Somebody is bound tuh want tuh laugh and play."

By this time, the wider meaning of the novel has begun to emerge. A dramatic tension has arisen between the sound business instincts of Janie's two husbands and her own striving toward a full life, which is later to take on flesh in the person of Tea-Cake. At first glance, what seems to be taking shape in the dramatic structure of the novel is the familiar cultural dualism of the Negro Renaissance. Although this Renaissance pattern is definitely present, Miss Hurston pitches her theme in a higher key. Janie rejects the Nanny-Killicks-Jody way of life because of its cramped quarters and narrow gauge: "Nanny belonged to that other kind that loved to deal in scraps." It is Janie's urge to touch the horizon which causes her to repudiate respectability.

Meanwhile, Janie's second marriage moves toward a culmination in Jody's illness and death. For many years their relationship has been purely perfunctory: "The spirit of the marriage left the bedroom and took to living in the parlor." Only on his deathbed does Janie confront her husband with the bitter knowledge of an inner life which she has been unable to share with him: "You done lived wid me for twenty years and you don't half know me atall." Taking stock after Jody's death, Janie senses in this repressed phase of her life an unconscious preparation for her great adventure: "She was saving up feelings for some man she had never seen."

If the first half of the novel deals with the prose of Janie's life, the latter half deals with its poetry. Not long after Jody's death, Tea-Cake walks into her life. First off, he laughs; next he teaches her how to play checkers. One afternoon he urges her to close up shop and come with him to a baseball game. The next night, after midnight, he invites her on a fishing expedition. Their relationship is full of play, of impulsiveness, of informality, and of imagination. Easy-going, careless of money, living for the moment, Tea-Cake is an incarnation of the folk culture. After a whirlwind courtship, he persuades Janie to leave Eatonville and to try his way.

On a deeper level, Tea-Cake represents intensity and experience. As Janie puts it in summing up her two years with him: "Ah been a delegate to de big 'ssociation of life." Their new life begins with a trip to Jacksonville, "and to a lot of things she wanted to see and know." In the big city, Tea-Cake deserts Janie for several days, while she suffers the torments and anxieties of a middle-aged lover. Upon his return she learns that he had won a large sum in a crap game and had immediately given a barbecue for his friends, in order to find out how it feels to be rich. When she protests at being left out, he asks with amusement, "So you aims tuh partake wid everything, hunh?" From that moment, their life together becomes an unlimited partnership.

From Jacksonville, Janie and Tea-Cake move "down on the muck" of the Florida Everglades for the bean-picking season. Janie goes to work in the fields in order to be with Tea-Cake during the long working day. They share the hard work and the hard play of the folk, laughing together at the "dickty" Negroes who think that "us oughta class off." In this milieu of primitive Bahaman dances, of "blues made and used right on the spot," and of "romping and playing . . . behind the boss's back," Janie at last finds happiness. In true Renaissance spirit, it is the folk culture, through Tea-Cake, which provides the means of her spiritual fulfillment.

One night, "the palm and banana trees began that long-distance talk with rain." As the winds over Lake Okechobee mount to hurricane force, the novel moves to a swift climax. Janie and Tea-Cake find themselves swept along with a crowd of refugees, amid awesome scenes of destruction and sudden death. In the midst of their nightmarish flight, Tea-Cake is bitten by a dog and unknowingly contracts rabies. Some weeks later, suffering horribly, he loses his senses and attacks Janie when she refuses him a drink of water. In the ensuing melee, Janie is compelled to shoot Tea-Cake to protect her own life. "It was the meanest moment of eternity." Not merely that her lover dies, but that she herself is the instrument—this is the price which Janie pays for her brief months of happiness. Her trial and acquittal seem unreal to her; without Tea-Cake she can only return to Eatonville to "live by comparisons."

As the reader tries to assimilate Janie's experience and assess its central meaning, he cannot avoid returning to a key passage which foreshadows the climax of the novel: "All gods dispense suffering without reason. Otherwise they would not be worshipped. Through indiscriminate suffering men know fear, and fear is the most divine emotion. It is the stones for altars and the beginning of wisdom. Half gods are worshipped in wine and flowers. Real gods require blood" (p. 215). Through Tea-Cake's death, Janie experiences the divine emotion, for her highest dream—to return to the opening paragraph of the novel—has been "mocked to death by Time." Like all men, she can only watch in resignation, with an overpowering sense of her own helplessness.

Yet if mankind's highest dreams are ultimately unattainable, it is still better to live on the far horizon than to grub around on shore. Janie does not regret her life with Tea-Cake, or the price which is exacted in the end: "We been tuhgether round two years. If you kin see de light at daybreak, you don't keer if you die at dusk. It's so many people never seen de light at all. Ah wuz fumblin' round and God opened de door" (p. 236). As the novel closes, the scene returns to Janie and her friend in Eatonville. Pheoby's reaction to the story she has heard is a clinching statement of the theme of the novel: "Ah done growed ten feet higher from jús' listenin' tuh you, Janie. Ah ain't satisfied with mahself no mo'."

William Attaway

William Attaway (1912–), the outstanding interpreter of the Great Migration, was himself a member of a migrant professional family. Born in a small town in Mississippi where his father practiced medicine, he moved North with the family while still a boy. Attaway was educated in the public schools of Chicago, and at the University of Illinois. "In Chicago," he writes, "I had all the advantages that a self-made man imagines are good for an only son. But after my father's death I rebelled and spent my time hoboing." Like Langston Hughes and Claude McKay, Attaway left college for the sea, and for two years led a vagabond life as seaman, and afterward as salesman, labor organizer, and hobo. In the end, he remarks, "I meekly returned . . . and got my B.A. as painlessly as possible."

Attaway's literary career began under the tutelage of his sister, who was interested in the theater and who eventually became a successful Broadway actress. While still in high school he tried his hand at script-writing for his sister's amateur dramatic groups. He experimented with both one-act plays and short stories at the University of Illinois, publishing a few pieces in literary magazines and newspapers. An interesting specimen of his early work appears in *Challenge* (June 1936), called "The Tale of the Blackamoor," in which a colored servant-boy of another era dances a minuet in fantasy with his mistress' Dresden China doll.

Attaway has written two novels: *Let Me Breathe Thunder* (1939) and *Blood on the Forge* (1941). The former is a record of his hoboing days; it is a run-of-the-mill proletarian novel strongly influenced by Steinbeck's *Of Mice and Men.* The latter is a novel of superior quality which portrays the disintegration of the folk culture under the impact of modern industrialism. Firmly rooted in Negro folk history, *Blood on the Forge* deals with the precipitous adjustment to factory life which was thrust upon thousands of Negro sharecroppers toward the end of World War I. By far the most perceptive novel of the Great Migration, it describes the transplanting of the folk from the familiar violence of Southern feudalism to the strange and savage violence of industrial capitalism.

The novel is formally divided into five parts, the first of which introduces the main characters in their natural habitat. In contrast to the Arcadian settings of Henderson and Hurston, Attaway's description of the rural South is harsh and realistic. On the Kentucky farm which the three Moss brothers work for shares, life is an unrelenting struggle for survival against a tired land and a tireless overseer. The Moss boys are bound, serflike, to the soil, for each crop leaves them deeper in debt than the last. Subject to every whim of a white landowner, they scarcely know where economic exploitation leaves off and racial oppression begins. Their status in Southern society is symbolized by the sack of hog entrails which literally stands between them and starvation.

In a society which would strip him of humanity, each of the three brothers has worked out his own means of self-realization. Melody, sensitive and thoughtful, with a rare gift of sympathy, "never had a craving in him that he couldn't slick away on his guitar." Chinatown, who is lazy, irresponsible, and playful as a child, has a gold tooth which "make everybody look when Chinatown smile." Big Mat, sober and industrious, but darker and more embittered than his younger brothers, has always wanted to preach the Word. Rendered inarticulate by his wife's failure to bear a child, which he interprets as a curse from God, Big Mat is a Joblike figure with a smoldering potential for violence and destruction. Symbolically, as Ralph Ellison has pointed out, the three brothers represent traditional aspects of the folk culture: Big Mat (Matthew), the religious; Chinatown, the pagan; and Melody, the artistic.

It is from Big Mat's inner tensions that most of the action of Part I flows. Through a series of events which symbolize the inexorable pressure of the white South, Big Mat is provoked into striking his "riding boss." His subsequent panic and flight coincide with the appearance of a Northern labor agent in search of recruits for the burgeoning steel mills of the Monongahela Valley. Forced to leave his wife behind because the steel companies refuse to transport women, Big Mat and his brothers join dozens of colored sharecroppers on a freight train heading North.

A bare summary of Part I may convey the impression of a typical protest novel, unless the texture and quality of the writing is taken into account. Attaway's style combines the stark language of social realism with poetic passages which express the imaginative faculty of the folk. The lean narrative prose and terse dialogue is balanced by lyrical interludes in a minor key. Attaway is able to hold the two attitudes in equilibrium because both are ultimately responses to human suffering. He takes his cue from the blues, an art form which allows for emotional freedom without losing touch with social reality.

Part II is a transitional section which describes the Moss boys' journey to the North. Nothing has altered in their status, for they are bunched up on the floor of the boxcar "like hogs headed for market." Transported in total darkness, they enter their new environment in blindness and in pain: "When the car finally stopped for a long time and some men unsealed and slid back the big door, they were blinded by the light of a cloudy day. In all their heads, the train wheels still clicked. Their ears still heard the scream of steel on the curves. Their bodies were motionless, but inside they still jerked to the movement of a bouncing freight car" (p. 49). Placed on an equal footing with the other major sections, Part II is made to seem, like the Moss boys' train ride, longer than it really is. The effect of this device is to create the feeling that an eternity divides the three brothers from their past.

Most of the novel's main themes are launched in Part III. The section opens with an effective counterpoint between the old way of life and the new. To the men from the red clay hills, Allegheny County looks like "an ugly, smoking hell out of a backwoods preacher's sermon." As they listen to bunkhouse tales of sudden death from the hot steel, they think inwardly, "What men in their right minds would leave off tending green growing things to tend iron monsters?" Apprehensive of their physical surroundings, they soon discover that they have entered a hostile human environment as well. Ancient hatreds take new form, as the colored men are stoned by white steelworkers who have learned that Negro labor is imported from the South whenever there is strike talk in the mills.

As the new men report for work, the massive operations of the mill are set forth in lively, imaginative prose: "Everywhere the metal was fighting to get loose. The shaping mills were far down the river, but he could hear the awful screams when the saw bit into the hot metal. The blast was a million bees in a drum. The open hearth was full of agony. . . . 'Sound like circus animals tryin' to git loose,' whispered Chinatown" (p. 67).

For twelve hours at a stretch, a deadly warfare is waged between the steel and its captors. The intensity of the conflict leaves the steelworkers taut and jumpy. At work, this tension may erupt in sudden outbursts of violence among the men. Away from the job, they still carry the pressure of the steel in their tired bodies. They seek catharsis by staging savage dogfights, by visiting the prostitutes in "Mex town," and by sporadic strike action which convulses the whole community.

As before, in their new industrial environment the Moss brothers must struggle to maintain their self-esteem. The racial attack aimed at the roots of their being has abated, for in the mills they can prove themselves in honest competition with the whites. But how are they to measure their human worth against the machine? "Like spiral worms, all their egos had curled under pressure from the giants around them. Sooner or later it came to all the green men: What do we count for against machines that lift tons easy as a guy takes a spoonful of gravy to his mouth?" (p. 66). Against this attack, the Moss boys' former defenses are useless. "The mills couldn't look at China's gold tooth and smile." Melody experiments tentatively with new rhythms, but eventually lays his guitar aside forever. Big Mat abandons his Bible, and with it all hope of sending to Kentucky for his wife. Under the pounding of the steel, the Moss boys' personalities begin to disintegrate.

Melody and Big Mat, who are more resourceful than Chinatown, try to restore their lost sense of worth through a woman. Melody first sees Anna in a shack in "Mex town." She has legs "as beautiful as fresh-split cedar," but Melody, inhibited by his artistic sensibilities, hesitates to make love to her. Shortly thereafter, Anna meets Big Mat at a dogfight and becomes his woman. As sex object, Anna is a symbol of Big Mat's rootlessness; more broadly, she echoes the main theme of the novel. Born a peon, she aspires to wear high heels in the American fashion. But like the Moss boys, she is denied self-realization by the circumstances of her life. Ironically, Big Mat and Melody seek to "count for something" through a woman whose life is as empty and as hopeless as their own.

By the middle of the novel a latent musical structure has begun to assert itself. Movement is linear; themes are introduced, developed independently, then woven together in a skillful counterpoint. Early in Part IV the most prominent of these motifs is the Big Mat – Anna – Melody tension. After Big Mat moves out of the bunkhouse to live with Anna, the two brothers gradually become estranged. Big Mat avoids Melody because he feels guilty for having deserted his wife; Melody feels uneasy in Big Mat's presence because he covets his brother's woman. By developing this breach between the brothers, Attaway is subtly laying the cornerstone of an ideological edifice. The pressures of industrial society, he suggests, divide brother from brother, as Negro and Slav are divided by the strike which materializes in Part V.

The latter half of Part IV is dominated by a sense of impending disaster in the mills. As suspense mounts, a Faulknerian note is introduced through the figure of Smothers, a disabled Negro who is regarded by his fellow workers as half insane. Possessing the intuitive powers ascribed by modern writers to madmen and idiots, Smothers interprets the violence in the mills as the steel's revenge for man's misuse of the land: "*It's a sin to melt up the ground.* . . . Steel bound to git ever'body 'cause 'o that sin. They say I crazy, but mills gone crazy 'cause men bringin' trainloads of ground in here and meltin' it up" (p. 178, italics in original). If Smothers is employed successfully as a dramatic device, it is only at some sacrifice of ideological clarity. His romantic pronouncements are given such fictional prominence that the novel almost sideslips into a sentimental revolt against modern industrialism.

Meanwhile, the mounting tension between the steel and the men erupts in a volcanic blast which takes fourteen lives and leaves Chinatown in eternal darkness. The tragic effect of this episode is heightened by a deliberate use of ambiguity: "That night, when a break came in the long shift, Chinatown walked out of the blast house. He saw the pointed stars of fire along the edge of the Monongahela. He looked up in the sky at the points of fire so much like those along the river. *He took his last look at all of these*" (p. 178, my italics). The reader is prepared for Chinatown's death; he learns with momentary relief of his survival, only to realize that in this case blindness is worse than death: "He had been a man who lived through outward symbols. Now those symbols were gone, and he was lost."

The first impression of this episode is dominated by suspense and shock; on second reading, an underlying tightness of style emerges. Chinatown's blindness, which plays a major symbolic role in the novel, is anticipated by the light imagery of Part I and by the dark boxcar of Part II. Less remotely, it is foreshadowed by the language with which the explosion is described: "It was deep night. . . . Then there came a blinding flash. . . . One of the black pop bottles had foamed over down there at the edge of the river." The latter image recalls Chinatown's childish addiction to red pop, now rendered colorless forever. The tight weave of Attaway's style is well illustrated by the climax of Part IV. The cumulative impact of this episode is no accident: suspense, ambiguity, and foreshadowing combine to produce a powerful dramatic effect.

Conceptually, Ralph Ellison has written of *Blood on the Forge*, "Attaway grasped the destruction of the folk but missed its rebirth on a higher level." In the last two sections of the novel the psychological destruction of the Moss brothers is carried to completion. The process is dramatized through an elaborate sexual metaphor, as each brother in turn is symbolically castrated. Melody "accidentally" smashes his "picking hand" at work, thus punishing himself for an unexpected sexual encounter with Anna. Chinatown's blindness so shatters his confidence that he can never again summon enough courage to face the ladies of "Mex town." Big Mat's outright sexual defeat at the hands of Anna reduces him to a hollow shell of a man.

Ellison's comment notwithstanding, *Blood on the Forge* is more than a novel of dissolution. Counterposed to the Moss brothers is the figure of Zanski, an old Ukrainian steelworker who represents a superior adjustment to the new industrial environment. Confronted with similar problems of acculturation, the transplanted Ukrainian peasants have been quicker to put their roots down than the Negro migrants. Zanski, knowing instinctively that no peasant can be happy unless he is growing things, insists at least upon having kids growing in his yard. In addition to realizing the importance of family life, the Slavs are overwhelmingly pro-union. Since Attaway will eventually part company with the Moss brothers on ideological grounds, Zanski helps to prepare the ground for this decisive shift in tone.

In the final section of the novel the action centers primarily around the figure of Big Mat. While Melody is occupied with nursing Chinatown back to health, Big Mat is drawn into the strike which divides Steeltown into two warring camps. The strike provides him with an opportunity to translate his private frustrations into public aggression. When Anna pulls the last prop from under him by returning to her former profession, Big Mat attempts to heal his ruptured ego with a brutal sense of power. Hurriedly "deputized," he joins a group of professional strike-breakers in a raid on union headquarters. In the ensuing struggle he kills an old Slav and is in turn beaten to death by a union sympathizer.

At this point it is essential to distinguish between the dramatic action of Part V and the author's attitude toward the action. Attaway relies upon tone to convey his own values, and thereby to control the reader's attitude toward Big Mat. Crucial to the establishment of this tone is a series of "blindness" and "vision" symbols, whose cumulative meaning is unmistakable. The burden of these symbols is that the Moss brothers move in darkness and in ignorance where their industrial environment is concerned. Big Mat cannot cope with the issues of the strike; he cannot see beyond his experience as a Southern Negro. For all intents and purposes, he is as blind as Chinatown.

The Moss brothers see the strike strictly from a racial point of view; there is nothing in their experience which would cause them to do otherwise. When Big Mat and Melody surprise a group of white strikers in the act of beating up a Negro foreman, they rush instinctively to his defense. Only later do they learn, somewhat incredulously, that he is a paid company spy. On the face of things, and especially to a Negro audience, Big Mat's course of action during the strike is made to seem highly plausible. It is clear from Attaway's tone, however, that he is playing devil's advocate; his aim is to discredit Negro nationalism, from a somewhat broader point of view. Ideologically speaking, *Blood on the Forge* represents the shift from race consciousness to class consciousness which so many Negro intellectuals experienced during the Red Decade.

In Part V Attaway in effect enters his own novel, not as a character but through his tone. The dramatic action is apprehended at one level by Big Mat, and at a more sophisticated level by the author. The failure of the novel is that Attaway tries to endow his protagonist with his own consciousness. The fiction demands that Big Mat should die as he lived, in blindness, but for didactic purposes Attaway arranges an eleventh-hour "revelation." In his last moments, as Big Mat staggers under the blows of a pickax handle, he dimly perceives what Attaway has known all along (pp. 273–74):

> It seemed to him that he had been through all of this once before. Only at that far time, his had been the arm strong with hate. Yes, once he had beaten down a riding boss. . . . Had that riding boss been as he was now? Big Mat went farther away and no longer could distinguish himself from these other figures. They were all one and the same. In that confusion he sensed something true. Maybe somewhere in the mills a new [owner] was creating riding bosses, making a difference where none existed.

By granting vision to Big Mat, Attaway reduces his protagonist from a tragic hero to a mere mouthpiece for his own political views. In the process he damages the aesthetic structure of the novel beyond repair. Thematically, *Blood on the Forge* deals with the struggle for self-realization waged by the Moss brothers against a hostile environment. In Part V this tension is resolved in terms of Big Mat's role in the strike. Ironically, Big Mat achieves self-realization, but only through antisocial channels; he gains his manhood, but only as a strike-breaker. But by bestowing insight upon his protagonist, Attaway has changed the *outcome* of Big Mat's inner struggle. Now he gains his manhood through a kind of social vision which has no real foundation in his experience. Instead of an ironic victory—which is really a defeat—he wins a facile, unearned victory over his environment.

In spite of an inept denouement, *Blood on the Forge* is an outstanding novel of the Depression era. In thematic complexity, style, and characterization, it ranks among the better novels of the proletarian school. One observation remains which is frankly impressionistic but which may serve to reinforce this judgment. In its over-all structure *Blood on the Forge* suggests a traditional jazz ensemble. Melody, as his name implies, plays trumpet; Chinatown, the light and frivolous clarinet; and Big Mat, the deep-voiced trombone. Now one, now another takes a "break," while often one brother plays against the other two. All three are set off against the steel, which supplies the basic beat. For those readers who can accept this extra dimension, jazz—the musical creation of the urban Negro—will seem most appropriate as background music for a novel of the Great Migration.

Richard Wright

Modern art in no small measure represents an attempt to cope with the chaotic formlessness and swift flux of the modern city. Romanticism was nature-centered; it was doomed by the tons of steel and brick and asphalt which have formed a buffer between modern man and his natural environment. It was replaced by an art which is city-centered, by a realism which is the product of too many subway rides. The modern novel, like most contemporary art forms, was spawned in those vast metropolitan centers which, for better or worse, have set the tone of 20th-century life. Paris, Dublin, and Chicago have left an indelible imprint on modern fiction.

The city entered American literature at about the turn of the century, through such novels as Crane's *Maggie, a Girl of the Streets* (1891), Dreiser's *Sister Carrie* (1900), and Sinclair's *The Jungle* (1906). It was the predominantly urban themes of these "scientific naturalists," treated with an unflinching realism, which precipitated the revolt against Victorianism and gentility in American letters. For obvious reasons, Negro fiction lagged behind this development by several decades. Around 1900, when the early naturalists had already begun to probe amidst the rubbish of the city, the Negro novelist was still a hostage to Southern feudalism, along with the overwhelming bulk of the Negro population. Prior to the Great Migration, the city was not an important influence on Negro life.

Even during the 1920's when the urbanization of the Negro had progressed sufficiently to be reflected in his literature, the resulting fictional image was shallow and distorted. To the writers of the Harlem School the urban scene was symbolized more by the crowded cabaret than by the crowded tenement. For another decade a shallow exoticism prevented the Negro novelist from coming to grips with the hard realities of city life. It was not until the Great Depression, with its strikes and evictions, its bread lines and its hunger marches, that the plight of the urban masses could no longer be ignored. Paradoxically, the first Negro novelist to deal with ghetto life in the Northern cities was a Southern refugee named Richard Wright.

Wright (1909–1960) was born on a plantation near Natchez, Mississippi. His father was a black peasant; his mother, a devout woman who was forced to support her family as best she could, after the desertion of her husband. Wright's childhood consisted of intermittent moves from one Southern town to the next, of part-time jobs and sporadic schooling, and of sharp lessons in what he was later to call "The Ethics of Living Jim Crow." At fifteen he struck out on his own, working in Memphis while he accumulated enough savings to go North. Arriving in Chicago on the threshold of the Great Depression, he worked at a succession of odd jobs, until his association with the Communist party lifted him to a new plane of consciousness.

From an early age Wright had dreamed of becoming a writer.

In Memphis he developed a passion for reading, cutting his teeth on such authors as Dreiser, Mencken, Lewis, and Anderson. "All my life," he writes in *Black Boy,* "had shaped me for the realism, the naturalism of the modern novel." A long apprenticeship ensued, however, before Wright was to attempt a full-length novel. His first published pieces were poems, articles, and stories, written for what may loosely be termed the Communist party press. While Wright was employed on the Federal Writers' Project, *American Stuff* carried one of his stories, which resulted in the publication of his first book, *Uncle Tom's Children* (1936). These five novellas of anguish and violence clearly reveal the strength of Wright's emotional ties to the deep South. His other major publications include a novel (*Native Son,* 1940), a pictorial history (*Twelve Million Black Voices,* 1941), an autobiography (*Black Boy,* 1945), and a posthumous collection of stories (*Eight Men,* 1961).[1] Richard Wright's *Native Son* marks a high point in the history of the Negro novel, not only because it is a work of art in its own right but because it influenced a whole generation of Negro novelists. To the average well-read American, and not without justice, *Native Son* is the most familiar novel—and Bigger Thomas the most memorable character—in Negro fiction. The book was an instantaneous popular success, and as a result Wright became the first fully professional Negro novelist. A best-seller and Book-of-the-Month Club selection, *Native Son* was successfully adapted to the Broadway stage by Orson Welles and was later revived as a movie by Wright himself. Since its appearance in 1940, the novel has inspired a host of imitators who may be said to constitute the Wright School of postwar Negro fiction.

By way of preliminary remarks, three important influences on *Native Son* should be considered. In terms of literary lineage the novel derives from the early American naturalists, by way of Dos Passos, Farrell, Steinbeck, and the late Dreiser. *An American Tragedy* (1925) in particular seems to have been a model for *Native Son.* Both novels make use of criminality as their chief dramatic device, and in each case the crime is the natural and inevitable product of a warped society. Both authors draw

1. In 1953 Wright published a second novel, *The Outsider*, a work strongly influenced by French existentialism and far inferior to *Native Son.* This was followed in 1958 by *The Long Dream,* a still more disastrous performance.

the data for their trial scenes, in classic naturalist fashion, from authentic court records: Dreiser from a murder case in upstate New York, and Wright from the famous Leopold and Loeb kidnap-murder in Chicago. Both novels, through their titles, make the point that Clyde Griffiths and Bigger Thomas are native American products, and not, as Wright remarks, imported from Moscow or anywhere else. Both authors advance a guilt-of-the nation thesis as a corollary to their environmentalist view of crime.

Much of the raw material for *Native Son* was provided by Wright's personal experience in metropolitan Chicago. For several hard-pressed years he worked at all kinds of jobs, from porter and dishwasher to ditch-digger and post office clerk. One job as agent for a burial society took him inside the south-side tenement houses, where he saw the corrosive effects of ghetto life on the Negro migrant. During the depression a relief agency placed him in the South Side Boys' Club, where he met the live models from whom he was to sketch Bigger Thomas: "They were a wild and homeless lot, culturally lost, spiritually disinherited, candidates for the clinics, morgues, prisons, reformatories, and the electric chair of the state's death house." [2] Meanwhile, even as his empirical knowledge of urban life increased, Wright was introduced to the theoretical concepts of Marxism through the John Reed Club and the Communist party.

Wright joined the party in 1934, breaking decisively about ten years later. The extent of his involvement has been, to put it as kindly as possible, modestly understated in *The God That Failed* (1949). For several years, Wright acted as a dependable wheel horse in a wide variety of party activities. To his credit, however, a stubborn and uncorruptible individualism kept him in constant conflict with the party bureaucracy, leading eventually to his break and expulsion. Of his main motive for joining the party Wright has written in retrospect: "[The party] did not say 'Be like us and we will like you, maybe.' It said: 'If you possess enough courage to speak out what you are, you will find that you are not alone.' " [3] As an excluded Negro and an alienated intellectual, Wright needed above all to feel this sense of belonging.

2. Richard Wright, "I Tried to Be a Communist," *Atlantic Monthly, 174* (Aug. 1944), p. 68.

3. Ibid., p. 62.

That he was able to find it, however fleetingly, only within the ranks of the Communist party is a commentary on the failure of the democratic left.

Wright's debt to Marxism is quite a different matter from his personal history in the Communist party. The party, it must be understood, manipulates Marxism for its own ends, which are the ends of the Russian ruling class. Yet the basic ideas of Karl Marx, like those of Sigmund Freud, are capable of effecting so vast a revolution in the consciousness of an individual that he may never recapture his former state of innocence. For Richard Wright, Marxism became a way of ordering his experience; it became, in literary terms, his unifying mythos. It provided him with a means of interpreting the urban scene which the Harlem School had lacked. Above all, it provided him with an intellectual framework for understanding his life as a Negro.

Wright, more than any Negro author who preceded him, has a sense of the presentness of his racial past. This sense of history, which was part and parcel of his Marxist outlook, has been recorded in *Twelve Million Black Voices* (1941), published hard on the heels of *Native Son*. In this folk history of the American Negro, Wright sees the black ghetto as the end product of a long historical process (p. 93):

> Perhaps never in history has a more utterly unprepared folk wanted to go to the city; we were barely born as a folk when we headed for the tall and sprawling centers of steel and stone. We who were landless on the land; we who had barely managed to live in family groups; we who needed the ritual and guidance of established institutions to hold our atomized lives together in lines of purpose . . . we who had had our personalities blasted with 200 years of slavery had been turned loose to shift for ourselves.

It was in this perspective that Wright saw the life of Bigger Thomas.

The most impressive feature of *Native Son* is its narrative drive. From the outset the novel assumes a fierce pace which carries the reader breathlessly through Bigger's criminal career. Wright allows as little interruption of the action as possible, with no chapter divisions as such and only an occasional break to mark a swift transition or change of scene. At the same time, he writes with great economy, breaking with the comprehensive and discursive tradition of the naturalistic novel. He provides only three brief glimpses of Bigger's life prior to the main action of the novel: his relationship with his family, with his gang, and with his girl, Bessie. The reader must supply the rest, for Wright's presentation is not direct but metaphorical.

On a literal level *Native Son* consists of three Books, dealing with a murder, a flight and capture, and a trial. But the murder and the circumstances which surround it are in reality an extended metaphor, like the whale hunt in *Moby Dick*. The novel is not to be read merely as the story of a gruesome crime, though it is that. It is the hidden meaning of Bigger's life, as revealed by the murder, which is the real subject of *Native Son*. The novel is a modern epic, consisting of action on the grand scale. As such, it functions as a commentary on the more prosaic plane of daily living.

Book I is called "Fear." Its structure pulsates in mounting waves of violence, beginning with the opening rat scene, increasing during Bigger's fight with Gus, and culminating in murder. Each successive wave of violence is a means of reducing fear, for great fear automatically produces great violence in Bigger. He has been so conditioned that being found in a white girl's room is the ultimate fear-inspiring situation. When the blind Mrs. Dalton appears as a white blur in the doorway of Mary's room, Bigger is seized with hysterical terror, and he murders. It is both an accident and not an accident, for the first characteristic of Bigger's life which the murder reveals is his uncontrollable fear of whites.

The second aspect of Biggers's normal life to receive thematic stress is his bitter sense of deprivation: "We black and they white. They got things and we ain't. They do things and we can't. It's just like living in jail. Half the time I feel like I'm on the outside of the world peeping in through a knot-hole in the fence" (p. 17). Living on the margin of his culture, Bigger is constantly tormented by the glitter of the dominant civilization. "The Gay Woman," a movie which he watches while waiting to rob a neighborhood store, is emblematic of that world of cocktail parties, golf, and spinning roulette wheels from which he is forever excluded. To fill the intolerable void in his life he seeks "something big"—the "job" at Blum's which never comes off, his real job as chauffeur and handyman for the Daltons. He finally breaks through the confines of his daily life by committing murder.

Book II, "Flight," opens with a recapitulation of Bigger's relations with family and gang, to show how they have changed as a result of the murder. Bigger has now achieved heroic stature: "He had murdered and created a new life for himself." This is the dominant irony of Book II—that Bigger finds fulfillment only by the most violent defiance of the legal and moral precepts of the society which oppresses him. As a criminal, Bigger achieves a sense of purpose, a feeling of elation which is a measure of the meaninglessness of his former existence.

After the fact of Bigger's rebirth is established, the narrative proceeds with a series of interrogations by Peggy, by the Daltons, and finally by the police. Bigger's conduct throughout is determined by the heightened perceptions which he enjoys as a result of the murder: "The whole thing came to him in the form of a powerful and simple feeling; there was in everyone a great hunger to believe that made him blind, and if he could see while others were blind, then he could get what he wanted and never be caught at it" (p. 91). Bigger learns to exploit the blindness of others, "fooling the white folks" during his interrogation, and this is again something deep in his racial heritage, springing from a long tradition of telling whites whatever they want to hear.

At last comes discovery, flight, and capture. Once again the action of the novel serves as an oblique comment on Bigger's "normal" way of life: "But it was familiar, this running away. All his life he had been knowing that sooner or later something like this would come to him" (p. 187). No such fear-ridden sequence as Bigger's flight and capture is possible without a proportionate act of violence. Bessie's murder, compounding horror upon grisly horror, serves to dispel any lingering doubt concerning Bigger's guilt. Learning from Dreiser's mistake, Wright takes no chances that his audience may be diverted from his main point by quibbling over the "accidental" nature of Mary Dalton's death. At the same time, the audience knows intuitively that it is Mary's murder, and not Bessie's, for which society will demand Bigger's life.

The successful fusion of narrative and metaphorical levels in *Native Son* is only a sample of Wright's craftsmanship. Not the least of his problems is to induce his readers to identify with Bigger in spite of his monstrous crimes. This he accomplishes by a tone which subtly controls and defines the reader's attitude toward Bigger. It is a tone of anguish and despair, established at the outset by Wright's epigraph from the Book of Job: "Even today is my complaint rebellious; my stroke is heavier than my groaning." Thus the stark horror of *Native Son* is balanced by the spiritual anguish which, in a sense, produced it. This note of anguish, which emphasizes Bigger's suffering, is so intense as to be almost physical in character. It is sustained by a style which can only be called visceral. The author writes from his guts, describing the emotional state of his characters in graphic psychosomatic terms. It is a characteristic device which has its source in Wright's aching memory of the deep South.

Notwithstanding Wright's professed naturalism, the symbolic texture of *Native Son* is exceptionally rich. The whole novel is contained in the first few pages when Bigger, in unconscious anticipation of his own fate, corners a huge black rat and kills him with a skillet. Much of Wright's meaning is conveyed by appropriate "objective correlatives" for Bigger's inner feelings and emotions. The icy gales and heavy snowfalls of Books I and II represent a hostile white environment: "To Bigger and his kind white people were not really people; they were a sort of great natural force, like a stormy sky looming overhead" (p. 97). Throughout Book II the red glow of the furnace appears as a projection of Bigger's guilt. A series of breathing and choking images anticipates the manner of the murder, linking it symbolically to Bigger's choked and stifled life. There is a constant play on blindness, focused around the figure of Mrs. Dalton but aimed ultimately at the reader, who is expected to grope his way to an understanding of Bigger's life.

A lesser artist would have directed Bigger's symbolic revolt against a brutal oppressor, but Wright understands that such an approach would only make his audience feel smug and superior. He chooses as Bigger's victim a girl who is "friendly to Negroes," but whose kindness under the circumstances is a bitter mockery. By this device, Wright means to suggest that Bigger's sickness is too deep to be reached by kindness, and at the same time to involve his audience in responsibility for Bigger's crime. The Daltons, who are people of good will, hire Bigger because they "want to give Negroes a chance." But they also own real estate on the South side, and have thus helped to make the black ghetto what it is. They are, in short, just as innocent and just as guilty as we.

Book I portrays the old Bigger; Book II, the new; Book III, the Bigger who might have been. The bare narrative is concerned with Bigger's fight for his life, but the dramatic tension of Book III is centered elsewhere. The important question is not whether Bigger will be spared, but whether he will be saved. Bigger's impending death in the electric chair is simply the crisis which forces a resolution of his inner conflict, thus revealing what is basic in his personality. After his talk with the lawyer, Max—the most intimate of his life—Bigger feels that he must make a decision: "In order to walk to that chair he had to weave his feelings into a hard shield of either hope or hate. To fall between them would mean living and dying in a fog of fear" (p. 305). On what terms will Bigger die; in hope or in hate? This is the tension of Book III.

Bigger's basic problem is to find someone or something he can trust. Kardiner and Livesey have written of the lower-class Negro family: "The result of the continuous frustration in childhood is to create a personality devoid of confidence in human relations, of an eternal vigilance and distrust of others. This is a purely defensive maneuver, which purports to protect the individual against the repeatedly traumatic effects of disappointment and frustration. He must operate on the assumption that the world is hostile."[4] This lack of relatedness appears above all in Bigger's relationship with Bessie. As Max points out, "His relationship to this poor black girl reveals his relationship to the world." It is a mutually exploitative affair, devoid of devotion, loyalty, or trust—

4. Abram Kardiner and Lionel Livesey, *The Mark of Oppression* (New York, Norton, 1951), p. 308.

luxuries which are denied to Bigger and Bessie by the circumstances of their lives.

Bigger's lack of relatedness is presented symbolically at the end of Book II, just before his capture: "Under it all some part of his mind was beginning to stand aside; he was going behind his curtain, his wall, looking out with sullen stares of contempt." This retreat, amounting almost to a catatonic trance, sets the stage for the dominant conflict in Book III. As Bigger slowly awakens from his trance, his fierce life-drive, set off perfectly by the death cell which he occupies, struggles toward some sort of relatedness with his fellows: "If he reached out his hands, and if his hands were electric wires, and if his heart were a battery giving life and fire to those hands, and if he reached out with his hands and touched other people, if he did that, would there be a reply, a shock?" (p. 307).

The structure of Book III is essentially a series of attempts by Bigger to realize this vision. He seeks desperately for a basis for hope but discards one alternative after another. He rejects his family ("Go home, Ma"); his fellow prisoners ("Are you the guy who pulled the Dalton job?"); the race leaders ("they almost like white folks when it comes to guys like me"); and religion. The old preacher tempts Bigger with the Christian explanation of suffering, but when the mob burns a fiery cross outside the jail, the cross of love turns to a cross of hate. Bigger finds it hardest to reject Jan and Max. These are the last symbols of relatedness to which he clings, and the main conflict of the novel occurs between them and Bigger's deepest experience as a Negro—his distrust of whites, his Negro nationalism.

Bigger's relations with Jan and Max cannot be understood apart from the context of Wright's experience in the Communist party. Most Negro Communists—and Wright was no exception—are Negro nationalists, for it is precisely the most embittered, anti-white Negroes to whom the party offers the possibility of revenge. But the vast majority of American Communists, after all, are white. Paradoxically, the most white-hating Negro is thrust, by his membership in the party, into what is surely, whatever else it may be, one of the freest arenas of interracial contact in America.

The result is an agonizing psychological conflict, as the Negro nationalist, newly won to Communism, struggles to relate to his white comrades. This is the conflict which is bothering Wright in Book III of *Native Son,* expressed on a somewhat primitive level through Bigger's relations with the white Communists, Jan and Max.

To Bigger, Communism is a matter not of ideology but of relatedness. Jan and Max are the flimsy base on which he tries to erect his shield of hope. Jan, through an act of understanding and forgiveness, evokes what is almost a religious response from Bigger, where the old colored preacher had failed: "The word had become flesh. For the first time in his life a white man became a human being to him." The resolution of the novel, however, comes in terms of Bigger's relationship with Max. Max serves as Bigger's father confessor as well as his lawyer, and Bigger comes closest to establishing a human contact with him.

After Max's speech fails, and after all avenues have been closed to Bigger, Max makes a final visit to Bigger's cell. Bigger seeks to recapture their former intimacy, but Max is too concerned with comforting him in the face of death. Max then tries to communicate his vision of Communism to Bigger, but fails. As his shield of hope slips from his grasp, Bigger takes up the shield of hate which is his destiny. The impact comes through Max's reactions: "Bigger saw Max back away from him with compressed lips. . . . Max lifted his hand to touch Bigger, but did not. . . . Max's eyes were full of terror. . . . He felt for the door, keeping his face averted. . . . He did not turn around. . . . Max paused, but did not look" (pp. 358–59). What terrifies Max is that Bigger, re-possessed by hate, ends by accepting what life has made him: a killer. Bigger's real tragedy is not that he dies, but that he dies in hatred. A tragic figure, he struggles for love and trust against a hostile environment which defeats him in the end.

Book III, and therefore the novel, suffers from a major structural flaw, flowing from the fact that Wright has failed to digest Communism artistically. The Communist party is simply not strong enough as a symbol of relatedness; Bigger's hatred, firmly anchored in his Negro nationalism, is hardly challenged. The contest is unequal, because there is nothing in Biggers' life that corresponds to "Communism." As a result, the conflict between love and hate, between universal brotherhood and Negro nationalism, cannot be successfully internalized. Wright is forced to go outside of Bigger, to Jan and Max, both of whom are more the mouthpieces for a thesis than credible characters in their own right. Wright is sure of Bigger, but Jan and Max elude him. In noting his failure to realize Communism artistically, it is not irrelevant to recall that for Wright himself, the party was no shield of hope.

Since Bigger is unable to bear the weight of political symbolism intended for him, Wright is forced to resort to rhetoric. The first two books of *Native Son* contain two levels of meaning; the bare action, and a running account of Bigger's feelings at the time. Now a third level is introduced: an interpretation of the action, undertaken by the author through the medium of Max's speech. This speech, with its guilt-of-the-nation thesis, throws the novel badly out of focus. The reader is likely to come away thinking that Bigger committed a horrible crime to which he was driven by a still more horrible environment, which I, the reader, have helped to create. Fictionally, however, the novel makes a different point: Bigger is a human being whose environment has made him incapable of relating meaningfully to other human beings except through murder.

Not satisfied with interpreting his own novel through Max, Wright tries again in his article "How Bigger Was Born": "Bigger, an American product, a native son of this land, carries within him the potentialities of either fascism or communism." [5] But Wright can only attempt in retrospect to impose a political symbolism on the novel which he fails to realize fictionally. He simply cannot fit the ideas of Bigger into those of the Communist party. A white Bigger could be a fascist; a colored Bigger with trade-union experience could be a Communist. But Bigger is a Negro without fellow workers and is therefore only Bigger, a memorable figure in contemporary literature whom Wright created in spite of his own political ideology.

Of the Negro novelists who wrote during the Great Depression, Richard Wright came closest to expressing the essential spirit of the decade. At bottom, the Depression years witnessed a continua-

5. *Saturday Review,* 22 (1940), 1–4, 17–20.

tion of the cultural dualism of the Negro Renaissance. During the thirties the Negro novelist maintained an active interest in his Negro heritage, systematically exploring the racial past in his search for distinctive literary material. Upon this base, in accordance with the climate of the times, was superimposed the formula of "proletarian art." Wright's contribution to the Negro novel was precisely his fusion of a pronounced racialism with a broader tradition of social protest.

The Red Decade was brought to an abrupt close by America's entry into World War II. As the unemployed workers were gradually absorbed into war industry, and as New Dealers and Communists alike raised the slogan of "national unity," the radicalism of the thirties faded into oblivion. The intelligentsia's brief excursion into proletarian art was over. During the war years, in any case, literary activity became a luxury and like so many aspects of the national life was laid aside for the duration. The Negro novel entered a period of wartime quiescence, from which it emerged into a vastly altered postwar world.

PART IV. *The Revolt against Protest: 1940–1952*

PEOPLE who want to write sociology should not write a novel.

RALPH ELLISON

8. *Postwar Expansion*

In treating the recent history of the Negro novel, some loss of perspective is inevitable. We are dealing with a period which has a beginning but no end, and like an audience waiting for the last act of a new play we are forced to suspend final judgment. Nevertheless, the major trends are clear, and historical influences can be described, at least in general terms. Perhaps the best way to focus such a discussion is to consider the formative years of the postwar generation of Negro novelists.

They were born—almost half of them—between 1911 and 1916. That made them twenty-five or thirty years old at Pearl Harbor. Of the men, seven were members of the armed forces; one joined the merchant marine; three were war workers. The women, like others of their age group, watched husband or brother or lover vanish, and with him family stability and emotional security. But the war was not the first time that their lives had been disrupted. If they were thirty at Pearl Harbor, they were twenty in 1931. They had reached adulthood at the depth of the Depression; almost none was young enough to recall it merely as a childhood trauma. They were not, like the writers of the 1920's, simply a lost generation; they were two-time losers, and their double catastrophe left a characteristic imprint on their work.

Their first and basic impulse was social protest—a natural product of their depression experience. But for want of an appropriate idiom their protest novels never materialized during the depression years. No sooner had Richard Wright supplied them with a model than their literary efforts were interrupted by the war. Five years later, when literary activity was again possible, the accumulated grievances of an earlier decade burst forth in a flood. The immediate postwar years were dominated, as a result, by what a hostile critic has called "the puerile imitators of Richard Wright." The Wright School was a carryover from the thirties—a delayed response to the potentialities of literary naturalism revealed through *Native Son.*

But if the Depression left its mark on the postwar generation, their wartime experience was no less momentous. After Pearl Harbor the American Negro lived through a period of rapid social change, with dramatic consequences for the racial status quo. In spite of the wartime riots, the social climate of the war years was distinctly favorable to the Negro's cause. Although the war in the Pacific had unmistakable racial overtones, the war against Hitler called forth a sharp attack on the very concept of a master race. Government spokesmen, inspired by the manpower shortage and the need for national unity, proclaimed a new era in American race relations. Sensing their tactical advantage, American Negroes demanded—and received—a fuller share in the national life.

The war years were only the beginning of a trend which has since culminated in a series of important Supreme Court victories. In response to this trend, the postwar novelists were forced to revise their literary goals. If Negroes were at last moving toward full integration, why not point the way by writing "integrated" novels? Superimposed on the old impulse to protest was a new impulse to expand their range, to transcend the parochial character of Negro experience. The attempts of the postwar generation to reconcile these conflicting impulses will become more meaningful after a closer examination of the period.

The Wright School

At the center of Richard Wright's art lies the impulse to protest; it determines both his content and his style. He was the first Negro novelist to depict the plight of the urban masses, and the first to approach this material in terms of the naturalistic tradition. His pioneer effort, *Native Son,* exerted an immense gravitational pull on subsequent Negro fiction. The source of its durability is not hard to determine: it links the Negro novel to a major tendency in modern art.

Urban realism did not originate, of course, with Wright. The basic innovations were made by Emile Zola; they were introduced into American literature by the early naturalists, and adapted to the needs of a later period by Farrell, Steinbeck, and Dos Passos. But before Wright, this tradition was untapped by the Negro novelist. Paradoxically, by the time the postwar generation mastered Wright's technique, the social conditions which evoked it had altered. The war boom had siphoned off the discontent of the 1930's, but the Wright School persisted as an anachronism. The work of Wright's disciples, which appeared belatedly in the mid-1940's, marks the peak of social consciousness in the Negro novel.

It is not surprising to discover that many of these authors served their literary apprenticeship as newspaper writers. Journalism has traditionally provided a training ground for naturalistic fiction, and the Negro novel is no exception. Dreiser is a symbol of the reporter-novelist in American naturalism, and there is a direct line of descent, through *Native Son,* from Dreiser to the Wright School. Ann Petry, Chester Himes, and William Gardner Smith, for example, have all had newspaper experience. Concerned as newspapermen with the sordid side of city life, they were forced to develop that respect for objective detail which is the stamp of literary naturalism.

This affinity for journalism may help to explain the revolt against protest which the Wright School ultimately provoked. John Aldridge once remarked that "events occur in wars with such intensity that they need not signify or connote." If for war we substitute racial conflict, we can begin to appreciate journalistic saturation in the Wright School novels. The modern reader has ceased to react to events as such. They are losing their significance because of staggering events like those at Buchenwald, Vorkuta, and Hiroshima. A novelist who wishes to transcend the limitations of naturalism must seek the meaning of events, must try to convey their impact on his characters. And this is precisely the difference between Richard Wright and his disciples: Wright sees the significance of Bigger Thomas, while his imitators seldom rise above mere sensationalism.

For the Wright School, literature is an emotional catharsis—a means of dispelling the inner tensions of race. Their novels often amount to a prolonged cry of anguish and despair. Too close to their material, feeling it too intensely, these novelists lack a sense of form and of thematic line. With rare exceptions, their style consists of a brutal realism, devoid of any love, or even respect, for words. Their characterization is essentially sociological, but it may contain a greater attempt at psychological depth than is usually associated with the naturalistic novel. Their principal theme, reminiscent of Sherwood Anderson, is how the American caste system breeds "grotesques." The white audience, on perceiving its responsibility for the plight of the protagonist, is expected to alter its attitude toward race.

While the Wright School is still preoccupied with protest, it is a less parochial concern than in the past. The protest content of these novels can be plotted along a curve ranging from "pure racial" at one extreme to "pure social" at the other. On the racial end of the curve, the antagonist is Jim Crow; on the social end, the antagonist is ordinarily the city slum or, in some instances, the social order. Wright, who in a way created this continuum, has influenced both of its poles: the racial with his tone of searing anguish, and the social with his environmentalism and Marxism.

Closest to unalleviated racial protest is Chester Himes' *If He Hollers Let Him Go* (1945), a novel whose neurotic, race-conscious protagonist makes Bigger Thomas seem well adjusted by comparison. This story of racial discrimination in a wartime California shipyard has a kind of political sequel in Himes' second novel, *Lonely Crusade* (1947). Here his protagonist, a labor organizer by profession, struggles against discrimination in the unions, and exposes the wartime betrayal of the Negro by the Communist party.

Not far behind in its tone of torment is Willard Savoy's *Alien Land* (1949), a novel of passing which makes use of the tragic mulatto stereotype. William Gardner Smith's *Last of the Conquerors* (1948), which deals with discrimination in the American Army, is built around the paradox of a colored GI who has to go to Hitler's Germany to find racial democracy. Alden Bland's *Behold a Cry* (1947) is a novel of the Great Migration, not without some psychological subtlety, whose particular cry of anguish is evoked by the Chicago race riots of 1918. Carl Offord's *The White Face* (1943) is another novel of urban adjustment, set in Harlem during World War II. Like *Behold a Cry,* it treats of the conflict between race and class consciousness, but in linking Negro nationalism with German fascism Offord peddles the party line in its crudest form.

While the emphasis is still racial in the novels of Bland and Offord, the fetid breath of the slum is already apparent. Coming as something of an anticlimax after *Native Son,* a group of novels appeared in the early postwar period which depict the slum neighborhood as a breeding ground of delinquency and crime. The ash can and the alley lend themselves traditionally to naturalistic treatment, but beyond naturalism the very phenomenon of slum life invites political analysis. Here the ideological limitations of Wright's disciples become evident: they attack the slum without understanding the social system which produced it. Their novels fall between the stools of racial and social protest, lacking the historical sweep with which Wright synthesized the two.

Of these environmentalist novels, *The Street* (1946) by Ann Petry is perhaps the most important. It is the story of a colored woman with middle-class values who struggles to protect herself and her son from the pernicious influence of the street. Written in a similar vein, though with considerably less talent, are *Third Ward Newark* (1946) by Curtis Lucas, and *Taffy* (1950) by Philip B. Kaye. Two novels of prison life treat the jail as an extension of, and necessary adjunct to, the city slum: Lloyd Brown's *Iron City* (1951) is a propaganda tract inspired by the Foley Square trial and written by a Party stalwart who is an associate editor of *Masses and Mainstream;* Chester Himes' *Cast the First Stone* (1952), a more successful treatment of prison life, differs from the author's earlier endeavors by virtue of the fact that his main characters are white.

By the late 1940's the vein of literary material unearthed by Richard Wright had been all but worked out. The market for protest had become saturated, and in any case it was no longer fashionable to write about slums. More fundamental than this, however, was the impact of the war years on the generation of GI's. Having discharged their debt to the Great Depression, they were eager to translate their wartime experience into literary terms. Perhaps it is time to examine the war years more closely, with an eye to understanding what has happened to divert the main current of Negro fiction from protest into new and unfamiliar channels.

The War Years

The Wright School survived into the postwar period out of sheer inertia; the dynamic factor shaping the course of the Negro novel was the war. Unlike World War I, which brought only a renewal of racial oppression, the second World War and its aftermath have witnessed great advances in the field of civil rights. As a result, if one compares the war generation of the forties and fifties with its counterpart of the twenties, one finds not a resurgence of Negro nationalism but rather a wave of assimilationist sentiment. This sentiment is a direct response to the new era in race relations ushered in by the war.

Whatever one's impatience with the rate of change, no one can doubt that a revolutionary transformation is taking place. We are witnessing the slow disintegration of a caste system which has controlled race relations for approximately eighty years. This pattern of caste has persisted, without any apparent loss of vigor, down to the period of America's participation in World War II. In the past twenty-five years, however—roughly since 1940—the ram's horn has been sounded and the walls are tumbling down. For the first time since the Reconstruction era the federal government is intervening in American life on behalf of the Negro. To summarize the high points of this development will attest to its depth.

The first important blow to be struck against caste was Roosevelt's Executive Order of June 25, 1941. Forced upon a reluctant president by A. Philip Randolph's "March-on-Washington Movement,"[1] the order created a Fair Employment Practices Committee within the War Manpower Commission. It was the task of this committee to see that hiring under government contract in the nation's war plants was conducted without regard to race, creed, or national origin. Shortly after the war (1945–49), eight Northern industrial states adopted similar antidiscrimination laws in the field of employment—laws which often covered public accommodation as well.

In interstate travel, two important court decisions (*Morgan v. Virginia*, 1946, and *Henderson v. U.S.*, 1950) virtually abolished segregation in seating and dining-car arrangements. In housing, the Supreme Court (*Shelley v. Kramer*, 1948) outlawed the enforcement of restrictive covenants (though not the covenants themselves) through civil suits. In family law, by a California Supreme Court decision of 1948 a statute forbidding miscegenation was held unconstitutional. In politics, the white primary was outlawed (*Smith v. Allbright*, 1944). The poll tax continued to survive in only five Southern states. In military life, the integration of the armed forces was effected by President Truman's Executive Order of 1948. Above all, in education, the separation of the races was held invalid in a series of decisions starting with *Sweatt v. Painter* (Texas, 1950) and *McLaurin v. Oklahoma State Regents* (1950), and culminating in the historic Supreme Court decision of 1954.

To be sure, these are legal and formal victories, which have yet to be validated in the popular consciousness. It would be prema-

1. See Myrdal, *An American Dilemma*, p. 414, for the story of negotiations between Randolph and Roosevelt.

ture indeed to suppose that an attack on the legal foundations of caste will in itself eliminate the inferior status to which our social customs, if not quite so much our social forms, reduce the American Negro. The "Negro problem" is still very far from being solved; a society in which it can be assumed that one's fate or chances in life in no essential way depend on the color of one's skin is still far from being a reality in America. Nevertheless, in spite of the Negro's continuing experience of caste, the historical trend is unmistakable: the edifice of white supremacy is crumbling in every important cultural area.

The all-important matter of interpretation remains: why, in a few short years, were such immense strides made in the field of civil rights when, for example, the situation in regard to civil liberties was steadily deteriorating? Official liberalism maintains, in a mood of self-congratulation, that the democratic conscience of America has at last become aroused. Those who, in light of the hysterical legislation of the McCarthy period, view the democratic conscience of America with some misgivings will prefer to seek a more substantial explanation. Like all revolutions, this one involves both a weakening of the *ancien régime* from within and a thrust against it from without. The former has to do with vast changes in the economic life of the South; the latter, with America's role on the world scene, and with the emergence in this country of what C. Wright Mills has called a permanent war economy.[2]

Threatened from within by the modernization of the South, then, and from without by the emergence of an American empire whose military and diplomatic needs conflict with the shibboleths of white supremacy, the American caste system is beginning to disintegrate. The speed and scope of this development have been exaggerated in some quarters and underestimated in others. A guarded optimism, which recognizes the roots and therefore the limitations of the present trend, seems the best attitude to adopt. But whatever one's appraisal of the objective situation, the subjective impact of these events on the Negro literary world is clear.

2. For an elaboration and defense of this thesis see my "The Changing Status of the Negro," *Dissent*, 2, No. 2, (spring 1955), pp. 124–32.

The recent gains have led to an upsurge of assimilationism, a revolt against the protest novel, and, in some instances, a conscious abandonment of the materials of Negro life.

The new cosmopolitanism of the postwar generation was primarily a response to the new climate in American race relations. Several secondary causes were operative, however, not the least of which was the military experience itself. To be swept up in the draft from uptown Manhattan, or southside Chicago, or Kingstree, South Carolina, and thrust into basic training with white boys from all over America was for many Negroes the beginning of a new freedom. Widespread travel in the states; enforced intimacy of combat training, and later of the battlefield; unaccustomed status as members of a conquering army; contact with Europeans who did not raise the color bar; leaves and liberties in Rome, Paris, or Berlin—all these experiences had an enormous psychological impact on the colored soldier.

Not that he escaped segregation and discrimination in the armed forces—the ranks of the anti-Hitler crusade were notoriously Jim Crow. But the caste system of the feudal South simply cannot thrive at the technological level of a modern army. White supremacy was unable to hold the line in the Southern army camps, let alone overseas. An unparalleled opportunity arose for interracial contact, both among American troops and with European civilians, and some of the colored GI's exploited it to the full. Out of this experience came a handful of war novels, though none of the caliber of Mailer's or Jones'. In a less immediate sense, however, the war produced a generation of Negro writers who could see beyond their own sufferings as Negroes. The war prepared them to deal with human tragedy on a deeper level than race.

The war years also witnessed an advance in technical facility, based on the superior educational attainment of the postwar generation. Education and leisure became increasingly available through the Negro's share in the general wartime prosperity. Where private resources proved inadequate, the "GI Bill of Rights" brought first-rate colleges and graduate schools within reach. In some instances, similar opportunities were provided by foundation grants, which in themselves reflect a new willingness to recognize and encourage Negro accomplishment in the arts.[3] On the whole, these writers were better prepared for their craft than any previous generation of Negro novelists.

Even the Communist party, opposed in theory to "bourgeois cosmopolitanism," contributed inadvertently to its growth by virtue of its conduct during the war. After Hitler's invasion of the Soviet Union and the inauguration of the so-called Browder period, the party suspended all domestic quarrels in the interests of Russian foreign policy. For the duration of the wartime alliance between the Soviet and American governments, the American Communist party either abandoned or actively sabotaged the struggle for Negro rights. As a result of this betrayal, carried out under the slogans of "national unity" and "win the war first," the party lost most of its influence among the Negro intelligentsia. Disillusionment with the party, and often with left-wing politics as such, is the dominant tone of postwar Negro fiction.

We have seen that members of the postwar generation came to maturity during a period of double catastrophe. Their depression experience tended to attract them to the party; their wartime experience decisively reversed the trend. This development can be illustrated by what might be called the Wright-Himes-Ellison configuration. During the Depression these three novelists were brought into the party fold primarily through their quest for racial justice. But when the party adopted a "soft line" on the Negro question during the war, the very militancy which originally attracted them to the party now caused them to break away.

During the thirties the Communist party provided a broad arena of interracial contact for the Negro intellectual. But no sooner did he break out of his closed racial world into this new political milieu than he was directed by the party's commissars

3. Ralph Ellison, Willard Motley, and Owen Dodson were Rosenwald Fellows; Ann Petry held a Houghton Mifflin Literary Fellowship; J. Saunders Redding held both a Guggenheim Fellowship and a Rockefeller Foundation Grant; and Willard Motley received a grant from the Newberry Library Fund.

of culture to "rediscover" his Negro roots. As a writer, he was expected to contribute to "the Negro people's struggle for national liberation," that is, to write protest novels. Since party influence has always been exerted in behalf of protest, the wartime defections have militated against the protest novel. Insofar as the party's hold over an important group of Negro novelists has been broken, these novelists have been free to join the revolt against protest which has gathered momentum during the postwar years.

A good index to the general temper of the period is the lack of any center of gravity for a specifically Negro art. There are no little magazines in the forties and fifties to perform the function of *Fire* and *Harlem* during the Renaissance, or of *Challenge* and *New Challenge* during the Depression. The absence of little magazines emphasizes the fact that there is no cohesive "movement" in contemporary Negro literature. This is perhaps as much a reflection of the uncertainties of the atomic age as of the assimilationist tendency which has dominated the period.

The critical function of the little magazine has been partially performed by *Phylon*, a review published at Atlanta University. Especially influential was a symposium on Negro literature (fourth quarter, 1950) which in its majority sentiment both reflected and helped to create the dominant mood of the period. For a brief time *Negro Story*, patterned after *Story* magazine, attempted to provide an outlet for creative writing, but it has not managed to survive. Some authors like Chester Himes and Ann Petry have published stories in *Crisis* and *Opportunity*, thereby reviving a tradition which had lapsed during the thirties. On the whole, however, the younger writers have preferred to seek nonracial outlets for their work, including such magazines as *Esquire*, *Coronet*, *Common Ground*, *Horizon*, and *Tomorrow*.

Expansion of the Negro novel in the postwar period has been in many directions—literary productivity, experience and consciousness, range and subject matter. On all sides the tendency has grown to abandon the protest-centered fiction of the Wright

School and to strike out in the direction of a more universal art. Paradoxically, the revolt against protest has led in some cases to a dead end and in others to the best fiction of the period.

The Revolt against Protest

To recognize the limitations of protest literature is one thing; to discover a viable alternative is another. Roughly speaking, the postwar novelist has explored three possibilities. The first and least constructive of these is escapist literature—pulp fiction frankly regarded as a commercial venture. Serious about nothing whatever, it poses no problem concerning race. The second alternative is the assimilationist novel proper, which avoids racial conflict by avoiding Negro life. The third is the novel of Negro life which deals with race material but not necessarily with racial conflict, approaching the Negro concretely as a human being rather than abstractly as a protagonist in the racial struggle.

The pulpsters may be quickly disposed of. The Negro novelist has traditionally been more interested in educating than in entertaining the white folks. It was not until relatively late that the familiar cleavage between art and popular culture appeared. The early novelist was too occupied with protest and instruction to succumb to the minstrel tradition, while the Harlem School managed to combine the Negro fad of the 1920's with serious art. The depression years had an urgency of their own, but by the postwar period some Negro writers were eager to achieve a kind of integration by abandoning protest in favor of pot-boilers and best-sellers.

These writers are marked by their willingness at all times to sacrifice literary values for sales. Their plots are grounded in fantasy and wish-fulfillment, and the action takes place in what invariably turns out to be the best of all possible worlds. Being themselves fortune-seekers, they are able to affirm the central values of American culture with some enthusiasm. Their novels represent a revival on the fantasy level of the success story in Negro fiction.

Will Thomas has written a pertinent article in the *Negro Digest* (July 1950) called "Negro Writers of Pulp Fiction." "Commercial fiction," he begins, "is undeniably phony as a six-dollar bill." He then proceeds with a formula for succeeding in this "phony" trade which includes the following points: (1) conceal your racial identity with a pseudonym; (2) protest doesn't pay, for editors buy entertainment; (3) the time-tested ingredients of successful popular fiction are crime and sex; and (4) study the happy ending. Following his own advice in all but one respect, Thomas has written a novel under his own name (*God Is for White Folks,* 1947) which is not much worse than others of its genre.

The prince of pulpsters is of course Frank Yerby. For seven consecutive years (as of 1952), he has written an annual best-seller, at least three of which have been turned into second-rate Hollywood thrillers.[4] As a result, Yerby has won serious treatment, or at least friendly tolerance, in some unexpected quarters. In his defense it must be conceded that whomever else he has fooled, he has never fooled himself; on being told that he was the second most popular American author in France, he mischievously replied: "The reputation of the French for sophistication is highly overrated." [5]

All of Yerby's pot-boilers are historical novels which give a superficial impression of research and authenticity, in order to balance the fabulous element in his plots. His favorite recipe, as described by Hugh Gloster, contains a bold, handsome, rakish, but withal somewhat honorable hero; a frigid, respectable wife; a torrid, anything but respectable mistress; and a crafty, fiendish villain. Structurally (to use *The Foxes of Harrow* as prototype), the Yerby novel carries its hero from a sandbar in the Mississippi (symbol of the outcast, the pariah, the base-born, the bastard) to his Harrow (wealth, fame, and the founding of a dynasty). It is likewise customary for transient love to evaporate, as all obstacles which have separated the hero from his true love are removed. A dash of sadomasochism and a generous sprinkling of derring-do, and the formula is virtually complete.

4. The titles of Yerby's novels follow, with the Hollywood scenarios starred: * *The Foxes of Harrow* (1946), *The Vixens* (1947), * *The Golden Hawk* (1948), *Pride's Castle* (1949), *Floodtide* (1950), *A Woman Called Fancy* (1951), and * *The Saracen Blade* (1952).

5. Reported by David Dempsey in "In and Out of Books," *New York Times Book Review,* Jan. 20, 1952.

Frank Yerby's significance lies not so much in his work as in the use to which it has been put by overly tolerant critics. Gloster, for example, writes of Yerby: "His chief contribution . . . has been to shake himself free of the shackles of race and to use the treasure-trove of American experience—rather than restrictively Negro experience—as his literary province." [6] Gloster's trouble is that he does not know a shackle from a shekel. All that is proved by Yerby's "raceless" novels—and they are "raceless" only in the most superficial sense—is that Frank Yerby is interested in making money.

The shining image of Frank Yerby as the fully integrated Negro novelist is simply an hallucination. Yerby's early literary career reveals an embittered, race-conscious Southerner who as late as 1944–46 was still writing protest stories in a Wrightian vein.[7] If Yerby has since abandoned overt protest, it is strictly for commercial reasons. As a matter of fact, the *un*historical intrusion of race consciousness and of regional consciousness into Yerby's "historical" novels would itself provide interesting material for discussion.

Arguments concerning integration in the arts often cut two ways. If the Negro novel were really integrated, Frank Yerby would be taken no more seriously than Mickey Spillane. By the same token, if Yerby can be hailed as its chief prophet, we may be sure that the recent trend toward "raceless" fiction is basically extraliterary in character.

A more challenging alternative to the traditional orientation of the Wright School is posed by the serious novel of white life. What prompted this development was an understandable but unsophisticated desire for an "integrated" art. Reasoning by simple analogy, the assimilationists argued that Negroes were at last breaking out of their ghettoes and moving toward full participation in every phase of American life. Why not art? Let the Negro novelist demonstrate his cosmopolitanism by writing of the dominant majority.

6. "The Significance of Frank Yerby," *Crisis, 55* (1948), 13.

7. See "Health Card," *Harper's* (May 1944), pp. 548–53; "Roads Going Down," *Common Ground* (summer 1945), pp. 67–72 (O. Henry Memorial Short Story Prize for 1945); and "My Brother Went to College," *Tomorrow* (Jan. 1946), pp. 9–12.

Thirteen of the thirty-three Negro novels written between 1945 and 1952 have a predominantly or exclusively white cast of characters. Of these, seven were written by Frank Yerby. The "raceless" protest novels of Chester Himes and Willard Motley account for three more. So strong was the assimilationist impulse in the years following the war that not even the protest novel was exempt. Along with Himes' *Cast the First Stone* (1952), both of Willard Motley's novels, *Knock on Any Door* (1947) and *We Fished All Night* (1951), are illustrative of this tendency. Aside from the racial identity of the main characters, these novels are indistinguishable from the environmentalist novels of the Wright School. *Knock on Any Door* in particular, though it deals with Chicago's Italian immigrant community, is a lineal descendant of *Native Son.* Containing impulses both toward protest and toward "racelessness," these novels display in microcosm the central conflict of the period.

Three assimilationist novels remain. In her latest novel, *Seraph on the Suwanee* (1948), Zora Neale Hurston abandons Negro folk culture, but not the rural South. Yet in this clinical study of a neurotic, poor-white woman, Miss Hurston writes far less forcefully than of Janie and Tea-Cake. William Gardner Smith's second novel, *Anger at Innocence* (1950), is an unsuccessful morality play, with a Wright-School setting and strong environmentalist overtones. *Country Place* (1947), by Ann Petry, is a novel of crumbling values, set in contemporary New England. A forceful characterization, a tight and economical style, and a well-executed design combine to make *Country Place* the best of the assimilationist novels.

What emerges most strikingly from this brief survey is the curious fact that, with few exceptions, those Negro authors who have attempted a novel of white life are precisely those who have previously published a typical protest novel. This pattern is readily demonstrable in the work of Ann Petry, William Gardner Smith, and Chester Himes. Even Frank Yerby, in his early short stories and in an unpublished full-length novel, tried his hand at racial protest before making a career of best-sellers.

Actually the close relationship between the Wright School and the assimilationists is perfectly understandable. They are two sides of a coin. The apparent paradox is readily resolved in light of the double trauma of the postwar generation. An early tendency toward Negro nationalism, stimulated by the Depression and the work of Richard Wright, has been overlaid by a conflicting tendency toward assimilationism, evoked by the social gains set in motion by the war.

In spite of superficial differences, the basic kinship of the protest novel and the assimilationist novel should be apparent. Both are propaganda novels, though the "message" of the assimilationist novel is delivered with greater subtlety. All that has happened is that the Negro's propaganda needs have changed. It is more important today to demonstrate that the Negro is prepared for integration than that he is getting a raw deal. That is why the milder assimilationist novel has replaced the bitter jeremiad of the Wright School.

Even on the surface, the two kinds of novels are not so different as they seem. Racial protest, even overt protest, dies hard. Excluded from the front door when the author chooses a white protagonist, it may enter surreptitiously through the servants' quarters. Thus the interracial marriage which is introduced as a subplot into *Country Place*. Thus the Mexican who plays an important secondary role in *Anger at Innocence*. Thus the unobtrusive Negro jailbirds in Chester Himes' novel of prison life. Why bother, one wonders, to avoid Negro life in the large, only to deal with it *en petit?* Instead of mastering the materials of Negro life with style and form, these authors have evaded the issue by writing novels which deal, at least ostensibly, with life on the other side of the color line.

In a revealing phrase, Gloster has described the novelists of this tendency as "tillers of broader fields than the circumscribed areas of racial life." [8] The metaphor is suggestive. Confronted by the exhausted soil of racial protest, these writers proposed *extensive cultivation*—the opening up of new acres—as a way out. In contrast, a group of writers emerged during the postwar period who advocated *intensive cultivation* as a new direction for the Negro novel. Keenly aware of the failure of protest, they turned

8. Hugh Gloster, "Race and the Negro Writer," *Phylon* (fourth quarter 1950), pp. 369–71.

to a more intensive exploitation of race material for aesthetic ends.

J. Saunders Redding has expressed their mood in a passage from *On Being a Negro in America:*

> I hope this piece will stand as the epilogue to whatever contribution I have made to the "literature of race." I want to get on to other things. . . . The obligations imposed by race on the average educated or talented Negro (if this sounds immodest, it must) are vast and become at last onerous. I am tired of giving up my creative initiative to these demands.[9]

Creative initiative was their first concern. Motivated primarily by artistic considerations, they rejected protest because it circumscribed their art.

At the same time, they did not fall into the countererror of avoiding Negro life. Blyden Jackson writes of them, "They did not decry the Negro writer choosing a Negro theme. They were merely mindful of the number of Negroes who had chosen Negro themes not because they were artists, but because they were Negroes."[10] More or less consciously, these writers accepted the idea of a distinctive Negro culture in which the Negro artist must root himself. Responding instinctively to their own needs as artists, they were led to espouse a practicing cultural dualism.

Little remains to be said of these novelists as a group, for like all real artists, their work is highly individualistic. Not all of them succeed, for it takes more than sound aesthetic theory to make a work of art. But among them may be found the most promising writers in postwar Negro fiction. It is with such novels as Dorothy West's *The Living Is Easy,* Owen Dodson's *Boy at the Window,* William Demby's *Beetlecreek,* and Ralph Ellison's *Invisible Man* that the following chapter is principally concerned.

The revolt against protest, insofar as it was more than a money-making maneuver, has been fed by two distinct streams. Some of the younger novelists have revolted on aesthetic grounds, others

9. J. Saunders Redding, *On Being a Negro in America* (Indianapolis, Bobbs-Merrill, 1951), p. 26.

10. Blyden Jackson, "Faith without Works in Negro Literature," *Phylon* (fourth quarter 1951), pp. 378–88.

under the siren spell of assimilationism. In both instances, however, the aim has been to provide a wider base for Negro art than the protest motif will allow. Their common goal has been to break out of the narrow limits of racial protest into some kind of universality. Except where it has led to escapism and to a conscious avoidance of Negro life, this quest has had a liberating effect on the Negro novel. That it has often led to a false freedom is in a sense irrelevant. What matters is that the need for intellectual *Lebensraum* has been generally acknowledged.

9. The Contemporary Negro Novel

IN recent years, more interesting novels have appeared than can be dealt with justly in brief compass. Perhaps eight or so—approximately one-fourth of the total—will not overtax the reader's patience. Most of these novels have been chosen for their aesthetic value, though some have been widely celebrated without good cause. In general, they represent the highest accomplishment within each tendency of the period.

Protest Novels

Chester Himes' *If He Hollers Let Him Go* (1946) is an impressive failure—with accent on the adjective. It takes the novel of pure race consciousness to its utmost limit, where it strangles to death in its own contradictions. The novel is Wrightian to the core, which is hardly surprising in view of the author's background and experience. Himes, like Wright, is a product of the Great Depression, of association with the labor movement, the Federal Writers' Project, and the Communist party. A kind of

Yerby in reverse, he began his writing career with popular fiction but veered sharply in the direction of protest. He has published short stories in *Esquire* and *Coronet,* as well as in *Crisis* and *Opportunity,* and as of 1952 was the author of three full-length novels of which the present work is the most important.

The novel is no mere catalogue of grievances, though these are amply provided, within the context of a wartime California shipyard. Racial oppression is a *donnée;* Himes is interested in the personal adjustment of a sensitive Negro to the bitter fact of caste. For the most part, the conflict is successfully internalized, as the protagonist is forced to choose between revenge and moderation—a theme first treated in Negro fiction by Sutton Griggs and Charles Chesnutt. The alternatives are given concrete dramatic expression through the rebellious protagonist and his accommodationist fiancée.

As a psychological study of a man who is obsessed by race, the novel has power and authority. The protagonist lives on the verge of violence, one minute rebelling, the next conforming; one hating, the next loving; now despondent, now exhilarated by his girl or simply by driving his car—battered from emotional pillar to post by external pressures which he can't control. To render this inner agony, Himes has borrowed freely from the visceral style of Richard Wright: "I started drawing in my emotions, tying them, whittling them off, nailing them down. I was so tight inside, I was like wood. My breath wouldn't go any deeper than my throat and I didn't know whether I could talk at all. I had to get ready to die before I could get out of the house" (p. 122).

This characteristic hyperbole is perhaps appropriate, since the whole plan of the novel rests upon magnifying normal emotions to pathological intensity. It has the disadvantage, however, of all overstatement: the reader builds up a gradual immunity. Somewhat more successful is the dream device through which Himes gives us occasional glimpses of his protagonist's subconscious. Here—through a freely symbolic medium—his naked hatred of whites, his violent oscillation between energy and impotence, and his corrosive feelings of rejection, fear, and shame are vividly conveyed.

The problem with case-study fiction is to generalize successfully. Himes solves it by developing Bob Jones as a symbol of willlessness. By thematic repetition of key phrases ("beyond my control," "I didn't have a chance"), he conveys the feeling of helpless frustration which ensues whenever one surrenders control of his destiny to others. It is a feeling which every slave, every convict, every conscripted soldier knows intimately. Bob Jones knows it in those areas of his life where he is deprived of will by the whites: "I don't have anything at all to say about what's happening to me. I'm just like some sort of machine being run by white people pushing buttons" (p. 202).

It is in these terms that the main tension of the novel is resolved. "To accept being black as a condition over which you have no control" seems in the eyes of the protagonist an ignominious surrender. For most of the novel he resists, but experience convinces him that personal defiance is suicidal: "I knew with the white folks sitting on my brain, controlling my every thought, action, and emotion, making life one crisis after another, day and night, asleep and awake, conscious and unconscious, I couldn't make it. I knew that unless I found my niche and crawled into it, unless I stopped hating white folks and learned to take them as they came, I couldn't live in America" (pp. 181–82). The crowning irony is that Jones' decision to conform is—disallowed. He makes his truce, but the white world will not respect it: he is framed on a rape charge and nearly sent to jail for thirty years. By a quirk of fate he is set "free," providing he is willing to "volunteer" for the Army. As a result, he loses both his girl and his dream of manhood.

In its denouement the novel reveals a fatal structural flaw. Here is a black nationalist, hypersensitive, neurotic, unable to mobilize his energies for anything but the race war, driven by his obsession to the brink of murder. The whole novel moves inexorably toward the opposing view that some kind of accommodation is the price of sanity. The protagonist chooses; he is born again; but suddenly we are confronted with a chain of events whose logic seems to justify his former view of reality.

Earlier in the novel, Himes has argued convincingly that in every human being there is an inner world which lies within his power to control. Is it now his thesis that in all crucial matters concerning a Negro's fate, the will of society is decisive? If so, we feel put upon, for we have been following Jones' inner conflict as if it mattered. Suddenly it is revealed as meaningless—no matter what Jones decides, society will dispose of his future. Such a thesis requires that the tensions of the novel be resolved on a sociological plane; the very basis of a psychological novel is destroyed.

At bottom the trouble is ideological: neither revenge nor accommodation is acceptable to Himes, and as a result, the novel flounders to an inconclusive finish. Earl Conrad writes of *If He Hollers Let Him Go:* "the book is at war with itself, as is Jones, as is Himes, as is the American Negro." The novel suffers ultimately from a one-to-one correlation between form and content: in portraying a divided personality, Himes has written a divided novel. But formless and chaotic is precisely what art cannot afford to be.

Last of the Conquerors (1948), by William Gardner Smith, is an expatriate novel in the Wright tradition. Like Wright, Smith rejects America both as a Negro and as a social critic. "America's is a superficial civilization," he writes in *Phylon,* "it is a soda-pop land, a civilization of television sets and silk stockings and murder mysteries, and contempt for art and poetry." Unlike Wright, however, Smith's expatriate impulse has remained essentially literary, for after a tour of duty as a soldier in occupied Germany, he returned to his native Philadelphia, where, having graduated from Temple University, he now pursues a writing career.

The novel recounts the experiences of a young colored soldier in the American army of occupation. Initially suspicious of the Germans, he discovers values in their civilization which compare favorably with the life he has known at home. His pro-German sentiments are nourished by a love affair with a German girl; his anti-Americanism, by his encounters with racial discrimination in the American army. Wavering between conflicting loyalties, he finally decides to return to Germany as a voluntary exile.

The dramatic vehicle for this conflict is provided by a sharp contrast between two army posts. Dawkins' Berlin outfit has high morale, good food, lax off-duty regulations, and an understanding commanding officer. Bremburg, as one soldier puts it, is "nigger hell," where Southern officers bear down on the colored troops in order to keep them from fraternizing with German women. It is, so to speak, America transplanted to German soil. This structure is reinforced by occasional flashbacks to Dawkins' civilian life, and by minor characters who dramatize the alternatives facing the protagonist.

Smith has evidently given careful thought to matters of form, but his style is immature, reminding us constantly that *Last of the Conquerors* is a first novel, published when the author was only twenty-two. Individual passages are promising, to be sure. The love scene which crowns Book I is simple and robust; the countryside at Bremburg is used effectively to shift the tone of the novel; the final farewell is skillfully done: Ilse's prediction that Dawkins will never return introduces an element of doubt which transfers the burden to the reader's imagination. On the other hand, there are passages which are painfully inept. In the course of a discussion of German war guilt, for example, an American soldier slaps a German girl, who continues serenely as if nothing has happened! The girl, being a mere pea in Smith's ideological shell game, is without importance as a human being.

In certain elementary respects, Smith has simply not mastered his craft. His dialogue is often stilted, and he has not yet grasped the relationship between language and personality. As a result, even the major characters are flat. Ilse, for example, is more a product of adolescent fantasy than a real woman. Her pidgin English (reminiscent of Hemingway's stylistic debacle in *For Whom the Bell Tolls*) is especially distracting. Smith will not trust his reader with verbal echoes. When he echoes himself, he flags the reader down with an overt reference to the original passage. He has not learned to write by implication. Above all, his style is not his own. It is imitative and therefore inconsistent: an occasional attempt at stream-of-consciousness is grafted upon a basic journalese.

This story of a Negro soldier suspended between American and German civilization provides the author with powerful leverage for propaganda purposes. His white audience, within the framework of the novel, is forced to choose between racism and national pride. But in order to maneuver his audience into this dilemma, Smith employs a series of crude equations which contain half-truths at best. He must persuade us, in fictional terms, that the American North is no different from the American South: "Listen, patriot . . . there ain't no difference between the South and the North." He must persuade us that American racism is the moral equivalent of the Nazi death-camps: "In America they do almost the same thing with your people—the black Americans—as the Nazis did here to the Jews."

Let us hope it will not be taken as evidence of either Yankee or American chauvinism if we point out that there are in fact important differences between the Negro's status in Philadelphia and in Georgia; between the systematic genocide of the Hitler government and the Supreme Court decision of 1954. Surely Smith's contrast between old-world culture and the GI comic book doesn't tell the whole story? Only by taking the worst of America and the best of Hitler's Germany can the scales be tipped in favor of exile. And somehow one knows that the author's finger is on the scales. Smith's point is surely not to exonerate the Nazis but only to intensify the guilt of white America. He has not exaggerated American racism, but who can deny that he has idealized Germany in order to make a debater's point?

Raceless Novels

In a revealing scene from one of Willard Motley's novels, a minor character who "happens to be a Negro" moves to the far end of a cocktail party when another Negro enters the room. It is just so with Motley's fiction, which studiously avoids Negro life as a matter of principle. Born and raised in a polyglot neighborhood in Chicago, Motley peoples his novels with second-generation Italians, Jews, and Poles. Second-generation assimilationism is his theme, and there is no reason to doubt that it is a projection of his own inner conflict.

Knock on Any Door (1947) is the story of Nick Romano, a boy of Italian immigrant stock whose environment pushes him remorselessly along the path to delinquency and crime. The presentation is naturalistic, panoramic, often redundant. For ninety-two chapters Motley piles episode on whirling episode, overwhelming the reader with evidence of society's guilt in producing the likes of Nick. The style is journalistic, and occasionally brilliant. It is corrupted, however, by that dead-pan, pulled-punch, pseudo-Hemingway technique which plays all human emotion in a single key. This monotone, one suspects, is a product of the fact that Motley is more interested in the emotions of his readers than of his characters. What there is of psychological insight depends on a school of analysis best described as Hollywood Freud.

On the strength of sheer narrative power, the novel might have transcended these limitations, except for its lack of originality. The truth is that in its main outlines it leans so heavily on *Native Son* as to border on plagiarism. Nick Romano, like Bigger Thomas, is a bad "dago"—as bad as Motley can make him, in order to intensify the general guilt. Like Bigger, he commits a symbolic murder which gives his life meaning ("This is what I was born to do"). The chase, the trial, the speech of Nick's lawyer ("I accuse society") is simply *Native Son* stripped of racial implications. The difference is that where Wright's treatment is condensed and selective, Motley's is detailed and exhaustive. In effect, Motley has borrowed terse symbolic episodes from *Native Son* and inflated them to naturalistic proportions.

The measure of the two novels may be taken in the scenes where Nick and Bigger await death in murderer's row. Motley is concerned with the morbid details of the execution; Wright, with Bigger's inner conflict. One novelist asks, will my protagonist beat the rap; the other, on what terms will he die? The focus is consistently outside of Nick, on the courtroom spectacle, on the switch that will snuff out his life. Since redemption is never possible, no real conflict is allowed to develop. Instead of dramatic tension, we have only *suspense,* and the hackneyed emotions inherent in the death-cell situation. Motley exploits these emotions for all they are worth. Nowhere, in fact, do any subtleties appear which might have prevented the film version of the novel from becoming a box-office success.

A competent naturalistic novel, when *Knock on Any Door* appeared it was greeted with extravagant critical acclaim. Comparisons to the work of Dreiser and Farrell were not uncommon. Such illusions will be quickly dispelled by a second reading: deprived of the element of suspense, the novel reveals its essential formlessness. If this should not suffice, Motley's second novel, *We Fished All Night* (1951), will amply demonstrate the limitations of his talent. It is a rambling tract which deals with such matters as GI disillusionment with the war, political corruption in Chicago, and the struggle between the People and the Interests. In a word, it faithfully reflects the politics of the Wallace movement.

A more successful portrayal of white life than either of Motley's novels, Ann Petry's *Country Place* (1947) is in fact one of the finest novels of the period. *Country Place,* moreover, is a manifestation not so much of assimilationism as of versatility. Mrs. Petry's early work, which includes both short stories and a novella, is strongly racial in emphasis. Her first novel, *The Street* (1946), attracted considerable attention both here and abroad as an eloquent successor to *Native Son.* Actually, if *Knock on Any Door* suffers by comparison to Wright, *The Street* suffers even more.

The Street is a *roman à thèse* whose aim, in the words of the author, is "to show how simply and easily the environment can change the course of a person's life." The heroine is a declassed *bourgeoise* who is driven to murder by the corrupting influence of "the street." As in Wright and Motley, a whole bookful of sociological data is adduced to validate the murder. Of an environmentalist who chooses to focus on society we can demand more than a superficial social analysis. The trouble with *The Street* is that it tries to make racial discrimination responsible for slums. It is an attempt to interpret slum life in terms of *Negro* experience, when a larger frame of reference is required. As Alain Locke has observed, "*Knock on Any Door* is superior to *The Street* because it designates class and environment, rather than mere race and environment, as its antagonist."

Country Place is a novel of another magnitude, large enough to justify a better acquaintance with its author. Ann Petry (1911–) was born and raised in Old Saybrook, Conn., where her father was the local druggist. After graduating from the College of Pharmacy at the University of Connecticut, she disappointed family plans by abandoning small-town life for the big city. In New York she tried her hand at advertising, social work, and newspaper reporting. Evenings were occupied with courses in creative writing and planned readings in psychology. Her first short stories were published in *Crisis* and *Phylon.* One was reprinted in Foley's *Best American Short Stories of 1946;* another, which attracted the attention of talent scouts, led to a Houghton Mifflin Literary Fellowship. A novella, "In Dark Confusion," based on the Harlem riot of August 1943, completes her literary apprenticeship.

One senses in Mrs. Petry's life and art a tension between metropolis and small town, between New York and Old Saybrook. In *The Street* she explores New York from an Old Saybrook point of view; in *Country Place* she reverses the process. Reminiscent of *Winesburg, Ohio,* and *Spoon River,* the novel treats small-town life from the perspective of a refugee. Like the writers of the Chicago Renaissance who fled from Main Street to Fifty-Seventh Street, it was necessary for Mrs. Petry to renounce the village before she could realize its literary potential. A record of this experience, *Country Place* embodies both the struggle for emancipation and the desire, once liberated, to re-establish one's ties with the past through art.

Conceived in the spirit of revolt from the village, the novel probes beneath the quiet surface of a country town to the inquisitiveness, bigotry, and malice which are typical of its inner life. On the theory that village life revolves around the drugstore, Mrs. Petry introduces Doc, the druggist-narrator, who serves to "place" the action of the novel. To encompass the collective personality of the town, she employs a shifting point of view which rotates among the chief participants. The burden of conflict, however, is borne by Johnnie Roane, a returning veteran who has outgrown the town. His sole remaining tie is his young wife, Glory; when he discovers her infidelity with Ed, the town bull, he renounces his father's contracting business and embarks upon an apprenticeship as an artist in New York.

A second center of dramatic interest is provided by Mrs. Gramby, whose inner struggle parallels that of Johnnie Roane. Like Johnnie, she fights her way free of the town and achieves a kind of affirmation. With her old-fashioned virtues of dignity and formality, she represents the best of the town's traditions, about to be inundated by the cheap and brassy vulgarity of the modern age. Confronted with the obnoxious "pushing" of her son's wife, Lil, she wonders what can be done to stem the tide, to affirm the values of the past in the context of the present. In the end, she revises her will, passing judgment on the younger generation from beyond the grave. The will thus becomes an effective device for resolving the central value-conflict of the novel.

The fundamental clash of values occurs between those who exemplify the village mores and those who transcend them. Among the former are several minor characters with well-defined symbolic roles. The village cab driver, known locally as "the Weasel," typifies the town's spirit of petty vindictiveness. Glory, pretty but empty-headed, suggests the frustrated romantic yearnings of the townswomen. Ed Barrell—"good old Ed"—is a symbol of the town's pride in its own lechery. Glory's mother, Lil, with her hawklike appearance, suggests vulgar materialism and acquisitiveness. Her middle-aged husband, Mearns Gramby, represents wasted talent and sexual repression. The town is of course xenophobic: anti-Catholic, anti-Semitic, anti-Negro. As counterweights, Mrs. Petry provides Neola, Mrs. Gramby's colored maid; the Portegee, her gardener; and Rosenberg, the Jewish lawyer. The village outcasts are in touch with fundamental reality; they offer some hope of redemption to a declining Yankee tradition.

The most notable feature of village life is its resistance to change, its tendency toward stagnation. Smugness and complacency are the outer signs, but they are symptomatic of a stubborn commitment to live in the past, by the light of some outmoded ideal. Doc, who is cast in the role of village philosopher, makes the diagnosis and prescribes the remedy: "I remember when electric lights were first installed in the town of Lennox. My father, whose reaction was fairly typical of the period, objected to them as being a wicked invention of the devil, expressly designed to ruin man's eyesight—the light being too harsh—and to soften his moral fiber" (p. 223). Personally, Doc goes on, he prefers to have his moral fiber softened by using electricity. Doc's drugstore contains an old-fashioned ice-cream parlor where he still mixes his own fountain sirups, but he dispenses penicillin and the sulfa drugs as well. Striving for a balance between change and tradition, Doc combines the best of the old with the best of the new.

Individuals, like communities, may fasten their lives to the past, but then, like barnacles, they pay the price of stagnation. Consider the case of Johnnie Roane, who has lived through four years of war with only the memory of his young wife to sustain him. Returning from overseas, he clings desperately to that memory, even though it means the death of his ambitions: "You want Glory . . . but having her means Lennox. So you forget you ever heard of a paintbrush or a drawing pencil or a place known in some circles as Manhattan Island" (p. 129). Only when his image of the past is irrevocably shattered by the knowledge of his wife's infidelity does he revise his attitudes toward permanence and change. Losing Glory, he has gained New York; he has learned to weigh the pain against the possibility of growth. If change is not always desirable, he concludes, it is in any case inevitable, and it brings in its wake an admixture, if often an imbalance, of good and evil.

Mrs. Gramby, as a living embodiment of the New England tradition, is particularly prone to idealize the past. She has watched the town change under the impact of two world wars, and in her opinion largely for the worse: "As I get older, I keep going back to the past, comparing it with the present, making myself unhappy by remembering it as a more gracious time in which to have lived" (p. 89). In her personal life, moreover, she has sacrificed her son to the past, keeping him in Lennox against his will for the sake of family tradition. Through a crisis in her son's marriage, however, she is forced to revise her values. Her new-found wisdom consists in recognizing the inevitability of change and attempting to influence its direction. In a conscious effort to alter certain of the town's established ways, she revises her will, underwriting an interracial marriage and financing Johnnie Roane's apprenticeship in New York.

On its deepest level, the novel suggests that resistance to change is not a parochial trait but a universal human tendency. Seeking for certainty in a world of flux, man creates images or dreams which he tries to invest with timelessness. Each of the characters in *Country Place* pursues a "soapbubble dream"; each seeks to protect his heart's desire from the ravages of time. Glory and Lil defy time in the shallow fashion of the Hollywood glamor-merchant: Glory, by her restless search for romance and adventure; Lil, by her pathetic efforts to stave off middle age. Mrs. Gramby's defiance takes the form of a refusal to allow her son to grow up, to live his own life. Mearns Gramby tries to arrest time by making a middle-aged marriage; Johnnie Roane expects time to have stood still during his absence overseas. All, in the end, are stripped of their illusions, but the positive characters are able to transform their loss into a source of growth.

It is from the theme of lost illusion that the narrative structure of the novel flows. *Country Place* develops a strong narrative drive, paced by a storm whose intensity is reminiscent of the New England hurricane of 1938. The action of the novel takes place in a single week (one cycle of weather), reaching a climax along with the storm. Through a kind of Lear motif the storm reduces each character to moral (or literal) nakedness. Faced with the death of their dreams, they are forced to re-evaluate the past, balancing achievement with desire. The storm thus becomes considerably more than a narrative device; it suggests first of all the widespread uprootedness caused by the war. Ultimately it emerges as a symbol of time and flux, relentless killers of the dream.

Mrs. Petry's style, like her narrative strategy, supports her main intent. In the Wright School manner, she will describe a cat, mangled by an auto accident, without flinching. Her realism, however, expresses more than a conventional tough-mindedness; it is well suited to a novel so largely concerned with deflating the romantic attitude. Beyond this, she achieves a metaphorical depth virtually unknown among Wright's disciples. Concrete, poetic, her style persistently seeks an "objective correlative" to human emotion. In the following passage she captures Glory's restless frustration through a vivid description of a marshy cove: "It was black, sullen, bordered by a ripple of white foam that gnawed restlessly at the edges of the marsh. The foam retreated and returned, retreated and then returned; and as she watched it she got the feeling that she could hear it snarl because it could not get free of the marsh that confined it" (p. 54).

From individual descriptive passages, image patterns and symbols emerge as part of a total design. The stifling atmosphere of small-town life is evoked, for example, by a recurrent image of confinement and restraint: "the grated window made the ticket-seller look as though he were in a cage." Each character, in fact, has his personal "cage," and through this symbol the essential village psychology is revealed. The townsfolk strive for an equal distribution of frustration; it is this that accounts for their vindictiveness. If the cage symbol is closed and static, the tree symbol is open and expansive. Initially the trees are used to dramatize the destructiveness of the storm, but later on they acquire another significance. Concern or indifference to their fate divides the positive from the negative characters. "Trees will grow," Mrs. Gramby insists, "people will live here." The town recovers from the storm, and life goes on. In a subtle movement which parallels the main direction of the novel, what has been a symbol of uprootedness becomes a symbol of growth.

Because of Mrs. Petry's technical proficiency it is especially difficult to account for the incredible lapse of taste which mars the closing pages of the novel. Somehow she can never manage (it is equally true of *The Street*) to remove her villains gracefully from the stage. Glory is handled throughout with unexceptionable irony, but in the final scene, during the reading of the will, Lil becomes an object of the author's unrestrained invective. The root of the trouble lies, one suspects, in Mrs. Petry's New England heritage. She understands evil, motivates her villains well, but fails to achieve distance in the end. Evil cannot go unpunished, even if the author has to administer the lash in person. This momentary loss of poise is unfortunate, but it cannot seriously detract from Mrs. Petry's distinguished achievement in *Country Place.*

Novels of Negro Life and Culture

Owen Dodson's *Boy at the Window* (1951) is a quiet novel, devoid of melodrama. It is the story of a boy's sudden maturation, precipitated by the death of his mother and the disruption of his childish world. The novel has a Wright School setting, but its focus is distinctly psychological, with emphasis on the boy's family constellation and early religious development. The author, a teacher of dramatics at Howard University, grew up in a cosmopolitan neighborhood in Brooklyn, not unlike that of his young protagonist. Educated at Bates College and the Yale School of

Drama, Dodson is the author of several unpublished plays and a book of verse, *Powerful Long Ladder* (1946).

Coin Foreman grows up in a hostile environment from which he is protected by the gentle ministrations of his mother. As a result of her illness and death he is confronted prematurely with the perplexities of adolescence: with sex, with race, with God, with the problem of his own identity. In dramatic terms the boy moves from innocence to sophistication, from dependence to self-reliance. Bewilderment gives way to understanding, as a series of disillusioning experiences deepens his conception of reality. *Boy at the Window*, in short, is a case study of the onset of puberty. The whole novel, as the epigraph suggests, celebrates a boy's initiation into the mysteries of adult life: "and he will be so as a boat baptized for a brave journey."

Coin's relationship with his mother is the axis upon which the broader meaning of the novel turns. Who was his mother; what did she stand for; how can he keep her memory alive?—these are the questions which determine the direction of his growth. The catalytic agent is Ferris, a chance acquaintance of his own age who becomes a symbol of friendship, of sympathy and understanding, of imagination and love of beauty, of everything, in short, of which he has been deprived by his mother's death. It is Ferris who helps Coin to find his mother, by boasting that "My Mama's name is in the Bible." Not to be outdone, Coin searches for Naomi, and in the *Book of Ruth* he finds her, "saying the words of together." In the moving story of Naomi and Ruth, Coin finds guidance for his journey through the adult world.

Mr. Dodson's literary manner is essentially Joycean; he employs a highly disciplined stream-of-consciousness style within a loose narrative framework. The point of view is decidedly Coin's; we learn about him by sharing his thoughts, not by observing his actions. The time scheme is psychological rather than chronological; we are apprised of events not in the order of their occurrence but as they become important in Coin's consciousness. As in Joyce, fragments of church hymns, children's jingles, subway ads, and fourth-grade readers are introduced to establish psychological authenticity. The boyish diction and the bold metaphors, well within reach of an imaginative child, help further to validate the boy's consciousness.

A poet and a dramatist, Mr. Dodson does not wholly succeed in transposing his talent to the narrative mode. *Boy at the Window* contains both lyric and dramatic elements which have not been fully assimilated to the longer genre. In pursuit of lyric intensity, for example, the author slips occasionally into an extreme subjectivity bordering on Dada. Mr. Dodson's sense of form, moreover, is essentially dramaturgical; one can almost see the curtain coming down on certain scenes. Stylistic considerations aside, the novel is lacking in scope and significance. The burden of meaning intended by the author is simply too great for a child to bear. The problem of conveying an adult theme through the consciousness of a nine-year-old seems virtually insuperable, but Mr. Dodson has struggled with it valiantly. Perhaps in his next novel he will bring his virtuosity to bear on a less confining subject.

The Living Is Easy (1948), by Dorothy West, is a bitingly ironic novel which deals with the ruthless success drive of the Negro middle class and its staggering toll in ruined personalities. Boston's "counterfeit Brahmins" are the objects of Miss West's satire, and she belabors them with an enthusiasm born of personal rebellion. Yet in presenting her indictment, she never subordinates psychological interest to social criticism. Such is her gift for characterization that even her minor figures come alive, while Cleo, the protagonist of the novel, is unforgettable. Manipulative, domineering, unscrupulous, and yet in her selfish way, loving, this castrating female is the most striking personality in recent Negro fiction.

Dorothy West's literary career spans three decades in the history of the Negro novel. A native Bostonian, she was educated at Boston University and the Columbia School of Journalism. She began to write during the mid-1920's, publishing short stories in *Opportunity*, the *Boston Post*, and *The Saturday Evening Quill* (literary organ of the local "New Negro" group). During the 1930's, as editor of *Challenge* and *New Challenge*, she helped keep alive the idea of a distinctive Negro art. A depression job as relief investigator in the Harlem tenements introduced a sociological note into her work; eighteen months on the Federal Writers' Project and personal contact with Richard Wright drew her briefly into the orbit of the Communist party. During the forties, she contributed short stories regularly to a news syndicate, while completing work on her first full-length novel.

The Living Is Easy reflects most of this background. From the Renaissance period comes a touch of primitivism, a Freudian approach to personality, a positive attitude toward Negro folk culture and a negative attitude toward the Negro middle class. From the author's depression experience comes an ability to root her characters solidly in their social milieu. Hers, however, is a primarily Renaissance consciousness. The very title of the novel, though ironic, helps to define its essential spirit through association with Catfish Row. The novel, in fact, seems to have had its inception in a short story which appeared originally in *The Saturday Evening Quill.* "Prologue to a Life" (April 1929) contains the prototypes of Cleo and Bart, the central figures of the novel. Their names are changed in the later work, but the essential circumstances of their lives remain unaltered.

Cleo is an ambitious parvenu from "down home" who sacrifices the happiness of herself and her family for the sake of admission to the ranks of the Boston élite. In a flashback to her Southern childhood, Cleo's dominant personality traits are revealed. Her tremendous vitality, wildness, and daring are displayed in the episode of the roan stallion; her masculine protest, in her fight with a boy whom she defeats by butting him in the groin. Her warped values are anticipated by a querulous remark to her father: "I don't want a kiss, I want a copper." Proud and despotic, she tyrannizes over her weaker sisters, blackmailing them out of their share of penny candy without scruple or remorse. Her deepest motives, however, spring from her relationship to her mother. The dethroned eldest child, she wants desperately to be loved best, and this neurotic need sets the pattern of her adult personality.

As the present action commences, Cleo is well on the way to social success. Having left the South with no assets but a fair complexion, she enters a loveless marriage with Bart Judson, "the Black Banana King." In an unguarded moment she admits her husband to her bedroom; the result is Judy, a disappointing dark child who takes after her father. In spite of this setback, Cleo resolves to raise her daughter as a proper little Bostonian. She steals from her husband, lies to her friends, and deprives Judy of her childhood in order to accomplish this objective. In her treachery and deceit, her willfulness and ambition, her fierce self-containment and her infinite capacity for rationalization, Cleo's literary archetype is Iago. What makes her a more successful character is her humanity, her capacity for suffering as well as inflicting pain.

Cleo's inner conflict is developed along typical Renaissance lines: "You really had to love Bostonians to like them. And the part of Cleo that did like them was continually at war with the part of her that preferred the salt flavor of lusty laughter" (p. 44). In color, in social position, in personality Cleo hovers between two worlds. In order to enjoy the best of both, she gathers her sisters around her, destroying their marriages in the process. But the climax of the novel occurs when Cleo symbolically turns her back on the Negro struggle in the South. This is the final price of acceptance by a group whose "lives were narrowly confined to a desperate effort to ignore their racial heritage." Nemesis arrives in the form of the first World War, which ruins her husband's wholesale banana business. Cleo's power was her husband's money; now she can rule only "the young, the weak, and the frightened." Gradually she is deserted by her sisters, her daughter, and at last her husband.

Cleo mutilates her "Rabelaisian soul" in order to become a Bostonian. Similar mutilations in other characters serve to broaden the theme. There is the Duchess, who buries her Catholic heart in an unsanctioned marriage, in order to pour tea for Boston ladies who have scorned her mother. There is the Duchess' husband, Simeon, who relinquishes the editorship of a militant Negro newspaper, in order to secure his sister's social position. There is a young doctor, interested in cancer research, who turns to the abortion trade as a source of ready cash. All, like Cleo, have paid too high a price for belonging; their Spartan discipline in the face of personal tragedy is described in one of Miss West's early stories: "The race was too young, its achievements too few, for whimsical indulgence. It must not matter whom you loved; it must not matter what you desired; it must not matter that it broke your heart, if sacrifice meant a step forward toward the freedom of our people." [1]

Out of the dramatic structure of the novel comes a persistent thematic idea: "there can be no interlocking of separated worlds." The immediate reference is to the secular and religious worlds of Simeon and the Duchess, but the concept is universal in application. The clashing worlds of past and present, of child and adult, of male and female, of white and colored, of South Carolina and Boston fall within its scope. Cleo's tragic error is her determination to unite these worlds by sheer force of will. The result is universal misery. The novel thus becomes a plea to respect individual differences; an admonition against "easy" solutions which involve self-mutilation of any kind.

The most characteristic feature of Miss West's style is her use of verbal irony. The ironist is ultimately concerned with values, and in this instance her shafts are aimed at the specious values of the Negro middle class: "Mr. Hartnett failed in business and blew his brains out just like a white man. Everybody was a little proud of his suicide." The tone flows spontaneously from the nature of her material. Miss West writes of a time when "a tailor and a stable-owner were the leaders of colored society." A Negro élite whose economic base is so inadequate to its social aspirations invites ironic treatment. Only once, and at her peril, does the author abandon this steady perspective. In handling the subject of Southern injustice, she drops her ironic tone and immediately lapses into the wildest melodrama.

The Living Is Easy, in spite of occasional brilliance, is a diamond in the rough. There is little to distinguish its style, other than a certain neatness and economy. Serious difficulties on the narrative level prevent the novel from realizing its full potential. The plot falters more than once, as the author's inventiveness fails to keep pace with Cleo's capacity for bitchery. Perhaps most damaging is the novel's lack of proportion. The formal division into

1. "An Unimportant Man," *Saturday Evening Quill* (June 1928), pp. 21–32.

Part I (280 pages) and Part II (67 pages) is indicative of the problem. Part II is in fact an epilogue which ties up the loose ends of the plot on an incredibly eventful day some years after the main action. Somewhere in the course of a busy day the conflicts initiated in Part I are hastily resolved. What can be said in extenuation of such formlessness? Only the trenchancy of its satire and the vividness of its characterization save the novel from oblivion.

Beetlecreek (1950), by William Demby, is an existentialist novel whose central characters come momentarily to life, only to return in the end to somnambulance. It is, moreover, an expatriate novel, whose tone is dominated by pessimism and disgust, flowing from a robust rejection of American culture and of Negro life in particular. Viewed psychologically, it is a novel of cramped desire, considerably illuminated by a knowledge of the author's personal history.

William Demby grew up in Clarksburg, West Virginia, in the heart of the mining region which provides the setting for his novel. His education at West Virginia State College for Negroes was interrupted by two years with the American Army in Italy, where he wrote for *Stars and Stripes.* With the help of the GI Bill he completed his undergraduate career at Fisk (Class of '47). Interested in painting as well as literature, he returned to Italy to study art at the University of Rome, where he has remained to write screen plays for Roberto Rossellini. From Clarksburg to Rome is a good many spiritual miles, and this distance is primarily responsible for the tone of *Beetlecreek.*

At Fisk, Demby wrote short stories for a creative writing class, some of which saw print in the *Fisk Herald,* the official student publication. For two years he was assistant editor of the magazine, drawing the covers and illustrations as well as making regular contributions in the form of stories and reviews. These were the years when, under the guidance of the poet Robert E. Hayden, the *Herald* produced something of an intellectual renaissance at Fisk. The flavor of the magazine was definitely "GI," antiparochial, and cosmopolitan. Its politics were racially militant and vaguely Wallacite, but for the most part it was content to be rather belligerently intellectual. It was this milieu, wherein he did daily battle with the somnambulance of the Fisk campus, that formed the backdrop of Demby's literary apprenticeship.

One of his undergraduate stories, which appeared in the *Fisk Herald* of December 1946, contains the germinal idea of *Beetlecreek.* The story, entitled "Saint Joey," is strongly antifascist in intent. It concerns a white teen-age gang led by a young religious fanatic, which is suggestive in its attitudes and activities of the Ku Klux Klan or the Christian Front. In vigilante fashion the gang decides to murder an old recluse who has violated the racial mores of the community. Much transformed (for example, the gang becomes colored), this material provides the main action of the novel.

At its narrative core, *Beetlecreek* is the story of Bill Trapp, an eccentric old white man whose belated attempt to reach out to his neighbors is doomed in advance by the town's instinct for death. A retired carnival worker, he lives on a ramshackle farm between the Negro section and the white business district, in self-imposed isolation from both groups. As the novel opens, he terminates fifteen years of silence and solitude by an act of will, thereby displaying the celebrated "courage to be" of French existentialism.

His first awkward contact is with Johnny, a young colored boy whom he catches in his apple orchard, and with Johnny's uncle David, with whom he drinks beer in the local Negro tavern. Elated by his initial success, he donates some pumpkins to a colored church festival and plans a mixed picnic for Negro and white children. As an aftermath of the picnic, he is unjustly accused of sexual molestation, whereupon he becomes the scapegoat for all of the town's frustrations and animosities. It is Johnny's gang which vindicates the honor of the colored community through a wanton act of arson and murder. To this martyrdom there are distinct religious overtones, for Bill Trapp is variously compared to a biblical shepherd, a saint, and Christ himself. He represents the positive values of kindliness, sympathy, compassion, and love.

Against Bill Trapp's rather ineffectual strivings toward life, Demby sets the deathliness of Beetlecreek. It is conveyed dramatically through the barbershop crowd (narrowness and defeatism), the funeral scene (shallowness and hypocrisy), the persecution of Bill Trapp (cruelty), and above all the church festival, with its petty money-grubbing in the service of a venal clergy. It is conveyed symbolically, too, as the town is compared to a coffin or a hearse: "You're the only one ever knew what a coffin this town was." "And Black Enameled Death that he had seen represented everything of Beetlecreek." Nor does Demby neglect the socio-economic dimension which has made Beetlecreek a kind of death trap. Mined out long ago, what remains is a ghost town where Negro life in particular is even more circumscribed than usual. As a symbol, then, Beetlecreek represents life without fulfillment. Beetlecreek is a place where life crawls, with a kind of insectile loathsomeness.

The dramatic conflict of the novel develops not around Bill Trapp but around Johnny and David, or more precisely around David, for Johnny is essentially an echo. Through their relations with Bill Trapp, both are brought to the brink of a decision; each evades his responsibility at the crucial moment, choosing the way of death rather than of life. David, one suspects, is Demby's other self, who chose not to be.

David is a frustrated artist, trapped in the deadly backwater of Beetlecreek by circumstances which he regards as inevitable. Even in childhood his desire to draw was firmly discouraged by his parents, who regarded art as "impractical." Then there was the problem of being colored, "the feeling of being suffocated and unable to move." In college he had sought for a while to escape from this feeling through art, but increasingly he turned to the easier and more conventional means of escape through drinking and good-timing. A summer romance, a pregnancy, and a hasty marriage have trapped him in Beetlecreek. Here he has stagnated, until the advent of Bill Trapp, and of Edith.

Edith is a college sweetheart, who has returned to Beetlecreek for her guardian's funeral. Symbolically, the touch of death is upon her; though she has fled from Beetlecreek, hers is a big-city deadness. David, in his weakness and cowardice, is attracted to her strength and defiance: "But most of all he liked the daredevil in her." In a pathetic "daredevil" gesture he decides to run off with her for a week, seeking at least a furlough from the spiritual death of the town. But Edith is not the path to life; she represents his dream of the past rather than a positive commitment to the present. It is his relationship to Bill Trapp which demands of David a genuine act of moral courage.

David's basic philosophical error lies in his conviction that "There was no way, really, that he could shape himself." At the climax of the novel, therefore, when Bill Trapp becomes the victim of mass hysteria, he simply drifts, acquiescing in the poisonous prejudice of Beetlecreek. Intimidated by the jeers of the barbershop crowd, he refuses to defend his friend. In the clutch, David lacks the courage to be: "He had stepped outside himself by becoming friends with Bill Trapp, had upset the delicate balance of things as they were, had interfered with the smooth running of what had already been prepared for him. And by this interference he had made it necessary for himself to act for himself. And sitting there in the dusty crowded living room, he was panicky, afraid" (p. 183). This is the meaning of David's symbolic choice between Bill Trapp and Edith: in the face of the terrifying responsibility of freedom, he capitulates; in the face of the urgent decisions of his "now-life," he retreats to the dead past.

Like David, Johnny is alone and afraid, restless and ashamed, and in desperate quest of his own identity. Man and boy share a spiritual state which is, in the existentialist view, the natural condition of man. It is accentuated for Johnny, because he has been uprooted by his mother's illness from his normal surroundings in Pittsburgh, and packed off for a prolonged visit to his uncle. He is a strange boy in a new town, wanting above all to be accepted, to belong. His feelings of alienation draw him first to Bill Trapp, another outcast, and then to the gang.

In Demby's portrait of the gang, the political overtones of the original story persist, and perhaps they intrude to a degree upon his larger thematic concerns. The Nightriders, with their initiation ceremonies and their black robes, with their nameless Leader, brutal and sadistic, offer to Johnny a fascist extreme of "other-direction." Here is strength in which his weakness can seek refuge. It is thus that Johnny, who was the instrument of Bill Trapp's awakening, becomes the instrument of his death. He is compelled by the force of events to choose between Bill Trapp and membership in the gang, and from this decision the denouement of the novel flows. Johnny's initiation into the Nightriders requires "a brave deed," and at the height of community insanity he is instructed to burn down Bill Trapp's shanty. In panic and confusion as he tries to escape, he kills his former friend.

Thematically the novel has been moving toward an existentialist definition of evil: if no other confirmation of his existence is possible, man will attempt to assert himself in negative and destructive ways. It is so with Bill Trapp, who even as a child preferred to be tormented than ignored; it is true of the townspeople, who find in their malicious persecution of Bill Trapp relief from their empty lives. It is true above all of David and Johnny, who suffer their creative powers to be perverted, rather than endure a spiritual vacuum. Edith and the gang bring movement and excitement into their lives, but it is movement without direction, without purpose, without meaning. The question from which all of Demby's characters shrink is "What do I want of life?" In the absence of positive goals their attempts to assert themselves lead to their own destruction.

In an exposition of theme, style should not be slighted, especially when the two are closely entwined. Demby writes well, and in a functional, not merely decorative, sense. His style is appropriately realistic, for existentialism is nothing if not tough-minded. But literary realism is only a point of departure: "Hair began growing on his soul," Demby writes of Bill Trapp's retirement. It is realism transformed by an active imagination in pursuit of higher ends. Demby has a good eye for the image, and this visual quality enriches his descriptive passages: "In the yard, the shadows under the trees were like jigsaw puzzles suddenly broken." But beyond their descriptive content, such passages may point toward the larger meaning of the novel: "Often [David] would sit on the railing of the swinging bridge, looking down at the creek, watching the current. He would watch floating things—boxes, tin cans, bottles. He would watch how some of these things became trapped in the reeds alongside the shore. First there was a whirlpool to entice the floating object, then a slow-flowing pool, and finally, the deadly mud backwater in the reeds" (pp. 93–94).

Recurrent images assume symbolic value and are used extensively to buttress the theme. The frantic, swooping birds, for example, provide an objective correlative to David's and Johnny's feelings of restlessness and dissatisfaction. The mirrors (each of the main characters studies himself in a mirror) underscore the problem of identity, while the swinging bridge suggests the social separation between colored and white in Beetlecreek. The season in which the action takes place (Indian summer) is converted into a particularly rich symbol. On one level, it helps to dramatize the necessity of choice, of decision: "The birds swooped and swooped, all the time screaming, undecided what to do. The freak summer fooled everybody and everything." On another, it suggests that the crucial decisions faced by Bill Trapp, David, and Johnny represent their last chance for life.

In the last analysis, Demby handles race symbolically, too. It is in part a question of "realism," of rooting his characters in a recognizable social milieu. But on a deeper level he succeeds in transforming race into a universal symbol. Throughout the novel his readers experience racism chiefly on the rebound, through the antiwhite sentiments of Negro characters. It is a white man, for example, who becomes the victim of a colored "mob." Yet at the same time Bill Trapp is *identified* with the Negro: "Watching them secretly as he did he could see that they were always dodging something, were ashamed of something just as he was; they were the same breed as he" (p. 55). Man is an exile, an outcast in a hostile universe. The recluse and the Negro become in this view only special instances of man's estrangement from his world and from himself. Here is a creative solution to the problem of race material which anticipates Ralph Ellison's symbolic use of race in *Invisible Man.*

Invisible Man, which won the National Book Award as the best American novel of 1952, provides a fitting note on which to conclude the present chapter. Ellison is a writer of the first magnitude —one of those original talents who has created a personal idiom to convey his personal vision. It is an idiom compounded of fantasy, distortion, and burlesque, highly imaginative and generally surrealistic in effect. It possesses at bottom a certain mythic quality, to which Ellison alludes in his acceptance speech. He was striving, he recounts, for a prose medium "with all the bright magic of the fairy tale."

Though not in the narrow sense a political novel, *Invisible Man* is based on a cultivated political understanding of the modern world. The first half of the novel portrays the disillusionment of the protagonist with the shibboleths of American capitalism—a social system which he apprehends through the institutional structure of the Southern Negro college. The latter half treats of his disillusionment with Stalinism, which he encounters through a revolutionary organization known as the Brotherhood. By means of this carefully controlled parallel development, Ellison penetrates to the heart of the two great illusions of his time.

John Aldridge once remarked that "the quality and intensity of a literary work will depend upon the success with which the writer can find and communicate his private truth in the public truth of his age." Ellison's private truth is that his color threatens constantly to deprive him of individuality; the public truth to which this corresponds is that all men have been deprived of individuality in the machine age. Invisibility is Ellison's symbol for this loss of self. *Invisible Man,* then, is a stubborn affirmation of the worth and dignity of the individual in the face of forces which conspire to render him invisible. The novel is dedicated in spirit to the suffering, mangled, helpless, plucked victim of Authority, whose only defense against power is his own humanity.

Although the author denies that *Invisible Man* is autobiographical, it is clear that in main outline, if not in detail, the novel is rooted in personal experience. Ralph Ellison (1914–) was born in Oklahoma City and educated in its public schools. With the help of a scholarship from the State of Oklahoma, he attended Tuskegee Institute as a music major from 1933 to 1936. Leaving for New York with the aim of becoming a composer, he struck up a friendship with Richard Wright and was soon drawn into the orbit of the Federal Writers' Project and the Communist party. He worked with Wright on *New Challenge,* and then branched out in the *New Masses* with stories, articles, and reviews. In the mid-forties, and more recently, he published in *Horizon, Tomor-*

row, *Common Ground*, the *Reporter*, the *Saturday Review*, etc. His fugitive pieces have recently been collected in *Shadow and Act* (New York, Random House, 1964).

Ellison's early apprenticeship was dominated by Richard Wright, and the stories of this period yield to none in bitterness and stridency. Violent, brutal, and full of mutilation fantasies which reveal an intense fear of a hostile environment, they anticipate much of the emotional content but little of the overmastering form of *Invisible Man*. Ellison's break with the Wright School is all the more interesting because of this background, and not least of all because it illustrates so strikingly the historic shift described in the last chapter. For in this instance the revolt against protest was extended to include a revolt against the naturalistic novel as such.

In accepting the National Book Award, Ellison states his reasons for avoiding the "hard-boiled" Hemingway idiom.[2] There is first the problem of understatement, which "depends, after all, upon commonly held assumptions, and my minority status rendered all such assumptions questionable." Then there is the problem of the clipped, monosyllabic prose: "I found that, when compared to the rich babble of idiomatic expression around me, a language full of imagery and gesture and rhetorical canniness, it was embarrassingly austere." Finally, he feels compelled to reject "the rather rigid concepts of reality" which inform these works in favor of a more fluid, more mysterious, more uncertain conception: "Thus to see America with an awareness of its rich diversity and its almost magical fluidity and freedom, I was forced to conceive of a novel unburdened by the narrow naturalism which has led after so many triumphs to the final and unrelieved despair which marks so much of our current fiction."

In repudiating naturalism, Ellison turns to the broad tradition established by Joyce, Kafka, and Faulkner. Like them, he finds the shattered forms of postimpressionism most effective in portraying the chaos of the modern world. But Ellison apprehends this chaos through a particular cultural screen. It is precisely his vision of the possibilities of Negro life that has burst the bonds of the naturalistic novel. His style, like that of any good writer, flows from his view of reality, but this in turn flows from his experience

2. All quotations are from *Crisis, 60* (1953), 157–58.

as a Negro. His unique experience, Ellison insists, requires unique literary forms, and these he tries to provide from the raw material of Negro culture. It is a major contribution to the evolution of the Negro novel.

What stylistic resources can a folk culture offer the creative writer? To begin with, there is the rhetorical skill of the American Negro, whose verbal expression, under slavery, was necessarily oral. The revival meeting, the funeral sermon, the graduation address, the political speech are used to good account in *Invisible Man*. Then there are the sonorous biblical phrases which season the dialogue, along with the spicier ingredients of jive. To freshen up a jaded diction, a whole new vocabulary is available—terms evocative of the numbers racket, of voodoo charms, of racing sheets, of spiritualist cure-alls, of the jazz world, the boxing ring, the ball park, the bar-room—in a word, of Harlem.

One of the nuances of Negro speech exploited by Ellison is the sheer delight in verbal play, in pure *sound*, which might be experienced by a child—or a transplanted people—in learning a new language. This is more readily sampled than described: "Then came the squad of drum majorettes . . . who pranced and twirled and just plain girled in the enthusiastic interest of Brotherhood." Closer to its folk origin is this bit of dialogue: "I'll verse you but I won't curse you— My name is Peter Wheatstraw, I'm the Devil's only son-in-law, so roll 'em! You a southern boy ain't you?" Intellectualized once more: a college professor, lecturing on Joyce, remarks, "Stephen's problem, like ours, was not actually one of creating the uncreated conscience of his race, but of creating the uncreated features of his face."

In their spoken idiom a people may unwittingly betray their innermost thoughts and feelings. The things that they laugh at are equally revealing of their deepest values, and Ellison's treatment of in-group humor is masterful. He displays a true comic genius, ranging from his sly description of a belligerent colored bartender ("He sliced the white heads off of a couple of beers with an ivory paddle") to the raucous comedy of the riot scene (in which one looter asks indignantly, "With all them hats in there and I'm going to come out with anything but a *Dobbs?*"). With his heritage of laughter-to-keep-from-crying, Ellison balances adroitly on the thin line which divides comedy from tragedy, and this double vision, this ability to perceive events as at once poignant and faintly ridiculous, introduces a subtle emotional tension into the novel. The solvent for this tension is a pervasive irony, through which the author achieves a satisfactory distance from his experience.

Jazz and the blues form an important part of Ellison's consciousness (he has played jazz trumpet since high school) and consequently of his style. The tone of the novel, for example, is established in the prologue by Louis Armstrong's not-so-innocent question,

What did I do
To be so black
And blue?

The blue note is sustained by occasional snatches of blues lyrics, and by such passages as this: "I strode along, hearing the cartman's song become a lonesome, broad-toned whistle now that flowered at the end of each phrase into a tremulous, blue-toned chord. And in its flutter and swoop I heard the sound of a railroad train highballing it, lonely across the lonely night" (p. 135).

Jazz forms have also influenced what might be called the composition of the novel. Something is always going on in the background of Ellison's prose—something not quite heard at first, but nevertheless insistent, which produces a feeling of depth and resonance when finally perceived. The circling, diving, plummeting pigeons which hover in the background during the shooting of Tod Clifton will serve to illustrate the point. It is a passage thoroughly characteristic of Ellison's technique: he writes a "melody" (thematic line) and then orchestrates it.

Not to overstate the case for a distinctive Negro style, some general literary influences should be acknowledged. At farthest remove is Flaubert, to whom can be traced a tightness of style in which no detail is superfluous, no word or phrase without its place in the design. In sifting through his American tradition for evidence of a usable past, Ellison discovered our classical novelists of the 19th century, and especially Melville and Twain. In them, he notes, he found a greater sense of responsibility for the future of democracy than among his own contemporaries. But above all, he found a sense of the unknown and mysterious frontiers of American life which corresponded to his experience as a Negro. "In their imaginative economy," he writes, "the Negro symbolized both the man lowest down and the mysterious, underground aspect of human personality."

Closer at hand is his debt to Faulkner and Eliot. To the extent that Ellison's style is directly imitative, it is Faulknerian. The lengthy sentences, the rapid flow of consciousness conveyed by a string of participles, the series of abstract nouns joined together by an overworked conjunction—these are familiar trademarks. From Faulkner, too, comes a sense of the grotesque, the monstrous, the outrageous in Southern life. The incest scene in *Invisible Man,* for example, is unimaginable without the precedent of Popeye. On the whole, it is more the symbolist of *The Sound and the Fury* than the local colorist of *The Hamlet* to whom Ellison pays the supreme compliment, but both elements are present in his style to a degree.

There are direct echoes of Eliot, too, in *Invisible Man,* and one of the epigraphs (the other is from Melville's *Benito Cereno*) is from *Family Reunion.* But Ellison's real debt stems from Eliot's insistence upon the importance of tradition. It was this reassurance from a major contemporary that fortified him in his determination to anchor his fiction firmly in his Negro heritage. It was Eliot who taught him to value a past which was both painful and precious and, flinching neither from slavery nor incest nor prostitution nor chaos itself, to assimilate even his negative heritage, conquering it, transforming it into an asset, a weapon.

But if one were to pinpoint the influence of a particular literary work on this novel, it would be Dostoevsky's *Notes from Underground.* This book, as a matter of fact, stirred the imaginations of both Ellison and Wright, inspiring not only *Invisible Man* but a powerful short story of Wright's called "The Man Who Lived Underground."[3] The story preceded the final publication of the novel by several years, and without a doubt Ellison was familiar with it. It would be a mistake, however, to conclude that the germinal idea of the novel was borrowed from Wright. The debt still goes back to Dostoevsky, even though Richard Wright may

3. *Cross Section,* ed. Edwin Seaver (New York, 1944), pp. 58–102.

well hold a first mortgage on the property. In any event, Ellison succeeds in developing on a full scale themes which Wright treats only sketchily.

It is not very difficult to understand why Wright and Ellison were fascinated by this extraordinary book. Dostoevsky's protagonist is a man of morbid sensitivity, prone to resentment and offense and consumed with self-hatred. Convinced that he excites aversion, his constant fate is humiliation and his constant study is revenge. Yet on this score he feels quite helpless: "The mouse distrusts alike its right to wreak vengeance and the ultimate success of its scheme, since it knows in advance that its poor attempts at retribution will bring upon its own head a hundred times more suffering than will fall to the lot of the person against whom the vengeance is aimed."[4] Against the historical backdrop of 19th-century Russia, Dostoevsky is describing a socially patterned neurosis which has an obvious parallel in the psychic life of the American Negro.

But beyond this matter of insult and revenge, there are vaster themes in *Notes from Underground* which commanded Ellison's attention. In exploring the lower depths of human personality, Dostoevsky poses questions about the nature of reality, the meaning of social responsibility, and the limits of human possibility, all of which are pursued with lively interest in *Invisible Man.* Both authors, moreover, share a central concern with individuality, with that which enables man to insist upon himself in the face of all rational systems. Dostoevsky's attack upon science, his profound antirationalism, is likewise shared by Ellison, though it rests on Freudian rather than Christian premises.

Given these common philosophical concerns, some borrowing of literary forms was perhaps inevitable. The basic image of the novel—withdrawal from humanity into an underground den—is a case in point. So, too, is its basic strategy: the presentation of an abstract spiritual state (invisibility), followed by a flashback (the main body of the novel) which provides the concrete experience from which the psychic state evolved. The two protagonists, moreover, have much in common: both are anonymous victims

4. *Notes from Underground* (Everyman Edition, New York, Dutton, 1953), p. 15.

(*non*heroes), and both address the reader in the first person with a certain ironic familiarity. Both are dealers in paradox and ambiguity, and both have known a shame so intense that in recalling it their venom turns to jest.

Neither the underworld of Dostoevsky nor that of Ellison is a pleasant place. Both authors are invading those cavernous recesses of human consciousness which the civilized world has preferred to ignore. Yet below in those murky depths, unknown or unacknowledged by respectable society, they discover the healing power of love and of human fraternity. That Ellison undertakes this descent to the particular underworld of his time and circumstances is sufficient testimony to his creative powers. Whatever his debt to Dostoevsky, no one who reads *Invisible Man* will challenge his claim to originality.

The prologue of the novel finds the protagonist ensconced below ground in the basement of a building rented strictly to whites, in a section "shut off and forgotten during the nineteenth century." Here he lives in the glare of 1369 light bulbs, whose current is supplied from a tapped line of Monopolated Light and Power. Light, he explains, gives form to his invisibility, and this is quintessential to a man whose fellows refuse to see him as he really is. And so he remains for the present in a state of contemplative hibernation, summoning from the past events which have led to his invisibility.

The first of these is an episode from his adolescence, about the time of his graduation from high school. He is invited by the superintendent of schools to address a white businessmen's smoker, but once there he is forced to participate in an obscene ritual symbolic of the Negro's status in American society. A group of colored boys are confronted with a naked blonde and threatened equally if they look and if they avert their eyes. This scene, which expresses in sexual terms the basic ambivalence of Negro life, is followed by a battle royal in which the boys are thrust blindfolded into a boxing ring and forced to fight one another (rather than, symbolically, their real enemy). Then they are compelled to retrieve their prize money from an electrified rug. All of the prizes of white society (money, women) are thus held out to them, only to be denied.

In spite of this degradation, and swallowing his own blood, the boy, who thinks of himself as a potential Booker T. Washington, delivers his prepared address. As a reward he receives a scholarship to a Negro college, along with a gleaming new calfskin briefcase. In a dream which closes this nightmarish episode, the boy imagines that he opens the briefcase and finds an inscription which reads, "To Whom it May Concern: Keep this Nigger-Boy Running."

The next few chapters concern an incident which occurs in his junior year and results in his expulsion from college. Assigned as a driver to one of the visiting white trustees, he commits the unpardonable sin of taking him away from the "whitewashed" campus into the back country. Through the figure of Mr. Norton, the trustee, Ellison traces "the unseen lines that run from North to South," converging on the Southern Negro college. He is a banker, a Bostonian, a bearer of the white man's burden, who feels that the destiny of the Negro people is somehow bound up with his own. Viewed historically, he is emblematic of those enlightened Northern capitalists who, looking ahead to the industrialization of the South, joined with the Southern gentry and the conservative Negro leaders in founding such centers of technical training as Tuskegee Institute.

What Mr. Norton (Northern) discovers back in the quarters is chaos, in the form of a colored sharecropper who has had incestuous relations with his daughter. Trueblood (*pur sang*) is the full-blooded, half-assimilated African in whom historic circumstances of the past three centuries have neither encouraged nor indeed permitted the civilized amenities to develop. His story, which is rendered with an altogether convincing combination of humor, delicacy, and horror, is a narrative tour de force. The crucial point is that, far from becoming a pariah, Trueblood is treated by his white neighbors as something of a local celebrity. They lavish upon his infamy material benefits which they have always denied to his industry. Norton, moreover, whose Oedipal attachment to his own daughter has been subtly touched upon, acknowledges his kinship with chaos by a gift of a hundred dollars.

Severely shaken, Mr. Norton requests a stimulant, and the youth reluctantly drives him to the nearest source of supply—a colored roadhouse called the Golden Day. Unfortunately, it is the day when the inmates of a nearby veterans' hospital pay their weekly visit to the local prostitutes. Once more Mr. Norton encounters chaos.

The theme of this episode is repression: the hospital attendant Supercargo (Superego) is responsible for maintaining order, and *double* order with white folks present. But Supercargo is symbolically drunk upstairs, and "when he was upstairs they had absolutely no inhibitions." A wild brawl ensues, with the attendant the main target of its fury. He represents the internalization of white values (order as against chaos), and it is no accident that the hapless veterans whom he supervises have been doctors, lawyers, and teachers in civilian life. They are emblematic of the repressed Negro middle class; their spokesman is a former surgeon who was dragged from his home and beaten with whips for saving a human life. It is thus (Trueblood-in-reverse) that the white South rewards genuine accomplishment.

In the light—or perhaps one should say the darkness—of Trueblood and the Golden Day, the irony of the Southern Negro college, the irony of its very existence, is revealed. Its function is not to educate but to indoctrinate with a myth. This is why the vet calls Norton "a trustee of consciousness," "a lyncher of souls." Yet Ellison presents the myth in all its splendor in the Chapel address of the Reverend Homer Barbee, not wishing to minimize the power of the system to provide dreams. It is "the black rite of Horatio Alger" which is enacted from the podium, and its slogan is "We are a humble, but a fast-rising people." To the hope which the speaker holds out to the race, if only they will adopt the white man's success formula, the protagonist responds with a desperate conviction, for the alternative of bitterness, of revenge, of racial conflict seems hopelessly destructive. It is only toward the end of this magnificent speech that he realizes that Homer Barbee is blind.

In taking Norton behind the scenes, the protagonist has betrayed the myth, and the president of the college swiftly administers discipline. Dr. Bledsoe is a harsh but essentially accurate portrait of the Southern Negro educator—a pragmatist who holds his own in a ruthless power struggle by hard and cynical methods.

He possesses power without dignity, though the trappings of dignity are in ample evidence. It is the only kind of power available to the black man in the Deep South. Bledsoe suspends the youth but endorses his proposal that he seek employment in the North, in hopes of being reinstated in the fall. As a gesture of reconciliation he furnishes the youth with letters of introduction to several wealthy patrons of the school.

The youth leaves for New York, his success ideology still intact, and he makes the rounds with his impressive-looking letters. But somehow the formula doesn't work, and he receives only evasive answers from his prospective employers. At last he learns the truth from a disillusioned younger son who finds himself incapable of his wealthy father's cynicism. The contents of the Bledsoe letters are revealed, and the youth discovers that he has been not suspended but expelled. The letters contain instructions, in effect, to "keep this nigger-boy running."

Two densely symbolic chapters follow, which conclude Ellison's portrait of the status quo. The first of these embraces the experience of the protagonist with modern industry, as he hires out as an unskilled laborer to Liberty Paint. It is a large concern which thrives on government contracts; its trademark is a screaming eagle, and its slogan "Keep America Pure with Liberty Paints." The youth is put to work on a batch of paint which is headed for a national monument, and his task is a puzzling one. He is asked to measure ten drops of dead black liquid into each bucket of "Optic White," and stir until the black becomes invisible. It is a famous national formula, of which the company is justly proud: "That's paint that'll cover just about anything!" his foreman remarks. Unfortunately, the youth takes his refill from the wrong tank and dopes the paint with concentrated remover. By rendering visible that which is black (compare the Norton episode), he unwittingly sabotages the national whitewash.

On another level, this chapter recapitulates the Negro's historic experience in American industry. The youth is hired in the first place so that the company will not have to pay regular union wages. He goes to work for a "slave driver" named Kimbro, who introduces him to the regimentation and fundamental irresponsibility of factory life. Shortly he is sent to the basement to work for a colored foreman named Lucius Brockway, who represents the skilled stratum of Negro labor which has been entrenched in American industry from the beginning—the black base on which our industrial pyramid is reared. Brockway has made himself indispensable, for it is he who mixes the base of the paint, and yet he lives in constant dread of being replaced by skilled whites. For this reason he is an Uncle Tom, a loyal worker who is fanatically anti-union.

The bewildered protagonist is caught in a crossfire between Brockway and the union, for each party suspects him of harboring sympathies for the enemy. His first act of rebellion against the system occurs in this context, and significantly he strikes out at the Negro underling. In the course of a quarrel with Brockway they forget to check their pressure gauges. An explosion occurs (not to be taken too literally), and the youth finds himself in the factory hospital, a part of his personality blasted away.

The hospital scene is primarily symbolic of the protagonist's rebirth; it is a transitional chapter which prepares us for his new life in the Brotherhood. At the same time, the machine age begins to emerge as his true antagonist. Only half conscious, he is strapped into a strange machine and subjected to a painful shock therapy, whose purpose is "to produce the results of a prefrontal lobotomy without the negative effects of the knife." The atmosphere of antiseptic efficiency, of coldness and impersonality, of helplessness and passivity which one associates with a modern hospital is brilliantly evoked as a symbol of contemporary life. The diction, which is abstract and scientific throughout, contributes powerfully to this effect. The identity theme is sounded as he is asked to think of his name, and of his mother. When he fails to remember, thus relinquishing all claims to individuality, he is pronounced cured. The machine is opened, the electric cord to the stomach node is cut, and he is born again.

Part II of *Invisible Man* is at bottom a projection of the author's involvement with the Communist party. Ellison, more than most writers who have felt the party's branding iron, has survived the experience and mastered it artistically. And yet this section of the novel tends to slip back into the naturalistic mode, as if the author's imagination were stumbling over the rugged terrain of his political past. On the other hand, Ellison's satirical portrait of a movement not famous for its humor is as trenchant as it is amusing. In a more serious vein, he succeeds in drawing a pointed parallel between the protagonist's new life and his former existence as a victim of capitalist society. To their victims, after all, the two power systems look remarkably alike. This perception gives the novel a better balance and a sharper cutting edge than most of the current fiction of political disillusionment.

The protagonist's personal fate in the Brotherhood is representative of a whole generation of Negro intellectuals. Deeply wounded by society, he becomes aware of "a painful, contradictory, inner voice" which calls insistently for revenge. After leading a spontaneous demonstration against a sidewalk eviction, he is recruited by the Brotherhood and thereby catapulted into history. In the Brotherhood he finds a new identity, a new outlet for his ambition, and a new myth. He is initiated into the mysteries of the dialectic by Brother Jack, and assigned to agitational work in Harlem. Just as a mass movement begins to develop, the "line" shifts in emphasis from local to international issues, and the Harlem organization is left stranded. The protagonist now faces a dilemma well known to the captives of Stalinist ideology: to remain historically relevant, he must betray the Negro masses; to retain his integrity, he must break with the Brotherhood and consign himself to political limbo.

In the end he rejects the Brotherhood more on philosophical than racial or political grounds. Brother Jack's glass eye (he is half blind) cannot penetrate the dark waters of Harlem. His peculiar brand of unreality ignores the unpredictable element at the core of our humanity which transcends politics and science and history and is at once more fundamental and mysterious than these. In an organization which is proud of its willingness to sacrifice the individual on the altar of history, the protagonist remains as invisible as ever. His loss of individuality is felt most keenly when his sense of responsibility collides with the iron discipline of the Brotherhood. Eventually he realizes that behind the façade of party discipline Brother Jack has been "running" him no less cynically than Norton or Bledsoe. It is then that he takes to the cellar, in order to renew his sense of self.

His sense of self has in fact been threatened all along, by the ambiguous position of the Negro in the Communist movement. On the one hand, he is constantly reminded of his Negro heritage and encouraged to embrace it; on the other, he is warned against the dangers of black chauvinism and offered all the inducements of universal brotherhood. This conflict between assimilationism and Negro nationalism is not new to the protagonist: he has passed through a phase of "white" (bourgeois) assimilationism in which he regards the renunciation of pork chops and grits as some sort of moral victory. But this particular form of self-effacement is discarded early in Part II, together with the success formula which inspired it. Confronted by a steaming tray of baked yams, he surrenders to its pleasures with a new sense of freedom and self-acceptance.

The Brotherhood, however, upsets his equilibrium with an irresistible hope: "For the first time . . . I could glimpse the possibility of being more than a member of a race." He now enters a period of "red" (revolutionary) assimilationism, in which his racial ties are subtly weakened through identification with a broader cause. This phase is symbolized by his abandonment of Mary, his landlady-mother, and his acceptance of new "living quarters" provided by the Brotherhood. But he cannot shed his old skin so easily. The grinning statuette which he tries unsuccessfully to discard and the leg chain presented to him by Brother Tarp are symbolic links to his racial past.

The inner doubts and reservations of the colored Brothers are strikingly projected in the magnificent figure of Ras the Destroyer. Ras (race) is a black nationalist, a West Indian agitator modeled upon Marcus Garvey, who would ban the sale of chicken breasts in Harlem if he could. In an attempt to drive the Brotherhood out of Harlem, he engages the protagonist and his chief lieutenant, Tod Clifton, in a savage street fight. Winning the upper hand over Clifton, Ras is unable to kill him because they are blood brothers: "We sons of Mama Africa, you done forgot?" Pleading the case for Negro nationalism with great eloquence, he accuses them of selling out for white women and a good job (the fight takes place beneath a sign which reads "Checks Cashed Here"). Ras' strength lies in the fact that he is not far from the mark in his appraisal of the white race, and not least of the Brotherhood. It is his all-important margin of error, his black vengeance and unrelenting hatred, which makes him a Destroyer.

Tod Clifton now comes to the fore as Ellison's symbol of a tragically divided personality. When, as Ras predicted, the Brotherhood betrays the Negro struggle, Clifton cracks under the strain and takes "the plunge outside of history." The protagonist discovers him on a downtown sidewalk, peddling an obscene, self-mocking image called "Sambo the Dancing Doll." This spiritual death (*Tod*) is quickly objectified when Clifton is brutally shot down by a policeman while resisting arrest for a minor misdemeanor. Stunned by the murder, the protagonist stumbles into a subway station, where he notices two nuns, one colored and the other white. The rhyme which spins through his dazed consciousness expresses his final attitude toward even the most sincere of his white allies:

> Bread and Wine
> Bread and Wine
> Your cross ain't nearly so
> Heavy as mine.

Like Clifton, the protagonist is threatened by destruction from his own nationalist impulses; but in running from them, he discovers invisibility. Pursued one evening by Ras' thugs, he slips into a drugstore and, improvising a hasty disguise, buys a pair of dark glasses and a wide-brimmed hat. The disguise is an unqualified success; everyone takes him for a certain Mr. Rinehart, and he decides to play along as the instances of mistaken identity proliferate. Hipsters and zoot-suiters greet him; an old woman inquires about today's number; a cop tries to shake him down; a married woman makes a date and slips money into his pocket. Obviously Rinehart is a man of parts, but this is only the beginning. On the other side of town, the protagonist picks up a handbill which invites him to the store-front church of "Rev. B. P. Rinehart, Spiritual Technologist." Sensing that he is on the brink of a great discovery, he asks excitedly, "Could he be all of them: Rine the runner and Rine the gambler and Rine the briber and Rine the lover and Rinehart the Reverend?" As he pursues the implications of his discovery, the metaphysical depths of the novel are sounded.

The dark glasses provide a point of departure for his speculations. Through their murky green, the world appears as a merging fluidity of forms. "What on earth was hiding behind the face of things?" he wonders. How can one distinguish the outer from the inner, the rind from the heart? Rinehart's multiple personality seems to suggest an answer: "His world was possibility and he knew it. He was years ahead of me and I was a fool. I must have been crazy and blind. The world in which we lived was without boundaries. A vast, seething, hot world of fluidity, [where] Rine the rascal was at home" (p. 376). This fluid conception of reality, the protagonist now perceives, is far more accurate than the rigid categories of the Brotherhood. Here, he reflects, is the crux of his quarrel with the Communists. In a fluid universe nothing is impossible; freedom is the recognition not only of necessity but of possibility.

The final chapter of *Invisible Man* is a freely distorted version of the Harlem riot of August 1943. Against a surrealistic background of looting and shooting, the major conflicts of the novel are resolved. Rinehartism, to begin with, is discarded for a less manipulative form of invisibility. For a time the protagonist has toyed with the idea of sabotaging the Brotherhood from within, but during the riot, when he discovers the full extent of their perfidy, he abandons any attempt to beat power at its own game. Authentically enough, he withdraws not merely from Stalinist politics but from politics as such. His retreat from politics, however, is somewhat mitigated by the episode of the tenement fire. When a well-organized group of tenants deliberately burns down the filthy tenement in which they have lived and suffered, his faith in the masses, if not their self-appointed leaders, is restored.

Meanwhile Ras appears astride a great black horse, dressed in the costume of an Abyssinian warrior, complete with shield and spear. He is out to spear him a white cop, as one of the bystanders observes, and to convert the riot into a race war. In a symbolic encounter the protagonist effectively silences his inner Ras, but in fleeing the scene he meets a gang of white hoodlums armed with baseball bats. Running for his life, he plunges through an open manhole into a coal cellar, where he can at last enjoy the safety of invisibility. He falls asleep and dreams of being surrounded by his enemies—all those who in one way or another have run his life. When he announces grimly that he is through running, they reply collectively, "Not quite." They advance upon him with a knife, and at last they leave him in command of his own destiny—castrated, but free of illusion.

In the end, Ellison succeeds brilliantly in rendering blackness visible. By far the best novel yet written by an American Negro, *Invisible Man* is quite possibly the best American novel since World War II. In any event, Ellison has set a high standard for contemporary Negro fiction. There was a period in the history of the Negro novel when a simple literacy was to be marveled at. Now, a century after Brown's *Clotel,* historical relativity is no longer a valid attitude. With the appearance of such novels as *Cane, Native Son,* and *Invisible Man,* the reading public has a right to expect no less than the best from the serious Negro artist.

Postscript

GIVE not thyself up, then, to fire, lest it invert thee.

MOBY DICK

10. James Baldwin

THE most important Negro writer to emerge during the last decade is, of course, James Baldwin. His publications, which include three books of essays, three novels, and two plays, have had a stunning impact on our cultural life. His political role as a leading spokesman of the Negro revolt has been scarcely less effective. Awards and honors, wealth and success have crowned his career, and Baldwin has become a national celebrity.

Under the circumstances, the separation of the artist from the celebrity is as difficult as it is necessary. For Baldwin is an uneven writer, the quality of whose work can by no means be taken for granted. His achievement in the novel is most open to dispute, and it is that which I propose to discuss in some detail. Meanwhile, it may be possible to narrow the area of controversy by a preliminary assessment of his talent.

I find Baldwin strongest as an essayist, weakest as a playwright, and successful in the novel form on only one occasion. For the three books of essays, *Notes of a Native Son* (1955), *Nobody Knows My Name* (1961), and *The Fire Next Time* (1963), I have nothing but admiration. Baldwin has succeeded in transposing the entire discussion of American race relations from statistics and sociology to the interior plane; it is a major breakthrough for the American imagination. In the theater, he has written one competent apprentice play, *The Amen Corner,* first produced at Howard University in 1955, and one unspeakably bad propaganda piece, *Blues for Mister Charlie* (1964). In the novel, the impressive achievement of *Go Tell It on the Mountain* (1953) has not been matched by his more recent books, *Giovanni's Room* (1956) and *Another Country* (1962). Perhaps a closer acquaintance with the author's life will help us to account for this unevenness.

James Baldwin was a product of the Great Migration. His father had come North from New Orleans; his mother, from Maryland. James was born in Harlem in 1924, the first of nine children. His father was a factory worker and lay preacher, and the boy was raised under the twin disciplines of poverty and the store-front church. He experienced a profound religious crisis during the summer of his fourteenth year, entered upon a youthful ministry, and remained in the pulpit for three years. The second crisis of his life was his break with this milieu; that is, with his father's values, hopes, and aspirations for his son. These two crises—the turn into the fold and the turn away—provide the raw material for his first novel and his first play.

Baldwin graduated from De Witt Clinton High School in 1942, having served on the staff of the literary magazine. He had already discovered in this brief encounter a means of transcending his appointed destiny. Shortly after graduation he left home, determined to support himself as best he could while developing his talent as a writer. After six years of frustration and false starts, however, he had two fellowships but no substantial publications to his credit. This initial literary failure, coupled with the pressures of his personal life, drove him into exile. In 1948, at the age of twenty-four, Baldwin left America for Paris, intending never to return.

He remained abroad for nine years. Europe gave him many things. It gave him a world perspective from which to approach the question of his own identity. It gave him a tender love affair, which would dominate the pages of his later fiction. But above all,

Europe gave him back himself. Some two years after his arrival in Paris, Baldwin suffered a breakdown and went off to Switzerland to recover:

> There, in that absolutely alabaster landscape, armed with two Bessie Smith records and a typewriter, I began to try to re-create the life that I had first known as a child and from which I had spent so many years in flight. . . . I had never listened to Bessie Smith in America (in the same way that, for years, I would not touch watermelon), but in Europe she helped to reconcile me to being a "nigger."[1]

The immediate fruit of self-recovery was a great creative outburst. First came two books of reconciliation with his racial heritage. *Go Tell It on the Mountain* and *The Amen Corner* represent a search for roots, a surrender to tradition, an acceptance of the Negro past. Then came a series of essays which probe, deeper than anyone has dared, the psychic history of America. They are a moving record of a man's struggle to define the forces that have shaped him, in order that he may accept himself. Last came *Giovanni's Room,* which explores the question of his male identity. Here Baldwin extends the theme of self-acceptance into the sexual realm.

Toward the end of his stay in Paris, Baldwin experienced the first symptoms of a crisis from which he has never recovered. Having exhausted the theme of self-acceptance, he cast about for fresh material, but his third novel stubbornly refused to move. He has described this moment of panic in a later essay: "It is the point at which many artists lose their minds, or commit suicide, or throw themselves into good works, or try to enter politics."[2] Recognizing these dangers to his art has not enabled Baldwin to avoid them. Something like good works and politics have been the recent bent of his career. Unable to grow as an artist, he has fallen back upon a tradition of protest writing which he formerly denounced.

Baldwin returned to America in 1957. The battered self, he must have felt, was ready to confront society. A good many of the essays in *Nobody Knows My Name* record his initial impressions of America, but this is a transitional book, still largely concerned

1. *Nobody Knows My Name* (New York, Dial Press, 1961), p. 5.

2. *Ibid.*, p. 224.

with questions of identity. Protest, however, becomes the dominant theme of his next three books. In *Another Country, The Fire Next Time,* and *Blues for Mister Charlie,* he assumes the role of Old Testament prophet, calling down the wrath of history on the heads of the white oppressor.

Baldwin's career may be divided into two distinct periods. His first five books have been concerned with the emotion of shame. The flight from self, the quest for identity, and the sophisticated acceptance of one's "blackness" are the themes that flow from this emotion. His last three books have been concerned with the emotion of rage. An apocalyptic vision and a new stridency of tone are brought to bear against the racial and the sexual oppressor. The question then arises, why has he avoided the prophetic role until the recent past?

The answer, I believe, lies in Baldwin's relationship to his father and, still more, to his spiritual father, Richard Wright. Baldwin's father died in 1943, and within a year Baldwin met Wright for the first time. It is amply clear from his essays that the twenty-year-old youth adopted the older man as a father figure. What followed is simplicity itself: Baldwin's habit of defining himself in opposition to his father was transferred to the new relationship. If Wright was committed to protest fiction, Baldwin would launch his own career with a rebellious essay called "Everybody's Protest Novel."[3] So long as Wright remained alive, the prophetic strain in Baldwin was suppressed. But with Wright's death in 1960, Baldwin was free to *become* his father. He has been giving Noah the rainbow sign ever since.

Go Tell It on the Mountain

The best of Baldwin's novels is *Go Tell It on the Mountain* (1953), and his best is very good indeed. It ranks with Jean Toomer's *Cane,* Richard Wright's *Native Son,* and Ralph Ellison's *Invisible Man* as a major contribution to American fiction. For this novel cuts through the walls of the store-front church to the essence of Negro experience in America. This is Baldwin's earliest world, his bright and morning star, and it glows with metaphorical

3. See *Notes of a Native Son* (Boston, Beacon Press, 1955), p. 13-23.

intensity. Its emotions are his emotions; its language, his native tongue. The result is a prose of unusual power and authority. One senses in Baldwin's first novel a confidence, control, and mastery of style that he has not attained again in the novel form.

The central event of *Go Tell It on the Mountain* is the religious conversion of an adolescent boy. In a long autobiographical essay, which forms a part of *The Fire Next Time,*[4] Baldwin leaves no doubt that he was writing of his own experience. During the summer of his fourteenth year, he tells us, he succumbed to the spiritual seduction of a woman evangelist. On the night of his conversion, he suddenly found himself lying on the floor before the altar. He describes his trancelike state, the singing and clapping of the saints, and the all-night prayer vigil which helped to bring him "through." He then recalls the circumstances of his life that prompted so pagan and desperate a journey to the throne of Grace.

The overwhelming fact of Baldwin's childhood was his victimization by the white power structure. At first he experienced white power only indirectly, as refracted through the brutality and degradation of the Harlem ghetto. The world beyond the ghetto seemed remote, and scarcely could be linked in a child's imagination to the harrowing conditions of his daily life. And yet a vague terror, transmitted through his parents to the ghetto child, attested to the power of the white world. Meanwhile, in the forefront of his consciousness was a set of fears by no means vague.

To a young boy growing up in the Harlem ghetto, damnation was a clear and present danger: "For the wages of sin were visible everywhere, in every wine-stained and urine-splashed hallway, in every clanging ambulance bell, in every scar on the faces of the pimps and their whores, in every helpless, newborn baby being brought into this danger, in every knife and pistol fight on the Avenue."[5] To such a boy, the store-front church offered a refuge and a sanctuary from the terrors of the street. God and safety became synonomous, and the church, a part of his survival strategy.

Fear, then, was the principal motive of Baldwin's conversion: "I became, during my fourteenth year, for the first time in my life

4. *The Fire Next Time* (New York, Dial Press, 1963), p. 29-61.

5. *Ibid.*, p. 34.

afraid—afraid of the evil within me and afraid of the evil without."[6] As the twin pressures of sex and race began to mount, the adolescent boy struck a desperate bargain with God. In exchange for sanctuary, he surrendered his sexuality, and abandoned any aspirations that might bring him into conflict with white power. He was safe, but walled off from the world; saved, but isolated from experience. This, to Baldwin, is the historical betrayal of the Negro Church. In exchange for the power of the Word, the Negro trades away the personal power of his sex and the social power of his people.

Life on these terms was unacceptable to Baldwin; he did not care to settle for less than his potential as a man. If his deepest longings were thwarted in the church, he would pursue them through his art. Sexual and racial freedom thus became his constant theme. And yet, even in breaking with the church, he pays tribute to its power: "In spite of everything, there was in the life I fled a zest and a joy and a capacity for facing and surviving disaster that are very moving and very rare."[7] We shall confront, then, in *Go Tell It on the Mountain,* a certain complexity of tone. Baldwin maintains an ironic distance from his material, even as he portrays the spiritual force and emotional appeal of storefront Christianity.

So much for the biographical foundations of the novel. The present action commences on the morning of John Grimes' fourteenth birthday, and before the night is out, he is born again in Christ. Part I, "The Seventh Day," introduces us to the boy and his family, his fears and aspirations, and the Temple of the Fire Baptized that is the center of his life. Part II, "The Prayers of the Saints," contains a series of flashbacks in which we share the inmost thoughts and private histories of his Aunt Florence, his mother Elizabeth, and his putative father, Gabriel. Part III, "The Threshing-Floor," returns us to the present and completes the story of the boy's conversion.

Parts I and III are set in Harlem in the spring of 1935. The action of Part II, however, takes place for the most part down home. Florence, Elizabeth, and Gabriel belong to a transitional genera-

6. *Ibid.,* p. 30.
7. *Ibid.,* p. 55.

tion, born roughly between 1875 and 1900. *Go Tell It on the Mountain* is thus a novel of the Great Migration. It traces the process of secularization that occurred when the Negro left the land for the Northern ghettos. This theme, to be sure, is handled ironically. Baldwin's protagonist "gets religion," but he is too young, too frightened, and too innocent to grasp the implications of his choice.

It is through the lives of the adults that we achieve perspective on the boy's conversion. His Aunt Florence has been brought to the evening prayer meeting by her fear of death. She is dying of cancer, and in her extremity humbles herself before God, asking forgiveness of her sins. These have consisted of a driving ambition and a ruthless hardening of heart. Early in her adult life, she left her dying mother to come North, in hopes of bettering her lot. Later, she drove from her side a husband whom she loved: "It had not been her fault that Frank was the way he was, determined to live and die a common nigger" (p. 92).[8] All her deeper feelings have been sacrificed to a futile striving for "whiteness" and respectability. Now she contemplates the wages of her virtue: an agonizing death in a lonely furnished room.

Elizabeth, as she conceives her life, has experienced both the fall and the redemption. Through Richard, she has brought an illegitimate child into the world, but through Gabriel, her error is retrieved. She fell in love with Richard during the last summer of her childhood, and followed him North to Harlem. There they took jobs as chambermaid and elevator boy, hoping to be married soon. Richard is sensitive, intelligent, and determined to educate himself. Late one evening, however, he is arrested and accused of armed robbery. When he protests his innocence, he is beaten savagely by the police. Ultimately he is released, but half hysterical with rage and shame, he commits suicide. Under the impact of this blow, Elizabeth retreats from life. Her subsequent marriage to Gabriel represents safety, timidity, and atonement for her sin.

As Gabriel prays on the night of John's conversion his thoughts revert to the events of his twenty-first year: his own conversion and beginning ministry, his joyless marriage to Deborah, and his brief affair with Esther. Deborah had been raped by white men

8. All page references are to the Dial Press editions of the novels.

at the age of sixteen. Thin, ugly, sexless, she is treated by the Negroes as a kind of holy fool. Gabriel, who had been a wild and reckless youth, marries her precisely to mortify the flesh. But he cannot master his desire. He commits adultery with Esther, and, informed that she is pregnant, refuses all emotional support. Esther dies in childbirth, and her son, Royal, who grows to manhood unacknowledged by his father, is killed in a Chicago dive.

Soon after the death of Royal, Deborah dies childless, and Gabriel is left without an heir. When he moves North, however, the Lord sends him a sign in the form of an unwed mother and her fatherless child. He marries Elizabeth and promises to raise Johnny as his own son. In the course of time the second Royal is born, and Gabriel rejoices in the fulfillment of God's promise. But John's half brother, the fruit of the prophet's seed, has turned his back on God. Tonight he lies at home with a knife wound, inflicted in a street fight with some whites. To Gabriel, therefore, John's conversion is a bitter irony: "Only the son of the bondwoman stood where the rightful heir should stand" (p. 128).

Through this allusion, Baldwin alerts us to the metaphorical possibilities of his plot. Gabriel's phrase is from Genesis 21:9-10, "And Sarah saw the son of Hagar the Egyptian, which she had born unto Abraham, mocking. Wherefore she said unto Abraham, Cast out this bondwoman and her son: for the son of the bondwoman shall not be heir with my son, even with Isaac." Hagar's bastard son is of course Ishmael, the archetypal outcast. Apparently Baldwin wants us to view Gabriel and Johnny in metaphorical relation to Abraham and Ishmael. This tableau of guilty father and rejected son will serve him as an emblem of race relations in America.

Baldwin sees the Negro quite literally as the bastard child of American civilization. In Gabriel's double involvement with bastardy we have a re-enactment of the white man's historic crime. In Johnny, the innocent victim of Gabriel's hatred, we have an archetypal image of the Negro child. Obliquely, by means of an extended metaphor, Baldwin approaches the very essence of Negro experience. That essence is rejection, and its most destructive consequence is shame. But God, the Heavenly Father, does not reject the Negro utterly. He casts down only to raise up. This is the psychic drama that occurs beneath the surface of John's conversion.

The Negro child, rejected by the whites for reasons that he cannot understand, is afflicted by an overwhelming sense of shame. Something mysterious, he feels, must be wrong with him, that he should be so cruelly ostracized. In time he comes to associate these feelings with the color of his skin—the basis, after all, of his rejection. He feels, and is made to feel, perpetually dirty and unclean:

> John hated sweeping this carpet, for dust arose, clogging his nose and sticking to his sweaty skin, and he felt that should he sweep it forever, the clouds of dust would not diminish, the rug would not be clean. It became in his imagination his impossible, lifelong task, his hard trial, like that of a man he had read about somewhere, whose curse it was to push a boulder up a steep hill. [p. 27]

This quality of Negro life, unending struggle with one's own blackness, is symbolized by Baldwin in the family name, Grimes. One can readily understand how such a sense of personal shame might have been inflamed by contact with the Christian tradition and transformed into an obsession with original sin. Gabriel's sermons take off from such texts as "I am a man of unclean lips," or "He which is filthy, let him be filthy still." The Negro's religious ritual, as Baldwin points out in an early essay, is permeated with color symbolism: "Wash me, cried the slave to his Maker, and I shall be whiter, whiter than snow! For black is the color of evil; only the robes of the saved are white."[9]

Given this attack on the core of the self, how can the Negro respond? If he accepts the white man's equation of blackness with evil, he is lost. Hating his true self, he will undertake the construction of a counter-self along the line that everything "black" he now disowns. To such a man, Christ is a kind of spiritual bleaching cream. Only if the Negro challenges the white man's moral categories can he hope to survive on honorable terms. This involves the sentiment that everything "black" he now embraces, however painfully, as his. There is, in short, the path of self-hatred and the path of self-acceptance. Both are available to Johnny within the framework of the Church, but he is deterred from one by the negative example of his father.

9. *Notes of a Native Son*, p. 21.

Consider Gabriel. The substance of his life is moral evasion. A preacher of the gospel and secretly the father of an illegitimate child, he cannot face the evil in himself. In order to preserve his image as the Lord's anointed, he has sacrificed the lives of those around him. His principal victim is Johnny, who is not his natural child. In disowning the bastard, he disowns the "blackness" in himself. Gabriel's psychological mechanisms are, so to say, white. Throughout his work Baldwin has described the scapegoat mechanism that is fundamental to the white man's sense of self. To the question, Who am I?, the white man answers: I am *white,* that is immaculate, without stain. I am the purified, the saved, the saintly, the elect. It is the *black* who is the embodiment of evil. Let him, the son of the bondwoman, pay the price of my sins.

From self-hatred flows not only self-righteousness but self-glorification as well. From the time of his conversion Gabriel has been living in a world of compensatory fantasy. He sees the Negro race as a chosen people and himself as prophet and founder of a royal line. But if Old Testament materials can be appropriated to buttress such a fantasy world, they also offer a powerful means of grappling with reality. When the Negro preacher compares the lot of his people to that of the children of Israel, he provides his flock with a series of metaphors corresponding to their deepest experience. The Church thus offers to the Negro masses a ritual enactment of their daily pain. It is with this poetry of suffering, which Baldwin calls the power of the Word, that the final section of the novel is concerned.

The first fifteen pages of Part III contain some of Baldwin's most effective writing. As John Grimes lies before the altar, a series of visionary states passes through his soul. Dream fragments and Freudian sequences, lively fantasies and Aesopian allegories, combine to produce a generally surrealistic effect. Images of darkness and chaos, silence and emptiness, mist and cold—cumulative patterns developed early in the novel—function now at maximum intensity. These images of damnation express the state of the soul when thrust into outer darkness by a rejecting, punishing, castrating father figure who is the surrogate of a hostile society. The dominant emotions are shame, despair, guilt, and fear.

At the depth of John's despair, a sound emerges to assuage his pain:

> He had heard it all his life, but it was only now that his ears were opened to this sound that came from the darkness, that could only come from darkness, that yet bore such sure witness to the glory of the light. And now in his moaning, and so far from any help, he heard it in himself—it rose from his bleeding, his cracked-open heart. It was a sound of rage and weeping which filled the grave, rage and weeping from time set free, but bound now in eternity; rage that had no language, weeping with no voice—which yet spoke now, to John's startled soul, of boundless melancholy, of the bitterest patience, and the longest night; of the deepest water, the strongest chains, the most cruel lash; of humility most wretched, the dungeon most absolute, of love's bed defiled, and birth dishonored, and most bloody, unspeakable, sudden death. Yes, the darkness hummed with murder: the body in the water, the body in the fire, the body on the tree. John looked down the line of these armies of darkness, army upon army, and his soul whispered, *Who are these?* [p. 228]

This is the sound, though John Grimes doesn't know it, of the blues. It is the sound of Bessie Smith, to which James Baldwin listened as he wrote *Go Tell It on the Mountain.* It is the sound of all Negro art and all Negro religion, for it flows from the cracked-open heart.

On these harsh terms, Baldwin's protagonist discovers his identity. He belongs to those armies of darkness and must forever share their pain. To the question, Who am I? he can now reply: I am he who suffers, and yet whose suffering on occasion is "from time set free." And thereby he discovers his humanity, for only man can ritualize his pain. We are now very close to that plane of human experience where art and religion intersect. What Baldwin wants us to feel is the emotional pressure exerted on the Negro's cultural forms by his exposure to white oppression. And finally to comprehend that these forms alone, through their power of transforming suffering, have enabled him to survive his terrible ordeal.

Giovanni's Room

Giovanni's Room (1956) is by far the weakest of Baldwin's novels. There is a tentative, unfinished quality about the book, as if in merely broaching the subject of homosexuality Baldwin had exhausted his creative energy. Viewed in retrospect, it seems less a novel in its own right than a first draft of *Another Country*. The surface of the novel is deliberately opaque, for Baldwin is struggling to articulate the most intimate, the most painful, the most elusive of emotions. The characters are vague and disembodied, the themes half-digested, the colors rather bleached than vivified. We recognize in this sterile psychic landscape the unprocessed raw material of art.

And yet this novel occupies a key position in Baldwin's spiritual development. Links run backward to *Go Tell It on the Mountain* as well as forward to *Another Country*. The very furniture of Baldwin's mind derives from the store-front church of his boyhood and adolescence. When he attempts a novel of homosexual love, with an all-white cast of characters and a European setting, he simply transposes the moral topography of Harlem to the streets of Paris. When he strives toward sexual self-acceptance he automatically casts the homosexual in a priestly role.

Before supporting this interpretation, let me summarize the plot. David, an American youth living abroad in Paris, meets a girl from back home and asks her to marry him. Hella is undecided, however, and she goes to Spain to think it over. During her absence, David meets Giovanni, a proud and handsome young Italian. They fall deeply in love and have a passionate affair. When Hella returns, David is forced to choose between his male lover and his American financée. He abandons Giovanni to the homosexual underworld, which is only too eager to claim him. When Guillaume, whom Baldwin describes as "a disgusting old fairy," inflicts upon the youth a series of humiliations, Giovanni strangles his tormentor. He is tried for murder and executed by the guillotine. Meanwhile David, who has gone with Hella to the south of France, cannot forget Giovanni. Tortured by guilt and self-doubt, he breaks off his engagement by revealing the truth about himself.

At the emotional center of the novel is the relationship between

David and Giovanni. It is highly symbolic, and to understand what is at stake, we must turn to Baldwin's essay on André Gide.[10] Published toward the end of 1954, about a year before the appearance of *Giovanni's Room,* this essay is concerned with the two sides of Gide's personality and the precarious balance that was struck between them. On the one side was his sensuality, his lust for the boys on the Piazza d'Espagne, threatening him always with utter degradation. On the other was his Protestantism, his purity, his otherworldliness—that part of him which was not carnal, and which found expression in his Platonic marriage to Madeleine. As Baldwin puts it, "She was his Heaven who would forgive him for his Hell and help him to endure it." It is a drama of salvation, in which the celibate wife, through selfless dedication to the suffering artist, becomes in effect a priest.

In the novel Giovanni plays the role of Gide; David, of Madeleine. Giovanni is not merely a sensualist, but a Platonist as well: "I want to escape . . . this dirty world, this dirty body" (p. 35). It is the purity of Giovanni's love for David—its idealized, transcendent quality—that protects him from a kind of homosexual Hell. David is the string connecting him to Heaven, and when David abandons him, he plunges into the abyss.

We can now appreciate the force of David's remark, "The burden of his salvation seemed to be on me and I could not endure it" (p. 168). Possessing the power to save, David rejects the priestly office. Seen in this light, his love affair with Giovanni is a kind of novitiate. The dramatic conflict of the novel can be stated as follows: does David have a true vocation? Is he prepared to renounce the heterosexual world? When David leaves Giovanni for Hella, he betrays his calling, but ironically he has been ruined for both the priesthood and the world.

It is Giovanni, Baldwin's doomed hero, who is the true priest. For a priest is nothing but a journeyman in suffering. Thus Giovanni defies David, the American tourist, even to understand his village: "And you will have no idea of the life there, dripping and bursting and beautiful and terrible, as you have no idea of my life now" (p. 203). It is a crucial distinction for all of Baldwin's work: there are the relatively innocent—the *laity* who are mere appren-

10. See *Nobody Knows My Name,* p. 155-62.

tices in human suffering—and the fully initiated, the *clergy* who are intimate with pain. Among the laity may be numbered Americans, white folks, heterosexuals, and squares; among the clergy, Europeans, Negroes, homosexuals, hipsters, and jazzmen. The finest statement of this theme, in which the jazzman is portrayed as priest, is Baldwin's moving story, "Sonny's Blues."[11]

Assumption of the priestly role is always preceded by an extraordinary experience of suffering, often symbolized in Baldwin's work by the death of a child. Thus in *The Amen Corner* Sister Margaret becomes a store-front church evangelist after giving birth to a dead child. And in *Giovanni's Room* the protagonist leaves his wife, his family, and his village after the birth of a stillborn child: "When I knew that it was dead I took our crucifix off the wall and I spat on it and I threw it on the floor and my mother and my girl screamed and I went out" (p. 205). It is at this point that Giovanni's inverted priesthood begins. Like Gide, he rebels against God, but the priestly impulse persists. He retreats from the heterosexual world, achieves a kind of purity in his relationship with David, is betrayed, and is consigned to martyrdom.

The patterns first explored in *Giovanni's Room* are given full expression in *Another Country*. Rufus is a Negro Giovanni—a journeyman in suffering and a martyr to racial oppression. Vivaldo and the other whites are mere apprentices, who cannot grasp the beauty and the terror of Negro life. Eric is a David who completes his novitiate, and whose priestly or redemptive role is central to the novel. There has been, however, a crucial change of tone. In *Giovanni's Room* one part of Baldwin wants David to escape from the male prison, even as another part remains committed to the ideal of homosexual love. In the later novel, this conflict has been resolved. Baldwin seems convinced that homosexuality is a liberating force, and he now brings to the subject a certain proselytizing zeal.

Another Country

Another Country (1962) is a failure on the grand scale. It is an ambitious novel, rich in thematic possibilities, for Baldwin has at

11. See *Partisan Review* (summer 1957), p. 327-58.

his disposal a body of ideas brilliantly developed in his essays. When he tries to endow these ideas with imaginative life, however, his powers of invention are not equal to the task. The plot consists of little more than a series of occasions for talk and fornication. Since the latter is a limited vehicle for the expression of complex ideas, talk takes over, and the novel drowns in a torrent of rhetoric.

The ideas themselves are impressive enough. At the heart of what Baldwin calls the white problem is a moral cowardice, a refusal to confront the "dark" side of human experience. The white American, at once overprotected and repressed, exhibits an infuriating tendency to deny the reality of pain and suffering, violence and evil, sex and death. He preserves in the teeth of human circumstance what must strike the less protected as a kind of willful innocence.

The American Negro, exposed to the ravages of reality by his status as a slave, has never enjoyed the luxury of innocence. On the contrary, his dark skin has come to be associated, at some buried level of the white psyche, with those forbidden impulses and hidden terrors which the white man is afraid to face. The unremitting daily warfare of American race relations must be understood in these symbolic terms. By projecting the "blackness" of his own being upon the dark skin of his Negro victim, the white man hopes to exorcise the chaotic forces that threaten to destroy him from within.

The psychic cost is of course enormous. The white man loses the experience of "blackness," sacrificing both its beauty and its terror to the illusion of security. In the end, he loses his identity. For a man who cannot acknowledge the dark impulses of his own soul cannot have the vaguest notion of who he is. A stranger to himself and others, the most salient feature of his personality will be a fatal bewilderment.

There are psychic casualties on the Negro side as well. No human personality can escape the effects of prolonged emotional rejection. The victim of this cruelty will defend himself with hatred and with dreams of vengeance, and will lose, perhaps forever, his normal capacity for love. Strictly speaking, this set of defenses, and the threat of self-destruction which they pose, constitutes the Negro problem.

It is up to the whites to break this vicious circle of rejection and hatred. They can do so only by facing the void, by confronting chaos, by making the necessary journey to "another country." What the white folks need is a closer acquaintance with the blues. Then perhaps they will be ready to join the human race. But only if the bloodless learn to bleed will it be possible for the Negro to lay down his burden of hatred and revenge.

So much for the conceptual framework of the novel. What dramatic materials are employed to invest these themes with life? A Greenwich Village setting and a hipster idiom ("Beer, dad, then we'll split"). A square thrown in for laughs. A good deal of boozing, and an occasional stick of tea. Some male cheesecake ("He bent down to lift off the scarlet bikini"). Five orgasms (two interracial and two homosexual) or approximately one per eighty pages, a significant increase over the Mailer rate. Distracted by this nonsense, how can one attend to the serious business of the novel?

In one respect only does the setting of *Another Country* succeed. Baldwin's descriptions of New York contain striking images of malaise, scenes and gestures that expose the moral chaos of contemporary urban life. The surface of his prose reflects the aching loneliness of the city with the poignancy of a Hopper painting. Harassed commuters and jostled pedestrians seem to yearn for closer contact. Denizens of a Village bar clutch their drinks with a gesture of buried despair. The whir of cash registers and the blatant glare of neon signs proclaim the harsh ascendancy of the commercial spirit. The tense subway crowds and the ubiquitous police convey a sense of latent violence. The furtive scribblings on lavatory walls provide a chilling commentary, in their mixture of raw lust and ethnic hate, on the scope and depth of our depravity.

Structurally speaking, the novel consists of two articulating parts. Book I is concerned to demonstrate how bad things really are in this America. Books II and III encompass the redemptive movement, the symbolic journey to "another country."

The central figure of Book I is Rufus Scott, a talented jazz drummer who is driven to suicide by the pressures of a racist society. Sensitive, bitter, violent, he sublimates his hatred by pounding on the white skin of his drums. With something of the same malice, he torments his white mistress, ultimately driving her insane.

Crushed by this burden of guilt, he throws himself from the George Washington Bridge. Rufus, in short, is a peculiarly passive Bigger Thomas, whose murderous impulses turn back upon himself. Like Bigger, he was created to stir the conscience of the nation. For the underlying cause of Rufus' death is the failure of his white friends to comprehend the depth of his despair.

In the melting pot of Greenwich Village, Baldwin brings together a group of white Americans whose lives are linked to Rufus' fate. Rufus' closest friend is Vivaldo Moore, an "Irish wop" who has escaped from the slums of Brooklyn. Cass, a girl of upperclass New England stock, has rebelled against her background to marry an aspiring writer. Eric Jones, having left Alabama for an acting career in New York, has experienced a double exile, and is about to return from a two-year sojourn in France.

Each of these friends has failed Rufus in his hour of need. It is the moral obtuseness of the whites that Baldwin means to stress. Rufus stands in relation to his friends as jazzman to audience: "Now he stood before the misty doors of the jazz joint, peering in, sensing rather than seeing the *frantic* black people on the stand and the *oblivious,* mixed crowd at the bar" (pp. 4-5, my emphasis). The audience simply refuses to hear the frantic plea in an insistent riff which seems to ask, "Do you love me?" It is a failure of love, but still more of imagination. Vivaldo and the others fail to transcend their innocence. They are blinded by their fear of self. Meaning well, they acquiesce in Rufus' death.

Having killed off Rufus early in the novel, Baldwin pursues the theme of vengeance and reconciliation through the character of Ida Scott. Embittered by the death of her brother, on whom she had counted to save her from the streets of Harlem, Ida takes revenge on the nearest white man. She moves in with Vivaldo, ostensibly in love, but actually exploiting the arrangement to advance her career as a blues singer. Toward the end of the novel, however, Vivaldo achieves a new sense of reality. This enables Ida, who has come reluctantly to love him, to confess to her deception. In a gesture of reconciliation, she slips from her finger a ruby-eyed snake ring—a gift from Rufus, and a symbol of her heritage of hate.

Books II and III are dominated by the figure of Eric Jones, the young actor who has gone abroad to find himself. His adolescence in Alabama was marked by a homosexual encounter with a Negro youth. In New York he has a brief, violent, and radically unsatisfying affair with Rufus, from which he flees to France. There he falls in love with Yves, a Paris street boy, and through a chaste and tactful courtship wins his trust and love. As Book II opens, they are enjoying an idyllic holiday in a rented villa on the Côte d'Azur. Eric must soon leave for America, however, where he has accepted a part in a Broadway play. After a suitable interval, Yves will join him in New York.

Since the love affair of Eric and Yves is the turning point of the novel, we must pause to examine its wider implications. Book II commences with highly charged, symbolic prose:

> Eric sat naked in his rented garden. Flies buzzed and boomed in the brilliant heat, and a yellow bee circled his head. Eric remained very still, then reached for the cigarettes beside him and lit one, hoping that the smoke would drive the bee away. Yves' tiny black-and-white kitten stalked the garden as though it were Africa, crouching beneath the mimosas like a panther and leaping into the air. [p. 183]

Like Whitman, his spiritual progenitor, Baldwin tends to endow his diffuse sexuality with mythic significance. Here he depicts, in this Mediterranean garden, what appears to be a homosexual Eden. Then, in an attempt to fuse two levels of his own experience, he brings into metaphorical relation the idea of homosexuality and the idea of Africa. Each represents to the "majority" imagination a kind of primal chaos, yet each contains the possibility of liberation. For to be Negro, or to be homosexual, is to be in constant touch with that sensual reality which the white (read: heterosexual) world is at such pains to deny.

The male lovers, naked in the garden, are not to be taken too literally. What Baldwin means to convey through this idyllic episode is the innocence of the unrepressed. He has been reading, one would surmise, Norman Brown's *Life against Death*. "Children," Brown reminds us, "explore in indiscriminate fashion all the erotic potentialities of the human body. In Freudian terms, children are polymorphously perverse."[12] In this episode on the Mediterranean coast we are back in the cradle of man, back in the sexually and racially undifferentiated human past; back in the lost paradise of the polymorphously perverse.

On these mythic foundations, Baldwin constructs a theory of personality. The primal stuff of human personality is undifferentiated: "He was, briefly and horribly, in a region where there were no definitions of any kind, neither of color nor of male and female" (pp. 301-2). One must face this formlessness, however, before one can hope to achieve form.

At the core of Baldwin's fiction is an existentialist psychology. In a passage whose language is reminiscent of Genesis, he describes Vivaldo's struggle to define himself: "And beneath all this was the void where anguish lived and questions crouched, which referred only to Vivaldo and to no one else on earth. Down there, down there, lived the raw unformed substance for the creation of Vivaldo, and only he, Vivaldo alone, could master it" (pp. 305-6). As music depends ultimately on silence, so being is achieved in tension with nothingness. Sexual identity—all identity—emerges from the void. Man, the sole creator of himself, moves alone upon the face of the waters.

We can now account for Eric's pivotal position in the novel. Through his commitment to Yves, he introduces an element of order into the chaos of his personal life. This precarious victory, wrested in anguish from the heart of darkness, is the real subject of *Another Country*. Images of chaos proliferate throughout the novel. Rufus leaps into chaos when be buries himself in the deep black water of the Hudson River. Cass encounters chaos in the strange, pulsating life of Harlem, or in an abstract expressionist canvas at the Museum of Modern Art. To Vivaldo, chaos means a marijuana party in a Village pad; to Eric, the male demimonde that threatens to engulf him. Eric is the first of Rufus' friends to face his demons and achieve a sense of self. He in turn emancipates the rest.

From this vantage point, one can envision the novel that Baldwin was trying to write. With the breakdown of traditional stan-

12. Norman Brown, *Life against Death* (Wesleyan University Press, 1959), p. 27.

dards – even of sexual normality – homosexuality becomes a metaphor of the modern condition. Baldwin says of Eric, "There were no standards for him except those he could make for himself" (p. 212). Forced to create his own values as he goes along, Eric is to serve "as a footnote to the twentieth century torment" (p. 330). The homosexual becomes emblematic of existential man.

What actually happens, however, is that Baldwin's literary aims are deflected by his sexual mystique. Eric returns to America as the high priest of ineffable phallic mysteries. His friends, male and female, dance around the Maypole and, *mirabile dictu,* their sense of reality is restored. Cass commits adultery with Eric, and is thereby reconciled to her faltering marriage. Vivaldo receives at Eric's hands a rectal revelation that prepares him for the bitter truth of Ida's confession. The novel ends as Yves joins Eric in New York, heralding, presumably, a fresh start for all and a new era of sexual and racial freedom.

For most readers of *Another Country,* the difficulty will lie in accepting Eric as a touchstone of reality. Let us consider the overall design. Rufus is portrayed as the victim of a white society that cannot face unpleasant truths. The redemptive role is then assigned to Eric. But few will concede a sense of reality, at least in the sexual realm, to one who regards heterosexual love as "a kind of superior calisthenics" (p. 336). To most, homosexuality will seem rather an evasion than an affirmation of human truth. Ostensibly the novel summons us to reality. Actually it substitutes for the illusions of white supremacy those of homosexual love.

In any event, it is the task of a literary critic not to debate the merits of homosexuality but to demonstrate its pressure on the novel. Let us accept Baldwin's postulate that in order to become a man, one must journey to the void. Let us grant that homosexuality is a valid metaphor of this experience. We must now ask of Baldwin's hero: does he face the void and emerge with a new sense of reality, or does he pitch his nomad's tent forever on the shores of the burning lake? The answer hinges, it seems to me, on the strength of Eric's commitment to Yves. Baldwin describes it as total, and yet, within a few weeks' span, while Yves remains behind in France, Eric betrays him with a woman and a man. How can we grant to this lost youth redemptive power?

One senses that Baldwin, in his portrait of Eric, has desired above all to be faithful to his own experience. He will neither falsify nor go beyond it. Central to that experience is a rebellion against the prevailing sexual, as well as racial mores. But on either plane of experience, Baldwin faces an emotional dilemma. Like Satan and the fallen angels, it is as painful to persist in his rebellion as to give it up. Total defiance is unthinkable, total reconciliation only less so. These are the poles of Baldwin's psychic life, and the novel vacillates helplessly between them.

The drama of reconciliation is enacted by Ida and Vivaldo. Through their symbolic marriage Ida is reconciled to whites; Vivaldo, to women. This gesture, however, is a mere concession to majority opinion. What Baldwin really feels is dramatized through Rufus and Eric. Rufus can be neither fully reconciled to nor fully defiant of white society. No Bigger Thomas, he is incapable of total hate. Pushed to the limits of endurance, he commits suicide. Similarly, Eric cannot be fully reconciled to women, nor can he surrender to the male demimonde. So he camps on the outskirts of Hell. In the case of Rufus, the suicidal implications are overt. With Eric, as we shall see, Baldwin tries to persuade us that Hell is really Heaven.

In its rhetoric as well, the novel veers between the poles of reconciliation and defiance. At times the butter of brotherhood seems to melt in Baldwin's mouth. But here is Rufus, scoring the first interracial orgasm of the book: "And shortly, nothing could have stopped him, not the white God himself nor a lynch mob arriving on wings. Under his breath he cursed the milk-white bitch and groaned and rode his weapon between her thighs" (p. 22). With what economy of phrase "the milk-white bitch" combines hostility to whites and women! Nowhere is Baldwin's neurotic conflict more nakedly exposed. On one side we have the white God and the lynch mob, determined to suppress sex. On the other, adolescent rebellion and the smashing of taboo, hardening at times into Garveyism.

By Garveyism I mean the emotional and rhetorical excess, and often the extravagant fantasies, to which an embattled minority may resort in promoting its own defense. *Another Country* is doubly susceptible to these temptations, for it was conceived as a joint assault on racial and sexual intolerance. Apparently prejudice encountered in either context will evoke a similar response. The arrogance of the majority has a natural counterpart in exaggerated claims of minority supremacy.

In the racial sphere Baldwin employs defenses that go well beyond a healthy race pride or a legitimate use of folk material. His portrait of Ida, for example, leans heavily on the exotic, on that stereotype of jungle grace which flourished in the 1920s. To a touch of primitivism he adds flat assertions of superiority: Negroes are more alive, more colorful, more spontaneous, better dancers, and, above all, better lovers than the pale, gray, milk-white, chalk-white, dead-white, ice-hearted, frozen-limbed, stiff-assed zombies from downtown. Well, perhaps. One does not challenge the therapeutic value of these pronouncements, only their artistic relevance.

Coupled with these racial sentiments are manifestations of sexual Garveyism. Throughout the novel the superiority of homosexual love is affirmed. Here alone can one experience total surrender and full orgastic pleasure; here alone, the metaphysical terror of the void. Heterosexual love, by comparison, is a pale—one is tempted to say, white—imitation. In many passages hostility to women reaches savage proportions: "Every time I see a woman wearing her fur coats and her jewels and her gowns, I want to tear all that off her and drag her someplace, to a *pissoir,* and make her smell the smell of many men, the *piss* of many men, and make her know that *that* is what she is for" (p. 210).

It may be argued that these are the sentiments of Yves and not of Baldwin, but that is precisely the point. In *Another Country* the sharp outlines of character are dissolved by waves of uncontrolled emotion. The novel lacks a proper distancing. One has the impression of Baldwin's recent work that the author does not know where his own psychic life leaves off and that of his characters begins. What is more, he scarcely cares to know, for he is sealed in a narcissism so engrossing that he fails to make emotional contact with his characters. If his people have no otherness, if he repeatedly violates their integrity, how can they achieve the individuality which alone will make them memorable?

In conclusion, I should like to view *Another Country* from the perspective of the author's spiritual journey. Reduced to its essentials, this journey has carried Baldwin from a store-front church in Harlem to a Greenwich Village pad. His formative years were spent among the saints, in an environment where repressive attitudes toward sex were paramount. As a result, his sexual experience has always contained a metaphysical dimension, bearing inescapably on his relationship to God. To understand the failure of *Another Country* we must trace the connection between his sexual rebellion, his religious conceptions, and his style.

Baldwin has described the spiritual geography of his adolescence in the opening pages of *The Fire Next Time*. On a little island in the vast sea of Harlem stood the saved, who had fled for their very lives into the Church. All around them was the blazing Hell of the Avenue, with its bars and brothels, pimps and junkies, violence and crime. Between God and the Devil an unrelenting contest was waged for the souls of the young, in which the girls of God's party bore a special burden: "They understood that they must act as God's decoys, saving the souls of the boys for Jesus and binding the bodies of the boys in marriage. For this was the beginning of our burning time."[13]

Baldwin's adolescent rebellion began, it seems plain, when his dawning sensuality collided with his youthful ministry. At first he rebelled against the store-front church, then Harlem, seeking to escape at any cost. Ultimately he came to reject the female sex, the white world, and the Christian God. As his rebellion grew, he discovered in his gift for language a means of liberation. Like hundreds of American writers, he fled from the provinces (in his case, Harlem) to Greenwich Village and the Left Bank. There he hoped to find a haven of sexual, racial, and intellectual freedom.

He quickly discovered, however, that he had not left the Avenue behind. In Greenwich Village or its French equivalent, he peered into the abyss, the demimonde of gay bars, street boys, and male prostitutes. This he recognized as Hell and recoiled in horror. But what alternative does he offer to promiscuity and fleeting physical encounter? He speaks in the rhetoric of commitment and responsibility, but what he has in mind is simply a homosexual version of romantic love. It is a familiar spiritual maneuver. Baldwin has built a palace on the ramparts of Hell and called it Heaven. Its proper name is Pandemonium.

13. *The Fire Next Time,* p. 32.

In an effort to make Hell endurable, Baldwin attempts to spiritualize his sexual rebellion. Subjectively, I have no doubt, he is convinced that he has found God. Not the white God of his black father, but a darker deity who dwells in the heart of carnal mystery. One communes with this dark power through what Baldwin calls "the holy and liberating orgasm."[14] The stranger the sex partner, the better the orgasm, for it violates a stronger taboo. Partners of a different race, or the same sex, or preferably both, afford the maximum spiritual opportunities.

Baldwin imagines his new faith to be a complete break with the past, but in fact he has merely inverted the Christian orthodoxy of his youth. Properly regarded, *Another Country* will be seen as the celebration of a Black Mass. The jazzman is Baldwin's priest; the homosexual, his acolyte. The bandstand is his altar; Bessie Smith, his choir. God is carnal mystery, and through orgasm the Word is made flesh. Baldwin's ministry is as vigorous as ever. He summons to the mourners' bench all who remain, so to say, hardened in their innocence. Lose that, he proclaims, and you will be saved. To the truly unregenerate, those stubborn heterosexuals, he offers the prospect of salvation through sodomy. With this novel doctrine the process of inversion is complete.

These contentions are best supported by a look at Baldwin's style. Two idioms were available to him from the Negro world: the consecrated and the profane. They derive respectively from the church-oriented and the jazz-oriented segments of the Negro community. To Baldwin the church idiom signifies submission, reconciliation, brotherhood, and platonic love. Conversely, the hipster idiom conveys rebellion, defiance, retaliation, and sexual love.

The predominant mode of *Another Country* is the hipster idiom. For Baldwin it is the language of apostasy. In rejecting the God of his youth, he inverts the consecrated language of the saints. The general effect is blasphemous: "What a pain in the ass Old Jesus Christ has turned out to be, and it probably wasn't even the poor, doomed, loving, hopheaded old Jew's fault" (p. 308). Baldwin's diction is deliberately shocking; its function is to challenge limits, to transgress. In the sexual realm it exploits the fascination of the forbidden, like a cheap film aimed at the teen-age trade. Indeed,

14. See *Blues for Mister Charlie* (New York, Dial Press, 1964), p. 105.

if the style proclaims the man, we are dealing with an adolescent: who else gets his kicks from the violation of taboo?

Curiously, however, the language of the store-front church persists. For the hipster idiom is really Baldwin's second language, and in moments of high emotion he reverts to his native tongue. This occurs primarily when he tries to heighten or exalt the moment of sexual union. In the vicinity of orgasm his diction acquires a religious intensity; his metaphors announce the presence of a new divinity: "When he entered that marvelous wound in her, *rending and tearing! rending and tearing!* was he surrendering, in joy, to the Bridegroom, Lord, and Savior?" (p. 308, emphasis in original).

This sudden shift into the church idiom betrays on Baldwin's part a deep need to spiritualize his sexual revolt. Here he describes Eric's first homosexual encounter: "What had always been *hidden* was to him, that day, *revealed,* and it did not matter that, fifteen years later, he sat in an armchair, overlooking a foreign sea, still struggling to find that *grace* which would allow him to bear that *revelation*" (p. 206, emphasis supplied). This is the language of Pandemonium: evil has become Baldwin's good. The loss of meaning that ensues is both moral and semantic, and the writer who permits it betrays both self and craft.

Another Country is not simply a bad novel, but a dead end. It is symptomatic of a severe crisis in Baldwin's life and art. The author's popular acclaim, his current role as a political celebrity, and the Broadway production of his recent play have all tended to obscure the true state of affairs. But Baldwin must suspect that his hipster phase is coming to a close. He has already devoted two novels to his sexual rebellion. If he persists, he will surely be remembered as the greatest American novelist since Jack Kerouac. The future now depends on his ability to transcend the emotional reflexes of his adolescence. So extraordinary a talent requires of him no less an effort.

Epilogue

THE material which the Negro as a creative writer knows best comes out of the life and experience of the colored people in America.

JAMES WELDON JOHNSON

11. *Freedom for the Negro Novelist*[1]

FROM the beginning, the Negro novelist has been torn between the conflicting loyalties of race and art. On the one hand, he has sought to be a spokesman for his people; on the other, to be accepted on his merits as an artist. Historically speaking, the issue has seldom been in doubt: the urge to protest has all but stifled the urge to create.

In recent years, however, the traditional loyalties of the Negro novelist have been called into question. A controversy has arisen in Negro literary circles which for the most part revolves around the problem of source material. In the course of this debate the Negro writer has been urged to concentrate exclusively on racial protest, and to avoid it entirely; to exploit his distinctiveness as a Negro, and to abandon the materials of Negro life altogether. Seldom has he been encouraged simply to go about his business as an artist, free to choose his subject matter on aesthetic grounds alone.

1. Most of the material in this chapter has appeared in the *Bulletin of the College Language Association,* winter 1957.

Selection of source material is not a problem which can be solved with mathematical precision. A variety of subjects will yield good novels, and there is no touchstone which will guarantee success. It is nonetheless true in the history of the Negro novel that certain kinds of subject matter have consistently produced better results than others. With this in mind, let us consider two schools of thought that have allowed extraliterary concerns to govern their choice of material. Afterward it may be possible to suggest an approach based on sound aesthetic theory.

The "Art-as-Weapon" Fallacy

The first school—which by virtue of seniority alone must be recognized as the traditional one—maintains that freedom for the Negro novelist is inseparable from the freedom of the Negro people as a whole. The novelist is closest to freedom, therefore, when he plunges boldly into the social struggle, placing his art at the disposal of his cause. Two spokesmen will serve to illustrate this point of view: Nick Aaron Ford of the faculty of Morgan State College, and Lloyd Brown, associate editor of *Masses and Mainstream.* No guilt-by-association is intended: Ford is merely inclined toward Negro nationalism; Brown is the Communist party's latest commissar of Negro culture. Both, however, share the assumption that art is primarily a weapon in the racial (class) struggle.

Ford's approach is given fullest expression in his article in *Phylon* called "A Blueprint for Negro Authors." He begins by invoking the art of Tolstoy and Whitman, with its ethical overtones and its conscious aim of fostering human brotherhood. The American Negro community, he continues, should demand no less of its writers, whose stake in brotherhood is even more compelling. He then presents his "blueprint," which contains the following specification: "My third requirement for the Negro author is the use of social propaganda subordinated so skillfully to the purposes of art that it will not insult the average intelligent reader. I do not think it is sufficient for the Negro author to treat racial themes with no regard to their deeper social implications." [2]

2. "A Blueprint for Negro Authors," *Phylon* (fourth quarter 1950), pp. 374–77.

Let it be noted that social propaganda is a *requirement* for the Negro novel. It is not sufficient—in this connection Ford mentions Countee Cullen and Zora Neale Hurston—to deal with Negro life and culture unless social propaganda is introduced. Yet it must be introduced ever so skillfully, lest it be recognized by an intelligent reader for what it is. Symbolism, according to Ford, is an indispensable device for disguising propaganda: "By this means, the Negro author can fight the battles of his race with subtlety and popularity." The implications of this approach are clear. The younger Negro novelists may imagine that they stand on the threshhold of aesthetic realization, but Ford insists that they should stand at Armageddon, ready to do battle for the Lord.

A more sophisticated defense of the position has been made by Lloyd Brown. Stressing the nationalist character of Negro literature, Brown concurs emphatically with Ford's defense of the protest novel: "For nearly all Negro writers throughout American history the question of what to write about was compellingly simple: the pen was an essential instrument in the fight for liberation." [3]

Despite this compellingly simple historical solution, Brown is dissatisfied with the protest novel of the recent past. He takes particular exception to "the narrow range of frenzy, shock, brutality, and frustration" which he associates with the work of Richard Wright and Chester Himes. Perhaps the problem is not so simple after all, or at least not since the period when Wright and Himes broke with the Communist party. Now, clearly, theirs is a counterrevolutionary frenzy. But how can the Negro novelist specialize in protest and yet avoid the "narrow range" of Wright and Himes?

Unlike Ford, who wishes to "refine" the propaganda content of the Negro novel, Brown proposes to enlarge its scope. Conflict and struggle, he argues, themselves possess universality: "One of the greatest American and universal themes [is] the epic struggle, still unended, of the Negro people in our land." The Negro's fight, moreover, is part of a worldwide (that is, universal) struggle against American imperialism. By striking a judicious balance between Negro nationalism and class consciousness, the Negro

3. "Which Way for the Negro Writer?" *Masses and Mainstream* (March 1951), pp. 53–63; (April 1951), pp. 50–59.

novelist can achieve a true universality: "The narrowness of bourgeois nationalism, like the "broadness" of bourgeois cosmopolitanism, is a blind alley. I have in mind rather the Marxist-Leninist concept that a people's culture should be national in form . . . but workingclass in content." To this sterile formula the Communist party reduces the complexities of Negro art.

The arguments in refutation of the art-as-weapon fallacy are as old as the fallacy itself. They rest on the autonomy of art. To violate this autonomy is to destroy aesthetic standards entirely and to replace them with extraliterary criteria. The task of criticism becomes wholly ideological: a novel is good if it serves our cause. Nothing has done more to retard the growth of the Negro novel than this stubborn effort to reduce it to the status of a pamphlet on race relations.

The life of the imagination, while it feeds on reality, will always remain separate from it. Art is not life; it is not a branch of politics; it is not to be used as a front for any cause, however just. Art is a different kind of human activity from politics—more or less valuable, depending on one's point of view—but in any case, different. To respect this distinction is the beginning of wisdom for the Negro novelist. The color line exists not between the covers of a book but outside, in the real world. Its obliteration is a political, not a literary task. Let the Negro novelist as citizen, as political man, vent his fury and indignation through the appropriate protest organizations, but as novelist, as artist, let him pursue his vision, his power of seeing and revealing which is mankind's rarest gift.

The "Cultural Ghetto" Fallacy

There is a second and more fashionable school of thought which tends to equate freedom for the Negro novelist with the avoidance of Negro life. By writing "race novels," these critics claim, Negro writers segregate themselves in a cultural ghetto. To be free is to break out of the ghetto; the Negro novelist is therefore closest to freedom when he writes about whites. By turning to a more cosmopolitan source material, he avoids "the deadly trap of cultural segregation" and strikes a blow against Jim Crow aesthetics.

This approach has won many adherents and partial adherents in the tempting climate of the postwar years. Some, like Langston Hughes and Alain Locke, have confined themselves to greeting, a trifle too enthusiastically, fiction written by Negroes "in the general American field." Others, like Hugh Gloster, have attempted a more serious defense of the new trend.[4] But the case for "raceless" fiction has been stated most emphatically by Richard Gibson, in an article in the *Kenyon Review.* The Negro novelist, according to Gibson, is the victim of a conspiracy which impels him toward protest. He is under constant pressure from Negroes who are committed to the propaganda novel, from publishers who traffic in racial sensationalism, and from professional liberals who need a cause to defend. In art, as in life, he is not allowed to transcend his category: "You are not yet free, he is told. Write about what you know, he is told, and the Professional Liberal will not fail to remind him that he cannot possibly know anything else but Jim Crow, share-cropping, slum ghettoes, Georgia crackers, and the sting of his humiliation, his unending ordeal, his blackness."[5]

The race problem, the Negro writer is repeatedly advised, is his private domain. "About it, however, he may soon learn, is a high wall; *and the young writer would do well to realize his real problem is finding a way over that wall*" (my italics). The essence of Mr. Gibson's thought is contained in this metaphor. To escape from the ghetto, to leap over the wall, in fantasy if not reality—this is the dominant impulse of the assimilationist critics. And the means of escape is art. The Negro novelist, Mr. Gibson reminds us, is not cut off from the main stream of modern intellectual life. He is a contemporary of Joyce, Kafka, Eliot, and Pound, not merely of Himes and Hughes. Armed with a copy of *Finnegan's Wake,* he can resist any attempt to confine him to Negro source material.

Assimilationist theory, which is at bottom a rationalization of the impulse to assimilate, is easy enough to demolish. Lloyd Brown, who writes at his best when attacking the assimilationist critics, has exposed the basic fallacy in their reasoning: "There are some Negro writers who confuse the essential and all-impor-

4. See "Race and the Negro Writer," *Phylon* (fourth quarter 1950), pp. 369–71.
5. "A No to Nothing," *Kenyon Review, 13* (spring 1951), 252–55.

tant struggle to break out of the ghetto with the false idea of breaking away from the people who are confined in the ghetto."[6] It should be obvious that there is a common denominator of human experience to be found in all cultures, including Negro culture. Why, then, is a novel based on Negro life thought to be less "universal" than a novel based, for example, on life in a small New England town? Why indeed, unless the critic is convinced of the inherent superiority of all things white?

Under the banner of assimilationism, the Negro novelist is not free, because he is not free to deal with Negro life. For some little time, life in the ghetto is likely to proceed in all its variety and complexity. But if the most sensitive Negro intellectuals disappear over the wall, who will remain to interpret it? Such a course can only produce a hot-house art, truncated, rootless, and artificial. This is especially true for the novel where social milieu, in all its nuances, plays such a crucial role. Moreover, what are the proponents of an "integrated" art to do with the anything but integrated history of the Negro in America? As soon as one takes the importance of tradition into account, as soon as one adds an historical dimension to art, the shallowness of the assimilationist approach becomes apparent.

Basically it is the element of fantasy, the loss of contact with the realities of Negro life, which makes the assimilationist novel a blind alley. Written to demonstrate the author's personal emancipation (that is, his "whiteness"), it reveals too often the strength of his negative ties to the Negro group. Conscious avoidance of race is not freedom; it is merely an inverted form of bondage. It amounts in the last analysis to a kind of literary "passing," and like passing it is essentially an evasion. Sterling Brown has written of these novelists, "They do not want art to deal with Negro life whether truly or falsely, with revelation or caricature; they just want out."

The assimilationist novel is in more than one sense a "passing" fancy. Already there are indications that the present vogue has entered its decline. From the beginning its limitations were apparent, for the assimilationist novel is no less a propaganda effort than the most militant protest novel. It is simply that the propa-

6. "Which Way for the Negro Writer?" p. 62.

ganda slogans have been altered to accommodate the racial strategy of a new era. The novelist influenced by Negro nationalism has cried out in his anger: "Integrate us!" The assimilationist has adopted a more subtle appeal: "See how integrated we are!" (and thus how worthy of acceptance). Both approaches are based on political rather than aesthetic considerations. What has been lacking in the current controversy is an approach to Negro art which is free from the requirements of racial strategy.

Toward an Autonomous Negro Art

Freedom for the Negro *artist,* if it means anything at all, means freedom to create without succumbing to the demands of racial propaganda. But merely to affirm the autonomy of art will not suffice. If the Negro novelist is to be guided in his choice of material by literary criteria alone, of what do these criteria consist? Perhaps it is possible to establish a general procedure which is valid for most novelists, including Negroes. We can then follow this procedure to its logical conclusion in the specific case of the Negro novel.

To succeed aesthetically, a novel must possess both distance and immediacy. Distance enables the author to develop a theme of universal significance from an otherwise isolated segment of human life. Immediacy provides verisimilitude, the illusion of reality. This distinction between the universal and particular aspects of the novel is reflected in the technical concepts of theme and vehicle. Theme is abstract, timeless: a mold into which a variety of responses can be poured. Vehicle deals with the surface of life, with its concrete aspect. No novelist can afford to neglect these surface details, for narrative fiction must first of all be convincing on the literal level.

In choosing an appropriate vehicle for his theme, the author's first consideration must be familiarity with surface detail. It is no accident that Melville's masterpiece is based on his former profession: his intimate knowledge of whaling lends authenticity to his philosophical speculations on the nature of evil. Immediacy such as Melville achieves in *Moby Dick* is ultimately biographical in origin. Fictional characters are created not out of thin air but from shreds and patches of memory. Settings are not simply invented; they reflect actual or vicarious experience. That is why Yoknapatawpha County is located in Mississippi rather than California, and why Lilliput resembles nothing so much as 18th-century England. Every artist apprehends reality through a specific culture. Why should the Negro novelist imagine that he alone is exempt from the limitations of time and place?

No special burden is imposed on the Negro novelist by insisting upon immediacy in his work. Philip Butcher, a teacher of creative writing at Morgan State College, instructs his students to avoid stories far removed from their experience: "One must have a thorough understanding of human beings in order to create convincing fictional characters, and one must begin by knowing the people with whom one is in intimate association, whatever their race may be."[7] For most Negro writers the quest for immediacy will lead directly to Negro source material. The serious Negro novelist will write of Negro life not because of any mystical bond with his people, or through mistaken motives of racial loyalty, but simply out of fidelity to his deepest experience.

To invest his art with particularity, to anchor it firmly in a living culture, the Negro novelist must rely upon his special knowledge of Negro life. Within this broad framework, however, specific problems arise which cannot lightly be dismissed. Among them are the proper place of racial conflict and the proper treatment of white characters in Negro fiction.

The question of race *material* was settled definitively by the Renaissance generation; the present controversy concerns the treatment of racial *conflict* within the novel of Negro life. On both sides, extremist views have obscured the issue. Never to write of racial conflict is just as absurd as always to write of it. Social conflict is real; it has its complexities and is therefore a legitimate subject for the artist who is prepared to do them justice. Novelists like Malraux, Silone, and Orwell have demonstrated that aesthetic realization is not impossible within a context of social struggle. Most Negro novelists, as Alain Locke points out, simply do not

7. "Creative Writing in the Negro College," *Journal of Negro Education* (spring 1951), pp. 160–63.

realize "how much art it takes to hold in smooth suspension the heavy sociology of racial issues and inter-racial tensions."

This much is certain: to deal successfully with racial conflict a new style will be required, for the naturalism of the Wright School has lost its power. Ralph Ellison's symbolic treatment of race in *Invisible Man* seems to offer a viable alternative. Here the Negro's "invisibility" is enlarged to encompass the central dilemma of modern man. In Ellison's hands race becomes a metaphor through which larger meanings are conveyed. As a by-product, the reader may gain considerable insight into American race relations.

Once committed to race material, the novelist is forced to deal in some degree with racial conflict, if only for the sake of authentic characterization. But how far he allows conflict with the white world to impinge on the lives of his characters is a matter of artistic selectivity. No novelist is obliged to treat the life of his protagonist comprehensively. Depending on his theme, the author may concentrate on his character's boyhood, his career, his religious development, his love life, or his experience with racial prejudice. He may choose the latter not for propaganda purposes but to render the impact of caste on a human personality. Such a novel may be limited but nevertheless well executed. Even a cry of anguish can be highly organized, and rendered with style and form.

But suppose a Negro novelist has no wish to emphasize the social tragedy of Negro life. It is his prerogative to select a more personal aspect of his protagonist's experience. In point of fact, however, the Negro novelist is seldom confronted with clear-cut alternatives. He chooses rather from a gradient that ranges from Hurston's *Their Eyes Were Watching God* (abnormally low racial tension) to Himes' *If He Hollers Let Him Go* (abnormally high racial tension). A sensible solution would seem to lie along the middle ranges (tension where relevant). The question of relevance, however, is a matter of artistic necessity, to be decided on the level not of propaganda but of theme and characterization.

The treatment of white characters is a somewhat more complicated question. In the first place, it is indefensible to regard race material as the only "natural" province of the Negro writer. There is nothing to prevent a Negro novelist from writing about whites—or about Hopi Indians, for that matter—so long as his choice is governed by aesthetic considerations. The right of the Negro author to any material which he finds promising is beyond dispute. Nevertheless, every author, confronted with the vast spectrum of human experience, is forced to be selective. A wise choice, as we have seen, will reflect the author's intimate knowledge of his subject. But this does not exclude the possibility of a successful novel of white life. To select source material on the basis of familiarity is not to surrender the right to less familiar material, whenever the author is prepared to use it to best advantage.

Long before the recent fad of literary passing, in a review of William Attaway's *Let Me Breathe Thunder* (1939), Ulysses Lee discussed the conditions under which a Negro novelist might justifiably attempt a novel of white life. His conclusions, which have been fully validated by subsequent events, are worth reproducing at length:

> It is not because the writer has deserted Negro life that his characters fail to materialize; it is because he has deserted life itself. It does not matter what his characters' race may be so long as he can root them firmly in their social backgrounds and feel them with all the shades and nuances of psychological experience possible to them. This does not mean that he must eschew the use of white characters altogether, and, like the Negro films, patriotically people his novels with Negro G-men, judges, and governors, where none exist. It does mean though that . . . he will use white characters only when, as a result of careful study, he is certain that he is capable of their full realization.[8]

In general, the Negro author should not undertake a "white" novel unless his experience of white life is extraordinary. (The same applies, it goes without saying, to white authors who wish to write of Negro life.) But how can he acquire an extensive knowledge of white life except through a progressive lowering of caste barriers? The color line must be crossed in life before it

8. Review of *Let Me Breathe Thunder,* in *Opportunity,* 17 (1939), 283–84.

can be crossed in literature. For good and sufficient artistic reasons, the Negro novel must approximate the Negro's present experience. As conditions change for the better, the content of Negro fiction will automatically adjust. This dynamic relationship between art and experience has been well expressed by Philip Butcher: "As Negroes become more and more integrated into a democratic America, their range of experience will increase. When Negroes who are writers are intimately associated with whites in their daily living, the literature they produce will naturally encompass larger and larger segments of American society.[9]

For the Negro novelist who decides to attempt an imaginative interpretation of white life, what practical expedients are available? To begin with, the short story whose characters are principally or exclusively white might serve as a useful apprenticeship. Beyond this, timing is important. An early novel of white life is a dubious undertaking, since most Negro novelists will produce only one or two novels in any case.[10] On the whole, it seems best to approach the longer genre by introducing white characters, both minor and major, into a novel of Negro life. By walking, not running, toward the novel of white life, the Negro novelist can gain preliminary experience in handling white characters, and can guard against any tendency to exploit "white" material for extraliterary ends.

In exceptional circumstances, then, both the protest novel and the novel of white life are legitimate concerns of the Negro novelist. To restore perspective, however, it is necessary to restate the general rule: a high protest content is not likely to produce good fiction; a studious avoidance of Negro life is scarcely more promising; the treatment of race material, though not necessarily race conflict, is by all odds the likeliest alternative. The weight of historical evidence certainly supports this conclusion.

Freedom for the Negro novelist is not a simple concept to define. In negative terms, one can assert with some confidence that the problems of racial conflict and of white characterization are

9. "Creative Writing in the Negro College," pp. 160–63.

10. Of sixty-two novelists writing between 1853 and 1952, forty, or two-thirds, have published only one novel. Eleven more have published only two novels; only eleven have published more than two.

the principal obstacles to freedom. Once these problems have been solved on a sound literary basis, the Negro novelist will be free to develop to the limits of his capacity. Without a doubt, notable progress has been made in this direction, as more of the younger writers have learned to respect the difference between social controversy and art. In the long run, an art-centered Negro fiction will evolve, free from the crude nationalistic propaganda of the past and the subtler assimilationist propaganda of the present.

Recommended Reading List

Major (4):
Jean Toomer, *Cane*
Richard Wright, *Native Son*
Ralph Ellison, *Invisible Man*
James Baldwin, *Go Tell It on the Mountain*

Superior (4):
William Attaway, *Blood on the Forge*
Zora Neale Hurston, *Their Eyes Were Watching God*
William Demby, *Beetlecreek*
Ann Petry, *Country Place*

Good (7):
James Weldon Johnson, *The Autobiography of an Ex-Colored Man*
Countee Cullen, *One Way to Heaven*
Nella Larsen, *Quicksand*
Claude McKay, *Banana Bottom*
Arna Bontemps, *Black Thunder*
George Wylie Henderson, *Ollie Miss*
Dorothy West, *The Living Is Easy*

Bibliography

FOR specialists in the field of Negro literature I am aware that a mere list of titles will not constitute a satisfactory bibliography. Let me therefore indicate briefly the sources of information and the criteria used in compiling the check list that follows.

A fairly adequate bibliography was initially available in Hugh Gloster's *Negro Voices in American Fiction* (1948). This work, however, in addition to some minor omissions, closes accounts in 1940. It was supplemented by my own research in the James Weldon Johnson Collection at Yale University, the Spingarn Collection at Howard University, and the Schomburg Collection of the New York Public Library. A verification of the results was recently made possible (1955) by the publication of Maxwell Whiteman's comprehensive bibliography, *A Century of Fiction by American Negroes, 1853–1952.* In comparing notes with Mr. Whiteman's work, I found only a few discrepancies, chiefly involving questions of racial identity, as noted below. Both Gloster and Whiteman, however, have been concerned with the broader subject of Negro *fiction;* for my purposes, a more precise definition of terms was necessary. Like most critical definitions, the following are perfectly arbitrary, and are useful only in assuring accurate communication. By using a slightly different terminology, another writer might discover 113—or 153—Negro novels instead of the 103 included in this study.

My term "Negro novel," to begin with, refers to novels written by Negro authors, regardless of subject matter. Novels written by white authors about Negroes, while often relevant to the present work, do not fall formally within its scope. I am concerned, moreover, only with *full-length* novels written by *American* Negroes. Following Ira Reid, a Negro is a person whose physical characteristics or known ancestry identify him as a person of full or mixed African descent; who is defined as a Negro by law and custom; and whose behavior and experience are affected by, and result from, the above identification and definition. An American Negro author is a person who was born and raised in the continental United States, or whose novels deal with some significant aspect of the American scene. In short, this study is restricted to Negro authors whose artistic consciousness, as expressed in their novels, has been decisively shaped by their experience of American life.

On grounds of racial identity, national origin, or literary genre, a number of marginal titles have been eliminated. In the first category are George Hamlin Ross' *Beyond the River* (1938), Felice Swados' *House of Fury* (1941), and M. Virginia Harris' *Weddin' Trimmin's* (1949). All three authors are listed as Negroes by Maxwell Whiteman, but as whites at the Spingarn Collection. In cases of conflict (there are others), I have preferred to wait for unanimity. Also excluded on grounds of race is *The Interne* (1932), by co-authors Wallace Thurman (Negro) and A. L. Furman (white).

The problem of national origin arises chiefly in regard to West Indian authors. On grounds of national consciousness I have excluded Eric Rasmussen, who was born in the Virgin Islands, who has lived sporadically in New York, but who writes of Carribean life in *The First Night* (1951). For similar reasons I have excluded R. Archer Tracy, who was born in the British West Indies, who practiced medicine for a time in Georgia, but who writes of island life in *The Sword of Nemesis* (1919). Also excluded are Thomas E. Roach and W. Adolphe Roberts, two authors of West Indian origin whose inept fantasies and historical extravaganzas reflect little knowledge of American life. Included, however, are Nella Larsen, born in the Virgin Islands, and Claude McKay, born in Jamaica, because they participated actively in the Negro Renaissance and wrote primarily of the American scene.

Finally it may be difficult, at least in some instances, to determine whether a given work of fiction is a novel. The most obvious requirement of the genre is length. A novel implies sustained performance, and an ability to handle more than a single, isolated fictional situation. At some point a distinction between a full-length novel and a novelette becomes essential.

Our definition of a full-length novel ought to be both liberal and flexible, so as not to exclude achievement in the field. Let us begin with the concept of a standard novel of 300 pages, more or less. Let us then, for the sake of liberality and flexibility, require only 200 pages of a full-length novel. We should now feel fairly confident that the novelettes which we exclude are truly undersize. On this basis, thirty-five novelettes and one fragmentary novel have been eliminated. These titles may be found in Section B, below. The only work shorter than 200 pages which has been included is *Clotel* (1853), by William Wells Brown. This book, 193 pages long in the original English edition, is widely regarded as the first novel to have been written by an American Negro.

From this point, determination of genre becomes even more arbitrary, for there are always a few literary hybrids which defy classification. A work may combine, for example, fiction and biography, or fiction and history, or fiction and a topical problem in sociology. In such cases we must ask, "Are the fictional elements in the work subordinate or central?" Although in theory such distinctions may appear tenuous, in practice they are easily made. For these reasons I have excluded Richard Wright's *Black Boy* (1945), as an autobiography which contains incidental fictional elements, and Chancellor Williams' *The Raven* (1943) as essentially a biography of Poe. I have likewise excluded Lewis A. H. Caldwell's *The Policy King* (1945) as a topical treatise on the policy racket; Chancellor Williams' *Have You Been to the River?* (1952) as a sociological study of religious cults; and Adam Powell, Sr.'s *Picketing Hell* (1942) as an allegorical sermon on Church reform.

Special problems present themselves, however: is the detective story a novel or a separate genre? On the grounds that the whodunit must conform to conventions peculiar to itself, I have excluded Rudolph Fisher's *The Conjure-Man Dies* (1932). The case of a collection of short stories, united around a single theme, such as Eric Walrond's *Tropic Death* (1926), or Richard Wright's *Uncle Tom's Children* (1938), may seem clear enough, but what should be done with Langston Hughes' book, *Simple Speaks His Mind* (1950)? Originally appearing as a character in a newspaper column, "Jess B. Semple" has acquired a certain literary longevity, but I have excluded the book on the grounds that it is too disjointed, too much a series of sketches, to be regarded as a novel.

On the other hand, I have included Jean Toomer's *Cane* (1923)—a literary mongrel if there ever was one. I would justify this decision on historical grounds, since Toomer participated in a literary coterie which was consciously experimenting with the form of the novel. Moreover, contemporary critics referred to him as a "poet-novelist," and there is no book other than *Cane* on which to base the latter claim.

Finally, the case of Oscar Micheaux requires special attention. Ostensibly Micheaux has written seven separate novels, but on closer examination we find that his first novel has gone through several editions under different names. I have therefore eliminated *The Homesteader* (1917) and *The Wind from Nowhere* (1941) as essentially new editions of *The Conquest* (1913). I have also eliminated *The Masquerade* (1947), which is an acknowledged plagiarism of Charles Chesnutt's *The House behind the Cedars* (1900). How Micheaux managed to evade the copyright laws remains a mystery.

These minor difficulties in classification ought not to be exaggerated. In an overwhelming number of instances, there is no problem in recognizing a novel as such. Only a handful of marginal volumes, nearly all of which have been mentioned, present a special problem. When the foregoing distinctions have been drawn, 103 volumes remain which in my opinion can reasonably be regarded as the full-length novels written by American Negroes between 1853 and 1952.

In limiting the scope of the subject in this manner, it is no part of my intention to minimize the number of novels written by American Negroes. On the contrary, I have consciously undertaken an exclusive rather than inclusive treatment of the subject in order to establish certain minimum standards by which substantial achievement in the field of the novel can be measured.

A. Full-length Novels Written by American Negroes, 1853–1952

1853: William Wells Brown, *Clotel, or the President's Daughter*, London, Partridge and Oakey.

1857: Frank J. Webb, *The Garies and Their Friends*, London, G. Routledge.

1886: James H. W. Howard, *Bond and Free,* Harrisburg, Pa.

1892: Frances E. W. Harper, *Iola Leroy,* Boston, James H. Earle.

1894: "Sanda" (Walter H. Stowers and William H. Anderson), *Appointed,* Detroit, Detroit Law Printing.

1896: J. McHenry Jones, *Hearts of Gold,* Wheeling, W. Va., Daily Intelligencer Steam Job Press.

1898: Paul Laurence Dunbar, *The Uncalled,* New York, Dodd, Mead.

1899: Sutton E. Griggs, *Imperium in Imperio,* Cincinnati, Ohio, Editor Publishing Co.

1900: Charles W. Chesnutt, *The House behind the Cedars,* Boston and New York, Houghton Mifflin.

Paul Laurence Dunbar, *The Love of Landry,* New York, Dodd, Mead.

Pauline Hopkins, *Contending Forces,* Boston, Colored Cooperative Publishing Co.

1901: Charles W. Chesnutt, *The Marrow of Tradition,* Boston and New York, Houghton Mifflin.

Paul Laurence Dunbar, *The Fanatics,* New York, Dodd, Mead.

Sutton E. Griggs, *Overshadowed,* Nashville, Tenn., Orion.

1902: Paul Laurence Dunbar, *The Sport of the Gods,* New York, Dodd, Mead.

Sutton E. Griggs, *Unfettered,* Nashville, Tenn., Orion.

G. Langhorne Pryor, *Neither Bond nor Free,* New York, J. S. Ogilvie.

1905: Charles W. Chesnutt, *The Colonel's Dream,* New York, Doubleday, Page.

Sutton E. Griggs, *The Hindered Hand,* Nashville, Tenn., Orion.

1908: Sutton E. Griggs, *Pointing the Way,* Nashville, Tenn., Orion.

1909: J. W. Grant, *Out of the Darkness,* Nashville, Tenn., National Baptist Publishing Board.

1910: Thomas H. B. Walker, *Bebbly,* Gainesville, Fla., Pepper.

Robert L. Waring, *As We See It,* Washington, D.C., C. F. Sudwarth.

1911: W. E. B. DuBois, *The Quest of the Silver Fleece,* Chicago, A. C. McClurg.

1912: James Weldon Johnson, *The Autobiography of an Ex-Colored Man,* Boston, Sherman, French.

1913: Oscar Micheaux, *The Conquest,* Lincoln, Nebraska, Woodruff Press.

1915: Oscar Micheaux, *The Forged Note,* Lincoln, Neb., Western Book Supply.

Otis M. Shackelford, *Lillian Simmons,* Kansas City, Mo., R. M. Rigby.

1917: Henry F. Downing, *The American Cavalryman,* New York, Neale.

1919: Herman Dreer, *The Immediate Jewel of His Soul,* St. Louis, Mo., St. Louis Argus.

1921: Mary Etta Spencer, *The Resentment,* Philadelphia, A.M.E. Book Concern.

1923: Jean Toomer, *Cane,* New York, Boni and Liveright.

1924: John T. Dorsey, *The Lion of Judah,* Chicago, Fauche.

Jessie R. Fauset, *There Is Confusion,* New York, Boni and Liveright.

Joshua Henry Jones, *By Sanction of Law,* Boston, B. J. Brimmer.

Walter White, *The Fire in the Flint,* New York, Knopf.

1926: Walter White, *Flight,* New York, Grosset and Dunlap.

1928: W. E. B. DuBois, *Dark Princess,* New York, Harcourt, Brace.

Jessie R. Fauset, *Plum Bun,* New York, Frederick A. Stokes.

Rudolph Fisher, *The Walls of Jericho,* New York and London, Knopf.

Nella Larsen, *Quicksand,* New York and London, Knopf.

Claude McKay, *Home to Harlem,* New York and London, Harper.

1929: Nella Larsen, *Passing,* New York, Knopf.

Claude McKay, *Banjo,* New York, Harper.

Wallace Thurman, *The Blacker the Berry,* New York, Macaulay.

1930: Langston Hughes, *Not Without Laughter,* New York, Knopf.

John H. Paynter, *Fugitives of the Pearl,* Washington, D.C., Associated Publishing.

1931: Arna Bontemps, *God Sends Sunday,* New York, Harcourt, Brace.

Jessie R. Fauset, *The Chinaberry Tree,* New York, Stokes.

William S. Henry, *Out of Wedlock,* Boston, Badger, the Golden Press.

George Schuyler, *Black No More,* New York, Macaulay.

——— *Slaves Today,* New York, Brewer, Warren and Putnam.

1932: Countee Cullen, *One Way to Heaven,* New York and London, Harper.

Wallace Thurman, *Infants of the Spring,* New York, Macaulay.

1933: Jessie R. Fauset, *Comedy American Style,* New York, Stokes.

John H. Hill, *Princess Malah,* Washington, D.C., Associated Publishers.

Claude McKay, *Banana Bottom,* New York, Harper.

1934: Zora Neale Hurston, *Jonah's Gourd Vine,* Philadelphia, Lippincott.

1935: George Henderson, *Ollie Miss,* New York, Stokes.

1936: Arna Bontemps, *Black Thunder,* New York, MacMillan.

1937: Zora Neale Hurston, *Their Eyes Were Watching God,* Philadelphia and London, Lippincott.

George W. Lee, *River George,* New York, Macaulay.

Waters Edward Turpin, *These Low Grounds,* New York and London, Harper.

1938: Mercedes Gilbert, *Aunt Sara's Wooden God,* Boston, Christopher.

1939: William Attaway, *Let Me Breathe Thunder,* New York, Doubleday, Doran.

Arna Bontemps, *Drums at Dusk,* New York, MacMillan.

Waters Edward Turpin, *O Canaan!* New York, Doubleday, Doran.

1940: Richard Wright, *Native Son,* New York, Harper.

1941: William Attaway, *Blood on the Forge,* New York, Doubleday, Doran.

1943: C. R. Offord, *The White Face,* New York, McBride.

1945: Chester B. Himes, *If He Hollers Let Him Go,* New York, Doubleday, Doran.

OSCAR MICHEAUX, *The Case of Mrs. Wingate,* New York, Book Supply.

O. P. WOOD, *High Ground,* New York, Exposition Press.

1946: GEORGE HENDERSON, *Jule,* New York, Creative Age Press.

CURTIS LUCAS, *Third Ward Newark,* New York and Chicago, Ziff Davis.

OSCAR MICHEAUX, *The Story of Dorothy Stanfield,* New York, Book Supply.

ANN PETRY, *The Street,* Boston, Houghton Mifflin.

FRANK YERBY, *The Foxes of Harrow,* New York, Dial Press.

1947: ALDEN BLAND, *Behold a Cry,* New York, Scribner's.

CHESTER B. HIMES, *Lonely Crusade,* New York, Knopf.

WILLARD MOTLEY, *Knock on Any Door,* New York, Appleton-Century.

ANN PETRY, *Country Place,* Boston, Houghton Mifflin.

WILL THOMAS, *God is for White Folks,* New York, Creative Age Press.

FRANK YERBY, *The Vixens,* New York, Dial Press.

1948: ZORA NEALE HURSTON, *Seraph on the Suwanee,* New York, Scribner's.

WILLIAM GARDNER SMITH, *Last of the Conquerors,* New York, Farrar, Straus.

DOROTHY WEST, *The Living Is Easy,* Boston, Houghton Mifflin.

FRANK YERBY, *The Golden Hawk,* New York, Dial Press.

1949: WILLARD SAVOY, *Alien Land,* New York, Dutton.

FRANK YERBY, *Pride's Castle,* New York, Dial Press.

1950: WILLIAM DEMBY, *Beetlecreek,* New York, Rinehart.

PHILIP B. KAYE, *Taffy,* New York, Crown.

J. SAUNDERS REDDING, *Stranger and Alone,* New York, Harcourt, Brace.

WILLIAM GARDNER SMITH, *Anger at Innocence,* New York, Farrar, Straus.

FRANK YERBY, *Floodtide,* New York, Dial Press.

1951: LLOYD BROWN, *Iron City,* New York, Masses and Mainstream.

OWEN DODSON, *Boy at the Window,* New York, Farrar, Straus and Young.

WILLARD MOTLEY, *We Fished All Night,* New York, Appleton-Century-Crofts.

FRANK YERBY, *A Woman Called Fancy,* New York, Dial Press.

1952: DOROTHY LEE DICKENS, *Black on the Rainbow,* New York, Pageant Press.

RALPH ELLISON, *Invisible Man,* New York, Random House.

CHESTER HIMES, *Cast the First Stone,* New York, Coward-McCann.

FRANK YERBY, *The Saracen Blade,* New York, Dial Press.

B. Novelettes, 1853-1952

ADAMS, CLAYTON, *Ethiopia, the Land of Promise,* New York, Cosmopolitan Press, 1917. 129 pp.

ASHBY, WILLIAM M., *Redder Blood,* New York, Cosmopolitan Press, 1915. 188 pp.

BLAIR, JOHN PAUL, *Democracy Reborn,* New York, privately printed, 1946. 182 pp.

BRUCE, JOHN EDWARD, *The Awakening of Hezekiah Jones,* Hopkinsville, Ky., Press of Philip H. Brown, 1916. 62 pp.

COLEMAN, A. E., *Rosy the Octoroon,* Boston, Meador, 1929. 121 pp.

DALY, VICTOR, *Not Only War,* Boston, Christopher, 1932. 106 pp.

DELANY, MARTIN R., "Blake, or the Huts of America," *Anglo-African Magazine, 1* (Jan.–July 1859). Fragmentary.

DURANT, E. E., AND ROACH, C. M., *The Princess of Naragpur,* New York, Grafton Press, 1928. 191 pp.

DURHAM, JOHN S., "Diane, Priestess of Haiti," *Lippincott's Monthly Magazine, 69* (April 1902), 387–466. 80 pp.

ELLIS, GEORGE W., *The Leopard's Claw,* New York, International Authors' Association, 1917. 172 pp.

FLEMING, SARAH LEE BROWN, *Hope's Highway,* New York, Neale, 1918. 156 pp.

GILMORE, F. GRANT, *The Problem,* Rochester, New York, Henry Conolly, 1915. 93 pp.

Gray, Wade S., *Her Last Performance,* Omaha, Nebraska, Rapid Printing and Publishing, 1944. 140 pp.

Hopkins, Pauline, *Of One Blood; or The Hidden Self,* in 12 installments in the *Colored American Magazine,* beginning Nov. 1902. Approximately 120 pp.

Jarette, A. Q., *Beneath the Sky,* New York, Weinberg Book Supply, 1949. 151 pp.

Jenkins, D. F., *It Was Not My World,* Los Angeles, Calif., privately printed, 1942. 104 pp.

Johnson, Mrs. A. E., *The Hazely Family,* American Baptist Publishing Society, 1894. 191 pp.

Johnson, E. A., *Light Ahead for the Negro,* New York, Grafton Press, 1904. 132 pp.

Jones, Yorke, *The Climbers,* Chicago, Glad Tidings Publishing, 1912. 191 pp.

Jordan, Moses, *The Meat Man,* Chicago, Judy Publishing, 1923. 96 pp.

Lee, John M., *Counter-Clockwise,* New York, Wendell Malliet, 1940. 103 pp.

Liscomb, Harry F., *The Prince of Washington Square,* New York, Stokes, 1925. 180 pp.

Lucas, Curtis, *Flour Is Dusty,* Philadelphia, Dorrance, 1943. 166 pp.

Morris, Earl J., *The Cop,* New York, Exposition Press, 1951. 126 pp.

Nash, T. E. D., *Love and Vengeance,* Portsmouth, Va., privately printed, 1903. 171 pp.

Nelson, Annie Greene, *After the Storm,* Columbia, S.C., Hampton Publishing, 1942. 131 pp.

——— *The Dawn Appears,* Columbia, S.C., Hampton Publishing, 1944. 135 pp.

Rogers, J. A., *From Superman to Man,* Chicago, M. A. Donahue, 1917. 150 pp.

Rosebrough, Sadie Mae, *Wasted Travail,* New York, Vantage Press, 1951. 90 pp.

Sanders, Tom, *Her Golden Hour,* Houston, Texas, privately printed, 1929. 167 pp.

Shaw, O'Wendell, *Greater Need Below,* Columbus, Ohio, Bi-Monthly Negro Book Club, 1936. 161 pp.

Turner, A. P., *Oaks of Eden,* New York, Exposition Press, 1951. 135 pp.

Walker, Thomas H. B., *J. Johnson, or The Unknown Man,* Deland, Fla., E. D. Painter Printing, 1915. 192 pp.

Wood, Lillian E., *Let My People Go,* Philadelphia, A.M.E. Book Concern, no date. 132 pp.

Wright, Zara, *Black and White Tangled Threads,* Chicago, privately printed, 1920. 193 pp.

——— *Kenneth,* Chicago, privately printed, 1920. A sequel of the above, approximately 145 pp.

C. Periodical Literature, 1853-1952

Barnes, Albert C., "Primitive Negro Sculpture and Its Influence on Modern Civilization," *Opportunity, 6* (1928), 139–40, 147.

Bland, Edward, "Social Forces Shaping the Negro Novel," *Negro Quarterly* (fall 1942), pp. 241–48.

Bontemps, Arna, "Famous WPA Authors," *Negro Digest* (June 1950), pp. 43–47.

Braithwaite, William S., "Negro America's First Magazine," *Negro Digest* (Nov. 1947), pp. 21–26.

——— "The Negro in Literature," *Crisis, 28* (1924), pp. 204–10.

——— "The Novels of Jessie Fauset," *Opportunity, 12* (1934), 24–28.

Brawley, Benjamin, "The Negro Literary Renaissance," *Southern Workman, 56* (April 1927), 177–84.

Brown, Lloyd, "Which Way for the Negro Writer?" *Masses and Mainstream 4* (March 1951), pp. 53–63; (April 1951), pp. 50–59.

Brown, Sterling, "Our Literary Audience," *Opportunity,* (1930), 42–46, 61.

——— "The Negro Author and His Publisher," *Quarterly Review of Higher Education among Negroes,* 9 (July 1941), 140–46.

Bullock, Penelope, "The Mulatto in American Fiction," *Phylon* (first quarter 1945), pp. 78–82.

Butcher, Philip, "In Print" (regular feature), *Opportunity, 25* (1947), 218–22; *26* (1948), 113–15.

——— "Creative Writing in the Negro College," *Journal of Negro Education* (spring 1951), pp. 160–63.

CHAMBERLAIN, JOHN, "The Negro as Writer," *Bookman, 70* (Feb. 1930), 603–11.

CHANDLER, G. LEWIS, "Coming of Age: A Note on American Negro Novelists," *Phylon* (first quarter 1948), pp. 25–29.

CHESNUTT, CHARLES, "Post-bellum, Pre-Harlem," *Crisis, 38* (1931), 193–94.

COHN, DAVID L., "The Negro Novel: Richard Wright," *Atlantic Monthly, 165* (May 1940), 659–61.

CONRAD, EARL, "The Blues School of Literature," *Chicago Defender,* Dec. 22, 1945.

DAVIS, ALLISON, "Our Negro Intellectuals," *Crisis, 35* (1928), 268, 284–86.

DE ARMOND, FRED, "A Note on the Sociology of Negro Literature," *Opportunity, 3* (1925), 369–71.

DUBOIS, W. E. B., and LOCKE, ALAIN, "The Younger Literary Movement," *Crisis,* 27 (1924), 161–63.

ELLISON, RALPH, "Richard Wright's Blues," *Antioch Review,* summer 1945.

——— "Recent Negro Fiction," *New Masses* (Aug. 5, 1941), pp. 22–26.

——— "Light on Invisible Man," *Crisis, 60* (1953), pp. 157–58.

FARRISON, W. EDWARD, "William Wells Brown, America's First Negro Man of Letters," *Phylon* (first quarter 1948), pp. 13–23.

FORD, NICK AARON, "The Negro Novel as a Vehicle of Propaganda," *Quarterly Review of Higher Education Among Negroes* (July 1941), pp. 135–39.

——— "A Blueprint for Negro Authors," *Phylon* (fourth quarter 1950), pp. 374–77.

FRAZIER, E. FRANKLIN, "The Garvey Movement," *Opportunity, 4* (1926), 346–48.

——— "The American Negro's New Leaders," *Current History, 28* (April 1928), 56–59.

——— "Racial Self-Expression," *Ebony and Topaz* (1927), pp. 119–21.

GIBSON, RICHARD, "A No to Nothing" *Kenyon Review* (spring 1951), pp. 252–55.

Glicksberg, Charles I., "The Alienation of Negro Literature," *Phylon* (first quarter 1950), pp. 49–58.

Gloster, Hugh, "Race and the Negro Writer," *Phylon* (fourth quarter 1950), pp. 369–71.

——— "The Significance of Frank Yerby," *Crisis, 55* (1948), 12–13.

Green, Marjorie, "Ann Petry Planned to Write," *Opportunity, 24* (1946), 78–79.

Holmes, Eugene C., "Problems Facing the Negro Writer Today," *New Challenge* (fall 1937), pp. 69–75.

Hughes, Langston, "The Negro Artist and the Racial Mountain," *Nation, 122* (1926), 692–94.

Hurston, Zora Neale, "What White Publishers Won't Print," *Negro Digest* (April 1947), pp. 85–89.

Ivy, James, "Ann Petry Talks about Her First Novel," *Crisis, 53* (1946), 48–49.

Jackson, Blyden, "Faith without Works in Negro Literature," *Phylon* (fourth quarter 1951), pp. 378–88.

——— "Full Circle," *Phylon* (first quarter 1948), pp. 30–35.

——— "An Essay in Criticism," *Phylon* (fourth quarter, 1950), pp. 338–43.

Jacobs, George W., "Negro Authors Must Eat," *Nation, 128* (1929), 710–11.

Jarrett, Thomas D., "Toward Unfettered Creativity: A Note on the Negro Novelist's Coming of Age," *Phylon* (fourth quarter 1950), pp. 313–17.

Johnson, James Weldon, "Negro Authors and White Publishers," *Crisis, 36* (1929), 228–29.

——— "Race Prejudice and the Negro Artist," *Harper's, 157* (1928), 769–76.

——— "The Dilemma of the Negro Author," *American Mercury, 15* (1928), 477–81.

——— "The Making of Harlem," *Survey Graphic* (March 1925), pp. 635–39.

Keith, Allyn, "A Note on Negro Nationalism," *New Challenge,* (fall 1937), pp. 65–69.

LASH, JOHN S., "The Race Consciousness of the American Negro Author," *Social Forces, 28* (Oct. 1949), 24–34.

——— "On Negro Literature," *Phylon* (third quarter 1945), pp. 240–47.

——— "The Literature of the Negro in Negro Colleges," *Quarterly Review of Higher Education among Negroes* (April 1948), pp. 66–76.

LEE, ULYSSES, "Criticism at Mid-Century," *Phylon* (fourth quarter 1950), pp. 328–37.

LOCKE, ALAIN, "American Literary Tradition and the Negro," *Modern Quarterly 3* (May–July, 1926), 215–22.

——— Series of annual reviews in *Opportunity: 7* (Jan. 1929), 8–11; *9* (Feb. 1931), 48–51; *10* (Feb. 1932), 40–44; *11* (Jan. 1933), 14–18; *12* (Jan. 1934), 8–11, 30; *13* (Jan. 1935), 8–12; (Feb. 1935), 46–48, 59; *14* (Jan. 1936), 6–10; (Feb. 1936), 42–43, 61; *15* (Jan. 1937), 8–13; (Feb. 1937), 40–44; *16* (Jan. 1938), 7–12, 27; *17* (Jan. 1939), 4–10; (Feb. 1939), 36–42; *18* (Jan. 1940), 4–10, 28; (Feb. 1940), 41–46, 53; *19* (Jan. 1941), 4–9; (Feb. 1941), 48–52.

——— "The Negro's Contribution to American Culture," *Journal of Negro Education, 8* (1939), 521–29.

——— "The Negro's Contribution to American Art and Literature," *Annals of the American Academy of Political and Social Science, 140* (1928), 234–47.

——— "Harlem," *Survey Graphic* (March 1925), pp. 629–30.

——— "Enter the New Negro," *Survey Graphic* (March 1925), pp. 631–34.

——— "Youth Speaks," *Survey Graphic* (March 1925), pp. 659–60.

——— "Apropos of Africa," *Opportunity, 2* (1924), 37–40, 58.

——— Series of annual reviews in *Phylon:* first quarter 1947, pp. 17–27; first quarter 1948, pp. 3–12; first quarter 1949, pp. 5–14; first quarter 1950, pp. 5–14; first quarter 1951, pp. 5–10; first quarter 1952, pp. 8–11.

——— "Our Little Renaissance," *Ebony and Topaz* (1927), pp. 117–18.

MINUS, MARION, "Present Trends of Negro Literature," *Challenge* (April 1937), pp. 9–11.

MOON, BUCKLIN, "A Literature of Protest," *Reporter* (Dec. 6, 1949), pp. 35–37.

PARKER, JOHN W., "Chesnutt as a Southern Town Remembers Him," *Crisis, 56* (1949), 205–6, 221.

REDDING, J. SAUNDERS, "The Negro Author: His Publisher, His Public, and His Prose," *Publisher's Weekly* (March 24, 1945), pp. 1284–88.

——— "The Negro Writer: Shadow and Substance," *Phylon* (fourth quarter 1950), pp. 371–73.

——— "The Fall and Rise of Negro Literature," *American Scholar* (spring 1949), pp. 137–48.

SCHUYLER, GEORGE, "Our Greatest Gift to America," *Ebony and Topaz* (1927), pp. 122–24.

——— "The Negro Art-Hokum," *Nation, 122* (1926), 662–63.

——— "What's Wrong with Negro Authors?" *Negro Digest* (May 1950), pp. 3–7.

——— "What Chance for Negroes in Journalism?" *Negro Digest* (Nov. 1948), pp. 15–18.

——— "What's Wrong with the NAACP?" *Negro Digest* (Sept. 1947), pp. 28–32.

SMITH, WILLIAM GARDNER, "The Negro Writer: Pitfalls and Compensations," *Phylon* (fourth quarter, 1950—literary number), pp. 297–303.

STARKEY, MARION L., "Jessie Fauset," *Southern Workman, 61* (May 1932), pp. 217–20.

TAUSSIG, CHARLOTTE E., "The New Negro as Revealed in His Poetry," *Opportunity, 5* (1927), 108–11.

THOMAS, WILL, "Negro Writers of Pulp Fiction," *Negro Digest* (July 1950), pp. 81–84.

THURMAN, WALLACE, "Negro Artists and the Negro," *New Republic, 52* (Aug. 31, 1927), 37–39.

VAN DOREN, CARL, "Negro Renaissance," *Century, 111* (1926), 635–37.

WALROND, ERIC, "The New Negro Faces America," *Current History, 17* (Feb. 1923), 786–88.

WEBB, CONSTANCE, "What Next for Richard Wright?" *Phylon* (second quarter 1949), pp. 161–66.

WHITE, WALTER, "The Negro Renaissance," editorial in all-Negro number of *Palms*, Oct. 1926.

WRIGHT, RICHARD, "How Bigger Was Born," *Saturday Review of Literature*, 22 (June 1, 1940), pp. 3–4, 17–20.

——— "I Bite the Hand That Feeds Me," *Atlantic Monthly*, *165* (June 1940), 826–28.

——— "I Tried to Be a Communist," *Atlantic Monthly*, *174* (Aug. 1944), 61–70; (Sept. 1944), 48–56.

——— "Blueprint for Negro Writing," *New Challenge*, (fall 1937), pp. 53–65.

See also *Challenge* 1934–37; *Harlem* (Nov. 1928); *Messenger* 1923–25; *Negro Digest* (Chicago), 1943–51; *Negro Story* (Chicago), 1944–46; *Negro World Digest* (New York) 1940; *New Challenge* 1937; *Opportunity*, the African Art issues, May 1924, May 1926; *Saturday Evening Quill*, 1928–29; *Stylus* (May 1921).

D. Biographies and Autobiographies

CHESNUTT, HELEN M., *Charles Waddell Chesnutt: Pioneer of the Color Line*. Chapel Hill, University of North Carolina Press, 1952.

DUBOIS, W. E. B., *Dusk of Dawn*, New York, Harcourt, Brace, 1940.

HUGHES, LANGSTON, *The Big Sea*, New York and London, Knopf, 1940.

HURSTON, ZORA NEALE, *Dust Tracks on a Road*, Philadelphia, New York, and London, Lippincott, 1942.

JOHNSON, JAMES WELDON, *Along This Way*, New York, Viking Press, 1933.

MCKAY, CLAUDE, *A Long Way from Home*, New York, Lee Furman, 1937.

REDDING, J. SAUNDERS, *No Day of Triumph*, New York and London, Harper, 1942.

WHITE, WALTER, *A Man Called White*, New York, Viking Press, 1948.

WRIGHT, RICHARD, *Black Boy*, New York and London, Harper, 1945.

Index